CITY OF THE DREAM

CITY

Volume Seven of a Series
on the Historic Birthplace of California

THE HISTORY OF SAN DIEGO

OF THE DREAM

Written by
RICHARD F. POURADE

Commissioned by
HELEN K. COPLEY

A COPLEY BOOK

PREVIOUS VOLUMES

The Explorers, 1960
Time of the Bells, 1961
The Silver Dons, 1963
The Glory Years, 1964
Gold in the Sun, 1965
The Rising Tide, 1967

ISBN 0-913938-19-X
LIBRARY OF CONGRESS CATALOG NUMBER: 77-020650

CONTENTS

DEDICATION

A City has a life unto itself. It generally rises, grows or wanes according to the pressures of time and events. The men who brought San Diego into being are long gone from the scene. But the City lives. The Seventh Volume of the History of San Diego is dedicated to another generation which sought to command events and assure a "City Beautiful" for those who would follow them.

HELEN K. COPLEY

"A certain Person among the Greeks being a Candidate for some Office in the State, it objected against him, That he was no Scholar. True, saith he, according to your Notion of Learning I am not; but I know how to make a poor City rich, and a small City great."

Jared Eliot

CHAPTER ONE

WAR EXTRA

WEATHER
Cloudy today and tomorrow; gentle winds, becoming southwesterly; little change in temperature.

The San Diego Union

AP WIREPHOTOS

Published daily and Sunday. Entered as second-class matter at the postoffice at San Diego, California, under the act of March 3, 1879.

ESTABLISHED 1868—SEVENTY-FOURTH YEAR | No. 28,495 | SAN DIEGO, CALIFORNIA, SUNDAY, DEC 7, 1941 | DAILY 5 CENTS—SUNDAY 10 CENTS

JAPS BOMBING HONOLULU, MANILA; SHIPS BATTLE

150 Nipponese Bombers Blast Naval Bastion at Pearl Harbor

RAID ON OAHU WITHOUT WARNING, WHITE HOUSE DECLARES; U. S. ARMY, NAVY ORDERED TO EXECUTE DEFENSE ORDERS

HONOLULU, Dec. 7 (U.P.) — Parachute troops were sighted off Harbor Point today.

HONOLULU, Dec. 7 (A.P.)—A naval engagement is in progress off Honolulu, with at least one black enemy aircraft carrier in action against Pearl Harbor defenses. Some aerial dogfights are in progress in the skies over Honolulu. At 9:30 a.m. (noon Pacific time) the attack was still in progress. One report said there were 150 attacking planes.

What damage was done by the swift surprise raid was not immediately apparent. But reports said enemy bombers scored a hit at Hickam field, army airport and another on an oil tank at the Pearl Harbor naval base.

At least two nine-plane formations of four-engined black bombers flew over Honolulu and Pearl Harbor. Each plane bore Japan's rising sun insignia. There was a report from persons who came past Pear Harbor that one ship there was lying on its side in the water and four others were on fire. This could not be immediately confirmed.

WASHINGTON, Dec 7 (A.P.)—Japanese airplanes today attacked American defense bases at Hawaii and Manila, and President Roosevelt ordered the army and navy to carry out undisclosed orders prepared for defense of the United States.

The White House said Japan attacked America's vital outposts in the Pacific — Hawaii and Manila and that so far as was known the attacks were still in progress.

Announcing the president's action for the protection of American territory, Presidential Secretary Stephen Early declared that so far as is known now the attacks "were made without warning— when both nations were at peace—and were delivered within an hour or so of the time that the Japanese ambassador had gone to the state departmen to hand to the secretary of state Japan's reply to the secretary's memorandum of Nov. 26.

Promptly, navy officers said that long prepared counter measures against Japanese surprise attacks had been ordered into operation and were "working smoothly." And within a few minutes the war department ordered all military personnel in this country into uniform.

There was a disposition in some quartershere to wonder whether the attacks had not been ordered by the Japanese military authorities because they feared the president's direct negotiations with the emperor might lead to an about-face in Japanese policy and the consequent loss of face by the present ruling factions in Japan.

A little later, the White House reported that an army transport loaded with lumber had been torpedoed 1300 miles west of San Francisco.

This is well east of Hawaii.

The first announcement did not say whether the ship was sunk or whether there was loss of life.

No official used the word war in reporting any of the developments, but with the series of events there could be no doubt that the Far Eastern situation had at last exploded, that the United States was at war, and that the conflict which began in Europe was spreading over the entire world.

Little information was immediately available regarding the strength of the Japanese air attacks.

Dispatches from Honolulu said, however, that at least two Japanese bombers, their wings bearing the insignia of the rising sun, appeared over Honolulu at 7:35 a. m. and dropped bombs.

The army's order affected not only the thousands of officers on duty in Washington, who have thus far performed their functions in civilian clothes to avoid a "militaristic" appearance, but all officers in every corps area, the United States' possessions and outlying bases.

Washington was expected to blossom tomorrow as a city of uniforms, because huge numbers of officers have been pouring into the city for months to perform the army's "overhead" functions.

Early said that so far as the president's information went, attacks were still in progress at Manila and in Hawaii. In other words, he said, "we don't know that the Japanese have bombed and left."

He went on to say:

"As soon as the information of the attacks on manila and Hawaii was received by the war and navy departments was flashed immediately to the president at the White House. There-

secretaries of navy and war. Steps are being taken to advise the congressional leaders."

Kichisaburo Nomura, the Japanese ambassador, and Saburo Kurusu, the special Japanese envoy, were at the state department at the time of the White House's announcement of the attacks.

The two Japanese went to Secretary of State Hull at 1:35 p.m. (10:35 Pacific Time) and remained about 20 minutes.

They handed to the secretary, Tokyo's reply to the statement of principles which he gave to them on Nov. 26.

After their departure, the state department announced that Hull had informed the Japanese that a document presented by them was "crowded with infamous falsehoods and distortions."

The blunt language Hull used in addressing the Japanese envoys was reflected in their faces as they left the state department.

There was no trace of a smile.

Hull kept them waiting for 15 minutes. Kurusu neatly dressed in well pressed blue, impatiently paced the floor, and engaged momentarily in whispered conferences with Nomura. The latter in rumpled gray had taken a seat on a leather

had been made of the bombings, endeavored to question them again.

"Is this your last conference?" one reporter asked Nomura.

He received no reply whatsoever.

"Will the embassy issue a statement later?"

"I don't know."

Followed by a swarm of reporters and photographers, the two Japa-

U. S. Air Center at Zamboanga Vital in Defense of Philippines

This U. S. army landing field, south of Zamboanga in the southern section of the Philippine islands, today was one of the centers for defense against the attacks started by Japan. Zamboanga is considered a vital army air center, not far from the equator.

All Naval Men Called to Duty

11th Area Personnel To Report at Once

LONG BEACH, Dec. 7 (A.P.)—Rear Adm. Charles A. Blakely of the 11th Naval district, today issued orders soon after announcement of the Japanese air attacks in the Pacific, requesting all officers and men attached to the district, or vessels of the district, to report to their stations or ships immediately.

The district embraces southern California from San Luis Obispo south to the Mexican border, and all of Arizona and New Mexico.

Winant, Churchill Confer on Isle Attacks

LONDON, Dec. 7 (A.P.)—Prime Minister Churchill and John C. Winant, United States ambassador to Britain, were in conference tonight a short time after President Roosevelt's announcement that Japanese planes had attacked Hawaii and the Philippines.

Bulletins

HONOLULU, Dec. 7 (U.P.)—Hawaii, including the great Pearl Harbor naval base, was attacked today by dive-bombing planes bearing the rising sun signia of Japan. The planes apparently were based on an aircraft carrier. They came in at great altitude but swooped low in dive attacks.

LONDON, Dec. 7 (U.P.)—The city was electrified tonight by news of the air attack on Hawaii. Official quarters had been alert for signs of the first outbreak in the Far Eastern warfare, but they had not expected it to come from that area.

NEW YORK, Dec. 7 (U.P.)—Pan American Airways officials said today that the Anzac clipper probably was in Honolulu when the Japanese bombing attack on Hawaii was launched. The clip-

SHIPS SHELL PEARL HARBOR; CANNON FIRE ROCKS ISLAND

Five Killed, Three Hurt in Early Raid On Hawaiian Capital; Citizens Flee

HONOLULU, Dec. 7 (A.P.)—Japanese bombs killed at least five persons and injured many others, three seriously, in a surprise morning aerial attack on Honolulu today.

NEW YORK, Dec. 7 (A.P.)—The Honolulu station of CBS reported by telephone today that 150 Japanese planes had attacked Hawaii.

The assault was delivered at night, it appeared.

The CBS representative said that the roar of anti-aircraft fire could be heard continuously and that the attack was continuing.

Two Planes Appear in Early Morning

By EUGENE BURNS

HONOLULU, Dec. 7 (A.P.)—At least two Japanese bombers, their wings bearing the insignia of the Rising Sun, appeared over Honolulu at 7:35 a. m. (Honolulu time) today and dropped bombs.

Unverified reports said a foreign warship appeared off Pearl Harbor and began firing at the defenses in that highly fortified post.

The sound of cannons firing comes to me here in Honolulu, as I telephone this.

The sound of cannonading coming from the direction of Pearl Harbor has been continuing for an hour and a half. So far, there are no reports of casualties. No bombs have fallen in Honolulu itself, so far as I could determine before making this call.

There is much commotion going on, with planes in the air and anti-aircraft firing.

The citizens of Honolulu have been cleared from the streets by military and naval units, assisted by civilian volunteers, all carrying arms.

But a lot of citizens have left the city for hills, to watch the planes and anti-aircraft, and get a general view of the excitement.

I heard one man say, as he passed me en route to the hills: "I'll bet the mainland papers are going to exaggerate this."

WATCH FOR SECOND EXTRA

A second extra of The Union will be issued later today as soon as additional news on the

Honolulu Reports Pearl Harbor Damage

NEW YORK, Dec. 7 (A.P.)—Untold damage has been done to the U. S. naval base at Pearl Harbor and to the city of Honolulu itself

U.S. Transport Hit in Pacific

Japan Naval Units East of Hawaii

WASHINGTON, Dec. 7 (A.P.)—The White House announced at 3:22 p.m. E. S. T. today that an army transport carrying lumber rather than troops had been torpedoed 1300 miles west of San Francisco. This placed Japanese naval action well east of Hawaii, toward the mainland.

There was no information whether the transport had been sunk or whether there was loss of life among the crew.

Ship Sends Call for Aid

WASHINGTON, Dec. 7 (A.P.)—The White House announced today that the army had just received word that an American vessel, believed to be a cargo ship, had been sending out signals of distress 700 miles west of San Francisco.

Whether it had been torpedoed was not immediately learned.

Germany Refuses Attack Comment

BERLIN, Dec. 7 (A.P.)—A German spokesman declared tonight there could be no reaction from Germany to the announced Japanese air attack on Pearl Harbor until all sides of the case were at hand.

Planes Shot Down At Pearl Harbor

NEW YORK, Dec. 7 (A.P.)—The British radio quoted the Reuters news agency tonight reporting from Honolulu that several planes were shot down in an attack on Pearl Harbor.

WASHINGTON, Dec. 7 (U.P.)—The federal bureau of investigation announced today that it is

This is how a new age unfolded for a City. War in the Pacific drastically altered life and times in San Diego. This is an extra edition of The San Diego Union *published on December 7, 1941.*

War — and the Shape of Things to Come

At the beginning of the great rush to Southern California the spirit of the "White City" was still very much alive. The World Columbian Exposition on the lake front in Chicago, just before the turn of the Century, with its canals and lagoons and buildings that shone in the sun like marble, had inspired the belief that man could shape the character and destiny of the cities in which he lived, and that disorder, congestion and decay were not inevitable.

Southern California was a kindly though fragile land and long before the Japanese bombs fell on Pearl Harbor in the Hawaiian Islands, its development had exceeded the capacity of its natural environment. And the impact of war — as well as the auto — would dramatically alter the course of its cities. But the idea of a "City Beautiful" would persist.

The Spaniards who arrived in the late 1700's had understood both the climate and the country, which were so similar to their own land. They were able to deal with it on its own terms and established an economy based on a pastoral way of life. They could succeed in this without doing violence to a natural environment which could support only a very limited number of people who had no assurance of unlimited survival.

It did not take Americans long, however, to find the key that could change the environment. That was water. It opened the gate to everything that happened to Southern California. The resource of water which the Americans first tapped, and which was unknown to the Spanish and Mexican settlers, was a store of underground water which had been collecting for millenia in sediments beneath the valleys. Here was water to supply the markets of the nation with the oranges, the grapes, and the out-

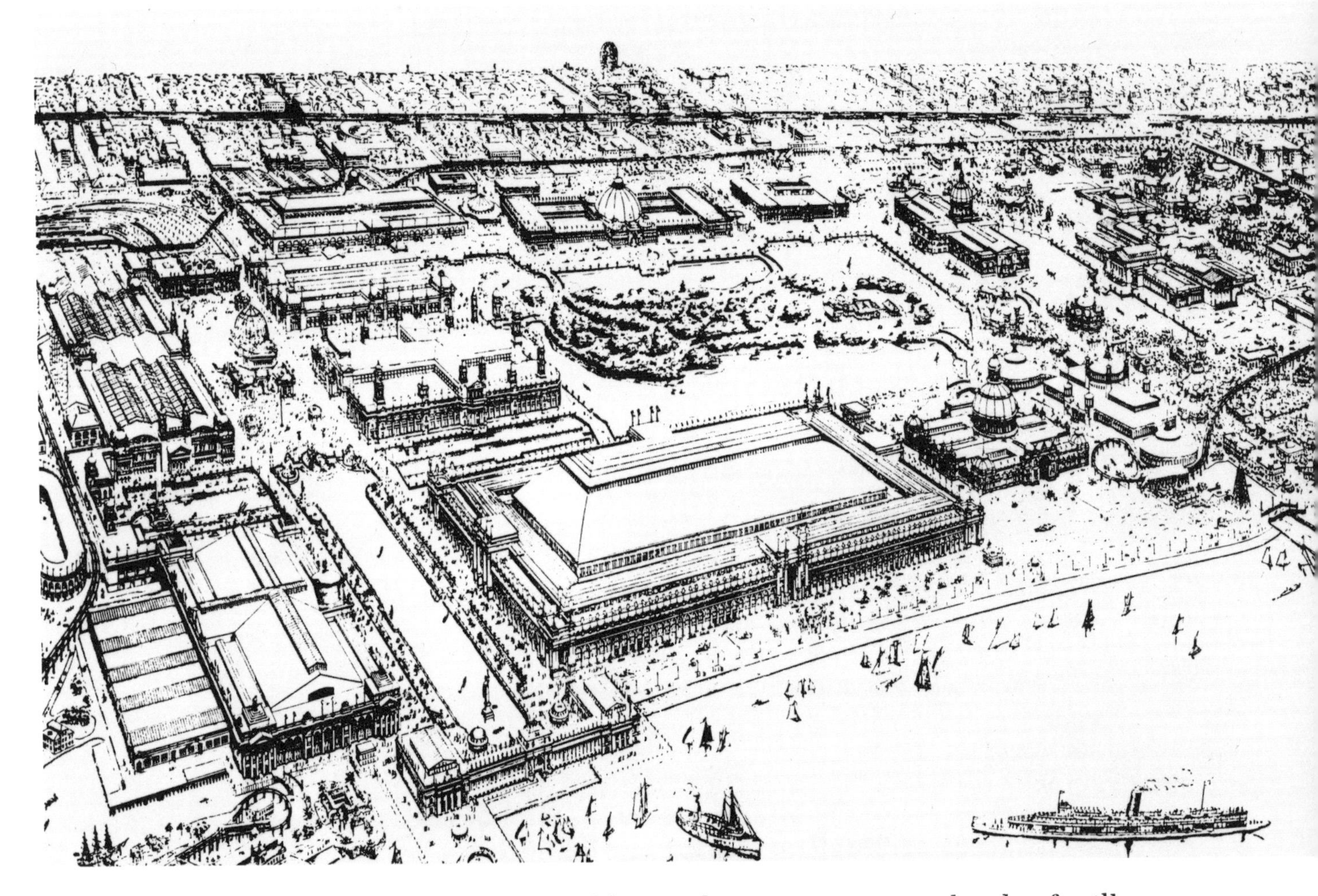

This is a sketch of the "White City" by which the World Columbian Exposition was known and which so influenced city planners for several generations in a search for a "City Beautiful."

of-season vegetables, and to water growing herds of milk cows. Besides, there was enough water to embark Los Angeles on the path of industrial success.

Southern California became one of the choice areas of the earth. To the natural advantages of a near-ideal climate, inspiring mountain ranges and a picturesque coastline, there had been added the thousands of square miles of palm trees and eucalyptus, decorative planting collected from all the continents and a system of highways unmatched in America. To move to California, by which was almost always meant Southern California, became the dream of millions of Americans across the land and for thousands of other people in Europe as well as in Japan and China. Southern California had become a phenomenon of progress and geography which was like nothing else anywhere.

In the decade of the 1920's, a million and a half people poured into Southern California. Most of them located in the Los Angeles area. That is where the jobs were. San Diego long since had lost out in the race to become the metropolis of the Pacific Coast. Its mountains to the west had not yielded to the railroads and to the south were the barren lands of Baja California.

San Diego was a quiet City, before the storm of 1941. Here is a scene looking up Fifth Avenue when street cars were the principal means of public transportation. Rain had dampened the street.

Its future would be different from that of its great neighbor to the north.

But San Diego's pioneer merchant, George W. Marston now reaching ninety years of age, was proud of the Civic Center which had risen on the waterfront and of other improvements such as Harbor Drive which reflected the suggestions made by the city planner from New England, John Nolen, whom he had brought to San Diego.

Marston had arrived in 1870, only three years after "Father" Alonzo Horton had laid out the site of much of the present downtown and summoned into existence a City distinct from the old settlement huddled around the Mexican Plaza in Old Town.

George W. Marston

Horton later recalled his first impression: "I thought San Diego must be heaven on earth, if it all was as fine as that. It seemed the best spot for building a city I ever saw." Marston wrote, early in 1941, before war came:

> "The present development of the City of San Diego is more nearly like what Horton and his associates dreamed of than at any other period in our history. Even as a village San Diego had great expectations and they are now being fulfilled. I count it a great privilege to have seen the City grow from 2,000 to 200,000 and I am more specially happy in the fine development of the waterfront."

In a losing campaign for mayor, Marston once stated that "I have been criticized for advocating the 'City Beautiful' idea, and I hereby plead guilty. I am for the 'City Beautiful.' I'm for it because it pays in dollars and cents. I believe in a 'City Beautiful' because we want more than selling real estate; we want comfort for our citizens."

The banker, Louis Wilde, represented another point of view, and said "Mr. Marston has been talking the 'City Beautiful' ever since I came here, and he has not managed to keep the streets clean." The struggle for the "City Beautiful" would be a long and often disappointing one.

Los Angeles became the first metropolitan area shaped by and for the users of the automobile. Autos permitted workers to live in garden communities far from their places of employment. Southern Californians were not constrained to build their homes along available street car lines. The results were the construction of towns and cities whose shopping areas, instead of being dense clusters in the manner of Eastern and European cities, spread out in lines many miles long and only two blocks wide, such as along Hollywood Boulevard in Los Angeles. Curbsides provided ample parking. Though much smaller, San Diego was being influenced in the same manner, to serve the auto, and had its University Avenue and El Cajon Boulevard which stretched for miles and were edged with small stores.

But all of the coastal Southern California ground water was being used more rapidly than it could be replaced and new sources had become necessary not only for growth but perhaps for mere survival. Without more water there could be no more homes built nor any more groves planted. Los Angeles reached 240 miles north and across the Sierra Nevada to tap the runoff from the high snows, and then began building another aqueduct eastward across the Coast Range and the desert to the Colorado River. San Diego was building more dams and creating reservoirs to capture and store uncertain surface runoff and had filed its own claim to a share of the water of the Colorado.

An engineering study in 1937 indicated that San Diego would not need the Colorado River water perhaps before 1970 if local sources were adequately developed. Otherwise, the metropolitan area, if agriculture continued to develop, might need additional water, and from the Colorado, sometime between 1950 and 1960. But the report did not foresee that the population of the City could exceed a half million until sometime between 1990 and the year 2000.

Even the Great Depression did not appreciably slow a Westward movement. San Diego, because of the availability of land along its protected bay and a temporate climate, became the location of numerous naval stations and developing aviation facilities, among them, Consolidated Aircraft Corp., which had moved west from Buffalo, New York, with large hopes and airplane designs adaptable to mass production. San Diego had not become a dominant industrial center and trading center, a promotional dream long since diminished by reality, and thus had not experienced the effects of the depression as severely as many other cities.

Before production for the spreading war in Europe, an educational system had begun to accept a philosophy that America was coming to the end of a road: the last frontier had been conquered, the tide of Westward discovery and settlement would be turning back on itself, and opportunity for individual enterprise would be diminishing. War would change everything, and the subsequent contributions of science and technology in the opening of vast new production and employment opportunities – a new Age of Discovery – could not be envisioned at the time. In this new age, San Diego would play a significant role.

In 1940 the population of Los Angeles City was more than a million and a half. San Diego's exceeded 200,000 and was expected to rise soon by at least 25,000. Both cities were beginning to feel the effects of the war in Europe and the determination of the national Administration to make the United States the arsenal of democracy. War goods poured across the sea in an effort to save England from defeat by the Axis powers. President Franklin D. Roosevelt set a production goal of 60,000 military planes in 1941 and 125,000 the following year. This meant producing a plane every eight minutes in 1941 and one every four minutes in 1942. San Diego's aircraft plants began a frantic expansion program. A $2,500,000 addition to the Consolidated plant was dedicated and it was then announced that the company's backlog of orders had reached $132,000,000.

Military forces were expanded, bases enlarged and new ones were rising almost overnight. The industrial development longed for by so many had arrived, though it was in restricted technical fields and not in consumer products.

A $15,000,000 Federal housing program in San Diego, approved by the President, was designed to create dwelling equivalent to a town of 30,000, and construction would call for 6,000 more skilled workmen. City laws were relaxed and private homes opened for rentals. In addition, the Navy was spending $3,000,000 on its own housing program.

By the beginning of 1941, San Diego's population growth was estimated to have exceeded 30,000 and by midSummer the City was expected to absorb 45,000 more residents in addition to

This was San Diego before the Great War. The sun is shining on the City while distant mountains glisten with snow. El Cortez Hotel was the beacon remembered by all who approached by sea.

16,000 military and naval personnel. Consolidated Aircraft had 16,500 employees and expected to hire 15,500 more by 1942. The smaller Ryan, Solar and Rohr production plants employed 3,400 workers and expected to hire 3,800 more. The San Diego Chamber of Commerce stressed the necessity of erecting 15,000 more dwelling units.

The Summer came and went, with occasional war scares, blackout tests and the practice mounting of aircraft guns atop the Consolidated plant which was turning out of a bombing plane almost daily, to be delivered to the Army Air Corps or flown across the Atlantic for the British. Other long-range planes were being delivered to the United States Navy.

On one occasion, the Navy picked up a rumor that a Japanese-manned private airplane was to lift off an airstrip somewhere in Southern California and crash with a load of explosives on warships in the port. Naval vessels were ordered out of the harbor. Nothing happened. However, the City's leading businessmen had formed a Civil Defense Council, with Lawrence Klauber as chairman. The Navy assigned Lieutenant Commander Max L. Black to serve as executive director.

Four days before the attack on Pearl Harbor, Consolidated Aircraft disclosed the largest employment program in the City's history, which would bring 10,000 more workers and their dependents, mostly from the Midwest and the South, into San Diego within five weeks.

Reuben Fleet

Two days later, while Japanese envoys presumably were negotiating for an agreement with the United States regarding the Far East, newspapers were publishing details of what was described as secret plans for the United States to raise an army of 10,000,000 men and an expeditionary force of 5,000,000. On Sunday morning, December 7, 1941, San Diegans read in their morning newspaper an article which comfortably insisted that the Japanese air force was limited to 5,000 planes and that there was a critical lack of experienced and capable pilots. But another news story disclosed that units of the Army Air Corps were being marshalled for a six-day test of San Diego's air defense capabilities.

War came on as peaceful a Sunday as San Diegans had enjoyed in many months. There was a warm Winter sun and thousands of persons were attending church services. Only a few persons in the Nation's capital knew of the belated warning of war dispatched to commanders in the Pacific, which, however, arrived by regular cable in Honolulu and was delivered too late to military headquarters.

Percy J. Benbough

A few minutes before noon in San Diego, those who had their radios turned on in their homes, or businesses, or in places of recreation, were stunned to hear that Pearl Harbor had been attacked and ships of the Pacific Fleet bombed. Some people on downtown streets were alerted by a sound truck but most of them had no information until newspaper extras appeared. Sailors and other military men hurried back to their ships or posts. The president of Consolidated Aircraft, Major Reuben H. Fleet, sent a message to President Roosevelt advising him that "we are on the job and at your command, sir." San Diego's Mayor, Percy J. Benbough, announced that "we are ready and awaiting orders. Firemen and policemen have been ordered to stand by." Within two hours after the strike at Pearl Harbor, orders had been issued bringing 1,200 men and women volunteers into action as enemy aircraft spotters. Protection plans were invoked for the water, telephone and power systems. Traffic was diverted from the vicinity of war production plants. The Civil Defense Council began the recruiting of 12,000 volunteers. A steel net was placed across the entrance to the harbor.

The office of the Federal Bureau of Investigation in San Diego acknowledged that it had a file of all alien Japanese in the County. Other reports placed the number of residents of Japanese descent at about 2,000, most of them associated with farming, with about 200 additional families believed to be farming between Tijuana and Mexicali in Baja California. They had

Japanese retained many of their customs and traditions when in San Diego, in the early days long before World War II. Like many ethnic groups of the time they lived a life apart.

turned to farming some of the poorest lands, or bottom lands subject to flooding, and over the years had prospered and were supplying a significant part of California's produce.

The news of war seemed to come as a shock to Japanese in San Diego County, as it did to most people. Many born in Japan chose to remain silent and remote. Others hesitated in answers as to their reactions. A few younger people on the streets merely smiled enigmatically. Those born in California, however, were largely willing to express their loyalty to the only land they had known. San Diegans generally with only limited experience and contact with Japanese were uncertain and many were apprehensive.

There was little general knowledge about Japanese residents. They had not been judged as rivals by most people, with the possible exception of some agricultural interests, but as a detached group living alongside of them and as yet out of the mainstream of American life. International travel was only for the few in those days and the little knowledge most San Diegans had of Japanese ways was in part from a legacy of two Expositions. That was the Japanese tea garden in Balboa Park. There were stepping stones, stone lanterns, pools, an arched bridge over a winding waterway and symbols of fish promising happy experiences. This seemed to offer a baffling contrast between charm and violence.

Many San Diegans knew of Japanese, or Japanese-Americans, only through visits to the delicate Japanese Tea Garden in Balboa Park. This photo was taken when it was being torn down to make more room for the Children's Zoo.

Newspaper reporters sought significance in attitudes and reactions. In a Buddhist temple which also served as a Japanese language school reporters found stacks of books and notices in the Japanese language. On a wall hung a large framed print of a Japanese aircraft carrier, with the flag of the Rising Sun flying at its stern and airplanes rising in flight from its deck. At a long table Japanese girls and women were silently engaged in the art of flower arranging. But at San Diego State College, a Japanese born in California and president of the college men's

Japanese children give the pledge of allegiance along with American friends at a school in California. A few months later they were to be removed with their parents to interior relocation camps.

glee club, proclaimed that "I am an American – as America goes, I go." Other students of Japanese descent who were members of the Japanese House of Pacific Relations took unequivocal stands as Americans in thought and action. The President of the San Diego chapter of the Japanese-American Citizens League said that send-off parties had been given for about twenty of their young men who already had joined the armed forces. Within three days 200 members of the Japanese-American Citizens League pledged to support the United States with their lives. *The San Diego Union* editorially advised restraint,

warning:

"It must be kept in mind that thousands of citizens of Japanese ancestry are loyal Americans and it is hoped there will be no witch-hunting directed against these people. They are no more responsible for the activities of the Japanese Government than are any of us and deplore the treachery of Japan as strongly as we do."

The San Diego Union was sure that competent authorities had the situation well in hand. Events moved swiftly. The Congress declared war on Germany and Italy as well as Japan. In San Francisco the headquarters of the Sixth Army, which embraced all West Coast Army commands, announced that war plans had gone into effect. Large units of Coast Artillery men who had trained at Camp Callan on pueblo, or city-owned, land on Torrey Pines mesa in San Diego, already had been deployed to man coastal defenses as far north as Alaska. San Diego's coast defenses at Fort Rosecrans on Point Loma had been heavily reinforced with larger guns, which, however, could not be used against air attacks launched from distant aircraft carriers. The Eleventh Naval District Headquarters assumed command of coordinated efforts of the Army, Navy and Marine Corps for the protection of San Diego. Anti-aircraft guns were manned at the Naval Air Station on North Island and aircraft patrolled far out to sea. Cavalry units from Camp Lockett near Campo moved out to assigned posts protecting the Barrett, Otay and Morena reservoirs which were near the International border.

At the outbreak of war, San Diego was the Navy's mightiest naval air base and grouped around the shore of San Diego Bay

Even before the attack on Pearl Harbor the United States had begun a buildup of its armed forces. Here, in March of 1941, the first recruits arrive to train at Camp Callan, with the Coast Artillery, on Torrey Pines mesa.

were more than 600 government buildings representing an investment in buildings and equipment of more than $50,000,000. Thirty-two thousand Navy men called San Diego home. The Naval Air Station on North Island was the base for 400 fighting, scouting, bombing and torpedo planes and was the repair base and operating base for the aircraft carriers Lexington, Saratoga, Ranger, Yorktown, Enterprise and Wasp, all of which had escaped the disaster at Pearl Harbor. In the area were the Naval Hospital, Marine Corps Base, Naval Training Station, Destroyer Base, Naval Air Station, Naval Fuel Depot, Naval Supply Depot and radio stations. A development program, before the bombs fell, had been estimated at more than $29,000,000.

However, response to the emergency was uncertain and at times erratic. The war in Europe had occupied most of the attention of the Administration and the military commanders and little had been done to physically prepare for war in the Pacific. While bases were being expanded, the coast was as wide open as Hawaii, or more so. In 1940 in the Eleventh Naval District, headquartered at San Diego but embracing a large area of the Southwest, there were only ten officers above the rank of lieutenant junior grade on the staff of the Commandant who were not either retired or in the Naval Reserve and summoned back to duty.

The United States had not been without knowledge of Japanese military ambitions, though not of all its actual plans, as the Navy had broken the Japanese most secret code late in 1940. It also was in 1940 that the U.S. Pacific Fleet was permanently based at Pearl Harbor and a line of defense marked out from Dutch Harbor in the Aleutian Islands to Pago Pago in the South Seas. Five years before that, however, Japan and Germany had agreed to exchange espionage information about the United States, and as a result, a Naval Intelligence officer reported Japanese were using radios in Guaymas, Mexico, on the Gulf of California, and at the tip of Baja California, to monitor maneuvers of the Pacific Fleet. The Japanese Navy assumed that the seizure of outposts along the American Ocean defense line, and the destruction of the Pacific Fleet, would force the power of the United States back to the mainland, where other thrusts could pin down its fighting units while Southwest Asia was brought under domination.

Intelligence services had not been unaware of Japanese espionage in the Islands and the identity of some of the agents. Ever since the American acquisition of the Islands the arrival of Japanese immigrants had provided a cover for slipping in espionage agents. By the time a decision had been reached to try and eliminate the Pacific Fleet, two systems were in operation. One was based in the consulate in Honolulu and depended on any information that could be obtained from hundreds of possible informants among the immigrants. Little information of value was produced, however, as the knowledge necessary to the Japanese Navy was readily available to anyone. Another system employed about a dozen secret agents directed by naval officers attached to the consulate. In this group was a Japanese-American taxi driver and a German drifter. This relatively small group easily gathered all the information necessary for a striking force on the positions of warships in the harbor, the range of aerial surveys, the most favorable time for an attack, and the information was sent to Tokyo by radio. Secret agents also were planted in cable company offices to read routine Fleet personnel messages.

Naval Intelligence considered San Diego the hub of Japanese espionage on the West Coast. Somewhat the same espionage system was used on the West Coast as in the Islands, with consulates as the main listening posts among Japanese immigrants. In addition, Japanese were aboard many fishing boats and visiting language students actually were officers in the Imperial Navy who coordinated all information on strategic West Coast defenses and sent them to the Embassy in Washington for dispatch to Tokyo. Their activities, however, were generally known to Naval Intelligence and to a certain extent to the Federal Bureau of Investigation. It was a deadly game of espionage and counter-espionage.

Although plans had been prepared for a war against Japan long before the attack on Pearl Harbor, and even though these plans were predicated on the assumption that the enemy would attack without a formal declaration of war, the Eleventh Naval District at San Diego was considered in a poor state of preparedness. The plans had been theoretical; there were neither the facilities nor funds to carry into effect the plans so laboriously made. The commandant of the District, Rear Admiral Charles A. Blakely, was in the Naval Hospital recuperating from a mild heart attack. On December 7, ammunition and ordnance depots were non-existent in the District, although the Naval Ammunition Depot at Fallbrook was nearing completion. There was insufficient housing for both civilian and military personnel. Only in the placing of nets and booms for closing the harbor entrance had there been thorough preparedness.

A blackout of the community was attempted the first night, December 7. There had been no real preparation and results were feeble. The lights at Consair continued to glow. When asked why, an official said "we're building airplanes – we haven't got time to play games." Under a threat of having a squad of Marines pull its power switches, Consair finally went dark. Tijuana, however, was blacked out quickly – the military merely pulled the power company switches.

Japanese carriers could have launched an attack on San Diego and the entire West Coast with impunity. The Army Air Force had only forty-five up-to-date fighter planes, ten heavy bombers and seventy-five medium bombers with which to defend the coast. The airplanes lacked proper equipment, bombs and ammunition. For detection, there were only six radar stations, the equipment was still crude, and there were no experienced operators.

The first day passed and by the second day discrimination in industry had come to an end. A class of women welders donned mechanic smocks and eye protectors and began training at San Diego's public Vocational School. Women had been refused entrance to mechanical classes for two years. Rosie the Riveter had arrived.

The first effective blackout was put into effect at midnight, December 8. It was described thusly in *The San Diego Union:*

> "Soft enveloping darkness, broken only here and there by the dimmed lights of an automobile or a slowly moving street car, brought the war – grim, real and challenging – to San Diego's doorstep last night. Exactly at midnight, while most of the City slept, all street lights, neon signs and big building lights suddenly were shut off as San Diego got its first taste of modern war's most fearsome experience – an air raid alarm."

The blackout followed hours of alerts concerning reports of enemy aircraft approaching the San Francisco area. Radio stations were restricted to brief announcements of blackout instructions and promptly at midnight all street lights were switched off as a signal to turn off all home and office lights. The blackout lasted until daylight. Reports of Japanese aircraft carriers off the coast of the mainland persisted and on the night of December 10 another blackout was signalled, this time embracing Southern California from Bakersfield south to the Mexican border and reaching as far inland as Las Vegas and Boulder City in Nevada. The blackout lasted about three hours and many San Diegans, caught away from home in the early evening hours by the sudden dousing of lights and warning blasts from gas company steam whistles, drove slowly homeward through silent and darkened streets. Thousands of workers were evacuated from the Consolidated Aircraft plant. Residents shuttered their windows with cloth or dark paper. Another limited alarm, called just before dawn two days later by the Fourth Interceptor Command, was attributed to vague reports of enemy airplanes over Point Loma.

E. Robert Anderson

In none of the situations were enemy planes actually identified. But the possibility of attack was there and the City of San Diego began a survey of buildings suitable for air raid shelters. The Navy augmented its patrol of the coast by chartering ten tuna clippers from the San Diego fleet for temporary duty. A San Diego-based airplane sighted an enemy submarine eight miles south of San Clemente Island, which was sixty miles west and slightly north of San Diego. The plane was from the Army Air Corps and assigned to assist the Navy in patrolling at sea. The sky was overcast with a ceiling of 2,000 feet. A large submarine appeared on the water's surface and the plane moved in to release its bombs. The attack was never made and the submarine slipped quietly beneath the choppy waves and disappeared. Air Corps regulations had stipulated that bombs had to be released from a height of 5,000 feet to avoid the possibility of damage to the aircraft.

The disaster at Pearl Harbor had not been fully revealed to the American people. Eighteen ships had been sunk or seriously damaged, including eight of the battleships which had been considered the backbone of the Pacific Fleet. But the nature of war was changing, and the aircraft carriers had been in the open sea.

Assigned to take command in the Pacific and of the decimated fleet was Admiral Chester W. Nimitz. To give himself

The warship came to its fighting end, for most purposes, in the Japanese attack on Pearl Harbor. One of the ships damaged was the U.S.S. Pennsylvania shown as she once led a battleship parade off San Diego.

time to consider plans and alternatives, he crossed the country by train and was met at Los Angeles by E. Robert Anderson, a commander in the Naval Reserve and Public Information Officer for the Eleventh Naval District. Nimitz was delivered to San Diego in Mayor Benbough's official sedan, which had been borrowed for the occasion, and private license plates substituted for official ones. From the Naval Air Station on North Island, he was flown to Pearl Harbor.

The day after Pearl Harbor, a National Guard unit from San Luis Obispo had moved into Balboa Park. Within a week the Navy brought about the removal of the Army and converted the park and its buildings, with one exception, into extensions of the Naval Hospital and Naval Training Station, for a Corpsman School and a Receiving Station. Later, the Army returned with units of its Air Defense Wing and the Women's Army Corps, among others.

Twice during those early days Japanese submarines lay within deck gun range of San Diego. Nine of Japan's most modern and powerful submarines had been dispatched across the Pacific

A soldier's life is not always a happy one. Here a soldier hurried up to wait for inspection at Fort Rosecrans, equipment at the ready. No guns were ever fired in anger at Fort Rosecrans.

to take positions by Christmas evening off the West Coast's important cities, with orders to shell radio and navigational stations. That same evening, however, before a shot was fired, new orders were received withdrawing them from attacks on land, for the time being, evidently in fear of counter-measures and the necessity of preserving the submarines for more important targets, especially shipping. Instead of firing their guns, the crew of one submarine off the Golden Gate listened to Christmas evening music broadcast by San Francisco radio stations. Two months later a lone Japanese submarine made a landfall at San Diego, after crossing the Pacific, but again no attack was undertaken. Instead the submarine proceeded northward to the Santa Barbara Channel, where it lobbed twenty-four shells onto shore at Goleta, near Santa Barbara. The shells did little damage but were the first to fall on American national soil since the war with Mexico almost a century before.

The first ship to be sunk off the coast was the oil tanker Emidio while it was returning in ballast from Seattle. It was shelled and torpedoed off Cape Mendocino on December 20, with a loss of six lives. Two more commercial ships were sunk in the same month, four others damaged and three others brought under attack. One of the ships attacked was the lumber carrier Samoa, out of Aberdeen, Washington, which was not damaged and made her way successfully to the San Diego Harbor. Other submarines shelled Fort Stevens in Oregon and Estevan Point in British Columbia. None of the attacking submarines were sunk in the eastern Pacific. In the United States no one was certain about Japan, and the fact that submarines were able to operate off the coast gave rise to fears of large-scale attacks by planes from aircraft carriers, as at Pearl Harbor, or even an attempt at invasion.

The 9,200 aliens who had been registered in the County in 1940 crowded the Post Office to acquire necessary identification cards; agents of the Federal Bureau of Investigation searched homes of aliens residing in Coronado which were within easy sighting of naval ships and bases. Subsequently all aliens were asked to voluntarily remove themselves from the vicinity of the waterfront. In the month following the attack on Pearl Harbor all the City and most of the County were declared prohibited areas by the Army, from which any or all persons could be excluded. Curfew regulations stipulated that aliens could not travel more than five miles from their homes except to places of employment. Of the people of German and Italian descent only a relatively few were detained or forced to leave the area. Of the latter, the most prominent was the resident manager of Hotel del Coronado, an Italian who had entertained many high-ranking American naval officers. Those forcibly removed as dangerous aliens and placed in confinement totalled seventy-one, and of them thirty-five were of Japanese ancestry.

Fears and suspicions were rife through the streets. The attack on Pearl Harbor obviously had been carried out by Japanese pilots with knowledge of the exact berthing or anchoring position of all United States warships in the harbor. What spying or mapping might have been done in San Diego, with its heavy concentration of military bases, ships and aircraft production plants, was not publicly known. There had been visitors from Japan. The Japanese who had migrated to this country had been barely assimilated, kept to themselves and often spoke only faltering English. The Neisi, or American-born Japanese, averaged only fifteen years in age. But most of them seemed to realize that the effect of the war on their lives was just beginning to unfold, just as it was unfolding for all San Diegans.

San Diego for decades had been a City with a large proportion of retired or elderly people. In 1930 the median age was estimated at almost thirty-three years. In 1940, with the median age of the national population placed at twenty-nine years, the average age of San Diegans, because of the influx of industrial workers, dropped under thirty-two years.

Though it had risen from the first White settlement on the Pacific Coast, with the early Spanish expeditions composed largely of people of dominant Mexican-Indian blood, its Mexican-American population was proportionately the lowest of any of the major cities of the Pacific Coast. Work in canneries and fields was not as available in San Diego as in Los Angeles.

Mexican-Americans, though their ancestors had been the founders of California, had never been influential in the affairs of the State or its large cities since the American conquest had brought to an end the Days of the Dons and the great rancho period. Most of them had been submerged quickly but had lived somewhat in harmony with their successors. It was not until World War II that Mexican-Americans began to become a factor in California, and this was due to heavy migrations, illegal or otherwise, from Mexico of a people who were fleeing their homeland in search of work and opportunity and had no real relationship with the old Californians of a bygone generation. The continuing infusion of cultural aspects from the homeland protected their language and customs and tended to make them a people apart. Assimilation would be slow and difficult. Few of them would remember that people of their blood long before them had once dominated San Diego and most of a great portion of California. But changing political attitudes would remind them of all of this.

The proportion of Blacks had remained low, too, at about two percent of the population, for somewhat the same reasons. Major Fleet, president of Consolidated Aircraft, had complained upon moving his plant to San Diego from Buffalo, that "there aren't any mechanics out here; only just a bunch of berry pickers." But assembly lines reduced the requirements for production skills. At Consolidated Aircraft the age of the average beginner was placed at less than twenty-one years, and in another twelve months 20,000 more workers under the age of twenty-one were expected to be hired and work for the first time in their lives. A second plant, financed by the Army Air Corps, for the production of parts for Consolidated planes, was being built on the tidelands north of the existing plant.

The housing situation had become acute and the City Manager, Walter Cooper, warned that it would become worse by Summer. Because houses couldn't be built fast enough, the Government had brought in about 650 trailers and connected them to City utilities. The estimates of new industrial workers, and number of the military, who would need housing, had been raised to more than 60,000.

Though the submarine threat somewhat dissipated, California's coast was long and exposed and the sea was considered a roadway for the same aircraft carriers that had taken the opening of war to the Hawaiian Islands. Another blackout was signalled in Southern California, and anti-aircraft fire was heard and searchlights sliced the skies over Los Angeles in an incident never fully explained. The only enemy plane to actually fly over the American West Coast was launched by a Japanese submarine off the coast of Oregon. It twice futilely attempted to set forest fires.

At San Diego, private bomb shelters were built and food, tents and clothing were stacked in autos for quick flights to the interior; store-bought fire-fighting equipment was stored in homes; schools conducted air raid drills; first aid classes were held and wardens stood guard over communications. The National Anthem was sung in theaters and at church services. On February 16, Navy officials called a meeting of tuna fishermen, who wanted to volunteer, and informed them that all boats suitable for service were to be taken into the Navy. More than 600 fishermen volunteered for service with their boats. Before the end of the month, fifty large tuna clippers were at sea to patrol against anticipated submarine attacks on the Panama Canal or as assigned to carry supplies between mid-Pacific islands.

The impact of the war in the Pacific soon began to shake people's confidence, especially when it was finally made public that 2,729 had been killed in the attack on Pearl Harbor, not just the several hundred that had been first announced. Rumors of what might actually have happened to the entire Pacific Fleet were fed by gossip brought to the mainland by evacuees from Hawaii. Stories also circulated that Japanese residents there had marked huge arrows in cane fields pointed toward military targets, that trucks had been used to block emergency roads, and that commercial fishermen had furnished supplies and gasoline to lurking Japanese submarines. In San Diego signs appeared everywhere: "Don't Gossip – the Enemy is Listening."

The City was considered safe from attack by land from the north because of the existence of the Army's Camp Callan on Torrey Pines and from the east by the mountains. To the south were the arid lands of Baja California with few roads. Only by sea could a blow be struck. The Coronado Islands were considered to be shields behind which enemy ships could approach the harbor by night to bombard installations or land a raiding force. The deep crevice in the ocean known as the La Jolla Canyon was considered an underwater passage available to submarines approaching from the northwest. The Coast Artillery mounted defensive guns at the Consolidated Aircraft plant but these units were relieved later by anti-aircraft forces from Texas and Georgia. Other guns were mounted along the southern beaches from Coronado to Imperial Beach. Anti-aircraft gun placements were dug into the hillsides of Point Loma and La Jolla Shores and concealed from view. Beaches were patrolled to thwart the landing of saboteurs.

Earl Warren

Fear of the unknown or unexpected fanned anew a resentment against Japanese which had lingered from the anti-Oriental attitudes which had in the past permeated many groups, particularly patriotic and farming organizations. The caution advised editorially by *The San Diego Union* vanished. On January 20, 1942, *The Union*, referring to the surprise attack on Pearl Harbor, stated editorially:

> "The treachery ... has been made a matter of record ... it has created a doubt in the minds of many persons in this country as to how far the Japanese who live here and are American citizens can be trusted."

Reluctance to move against the Japanese was still evident, however, in the action of the San Diego City Council. Instead of adopting a formal resolution it forwarded to the Federal Bureau of Investigation a report by one of its members, Fred W. Simpson, declaring that the presence of the Japanese was inimical to the best interests of the area. The City Council of National City demanded that Japanese be moved a hundred miles inland. The Councils of Chula Vista and La Mesa, however, refused to act. But anti-Japanese sentiments continued to mount. Action then was demanded by the League of California Cities and the California Association of Boards of Supervisors, the Congressional delegation on the West Coast, and a State Legislative Committee headed by Assemblyman Jack B. Tenney. The Board of Supervisors of San Diego County insisted that Japanese in Hawaii had aided the attackers and no one in California could distinguish between a loyal and a disloyal Japanese.

After a period of apparent indecision, the Attorney General of California, Earl Warren, a nominal Republican, made the rounds of all interested Federal agencies "trying to get some relief from this situation." In testimony before a Congressional committee holding hearings on the possibility of evacuation,

Aircraft detection instruments were mounted along the shoreline of California, and particularly off San Diego. Here is one "somewhere" on the California coast. A soldier warms his hands in sandbag dugout.

Warren stated:

> "Many of our people in other parts of the country are of the opinion that because we have had no sabotage and no fifth-column activities in this state since the beginning of the war, that means that none have been planned for us. But I take the view that that is the most ominous sign in our whole situation. It convinces me more than perhaps any other factor that the sabotage we are to get, the fifth-column activities, are timed just like Pearl Harbor was timed. ... If there were sporadic sabotage at this time ... the people of California or the Federal authorities would be on the alert to such an extent that they could not possibly have any real fifth-column activities when M-day comes."

General John L. DeWitt, military commander of the West Coast, said there was evidence that Japanese on the mainland already had been in radio communication with enemy ships. This was denied by J. Edgar Hoover, director of the Federal Bureau of Investigation. However, the director of the Federal Communications Commission acknowledged that personnel

Culbert L. Olson

and equipment on the West Coast were inadequate to assure detection of radio communications. Though the government of California at the beginning of war was a liberally-oriented one, no prominent voices were raised against evacuation. The Governor, Culbert L. Olson, a Democrat elected as a progressive, was certain that the Japanese would not report subversive activities of their own people because, he said, they had not done so as yet.

As February drew to a sad close, with more and more reports of defeats of the forces of the United States in the Pacific, a group of leaders of the Japanese-American Citizens League approved relocation and issued the following statement:

> "We are preparing our people to move without bitterness. We only jeopardize this country or our own people by trying to insist on staying or even by pursuing our legal rights as citizens."

The decision to re-locate them, however, was a military one. President Roosevelt signed an order authorizing the Secretary of War to establish military areas and to exclude from them, with no declaration of martial law, any or all persons. On March 1, General DeWitt proceeded to establish Military Area No. 1 and exclude all people of Japanese descent, both alien and citizen, but they were to remove themselves voluntarily. The Federal Reserve Bank in San Francisco was selected to assist Japanese in liquidating their possessions. By the end of the month, voluntary evacuation was abandoned in the face of refusal of many Japanese to leave and the reluctance of governors of Western states to accept their presence.

On April 1, almost four months after Pearl Harbor, a Civilian Exclusion Order announced that all Japanese aliens and citizens living south of the San Dieguito River would be removed. Within six days 306 family groups composed of 1,150 Japan-born Isei and American-born Nisei left San Diego by train, on April 7, bound for the Santa Anita racetrack near Los Angeles and then to be distributed to relocation centers in the interior. They were allowed to take only what they could carry in the way of daily necessities. About a month later a final group of Japanese from the North County boarded a train at Oceanside and left for Parker, Arizona. The special train carried 425 men, women and children, completing the evacuations. The total of evacuees from San Diego County was 1,919.

Carey McWilliams, then a State official and long-time spokesman for liberal causes, contended that in the long run the Japanese "will probably profit by this painful and distressing experience." Down through the years the defenders of Warren and McWilliams and other liberals who participated in bringing about the evacuation would argue that they acted in the interests of the Japanese themselves. A Japanese-American would argue the same way. He was S. I. Hayakawa, who came to California from the Midwest in 1950 and became president of San Francisco State University and then a United States Senator. He would write that if the war in the Pacific had gone against America, there would have been widespread anger and frustration and at best people would have beaten the Japanese in the streets, and at worst, they might have descended in mobs on Japanese communities, burning homes and killing people as had been done generations earlier with the Chinese.

The number of those evacuated throughout the state was 110,000, of which 70,000 were American citizens. As no general attack on the mainland took place, the question of loyalty was never put to a test, and allegations of sabotage in the Hawaiian Islands turned out to be false. Arguments against the evacuation centered on the fact that no such action had been found necessary in the Hawaiian Islands, where 35,000 Japanese were aliens and 124,000 others were American-born citizens, out of a total of 425,000 residents. But the Japanese had become so much a part of the economy of the Islands that to move them would have seriously crippled vital wartime functions.

The situation in Hawaii was investigated by the Institute of Pacific Relations and it concluded that it would have been manifestly impractical to transport 160,000 persons over 2,000 miles of water to isolated wartime camps on the mainland, and the Japanese were needed on the Islands as they constituted more than a third of all gainfully employed persons, including a half of all craftsmen, small farmers and fishermen, and operated a half of the retail food stores and restaurants.

The Hawaiian Islands were placed under martial law, all aliens considered dangerous removed, while others were free to come and go within certain limitations regarding travel and conduct. Japanese women laid away their kimonas, and commercial fishing ended.

Not all was peaceful, or fate accepted, in the internment camps in the United States. But by Thanksgiving leaders of the Japanese-American Citizens League were to send a telegram to President Roosevelt asking that their members be allowed to fight, and expressing the fear that relocation might become permanent and they would be confined like Indians on reservations.

While United States Cavalry patrolled the border and guarded nearby reservoirs, concern arose over the possibility of enemy use of airfields or bays of Baja California. Though Mexico had not declared war on Japan, the two naval bases and five airfields of Baja California were placed at the service of the United States, and a former president, General Lazaro Cardenas, was recalled from retirement to command the Pacific Zone. Troops in Baja California were reinforced, two battalions of 1,500 soldiers moving from Sonora through San Diego, by train, to Tijuana.

Early in January Presidents Roosevelt and Manuel Avila Camacho of Mexico had set up a United States-Mexico Defense Board and soon afterward Mexican aircraft began daily

One of the first military actions taken at San Diego was to protect the water supply, in particular the reservoirs lying near the border. Here cavalry from Camp Lockett is on patrol.

patrols from Cedros Island northward and Mexican gunboats aided in protecting minefields along the coast. Japanese farmers were moved inland from the coastal area.

After a conference in San Diego, on cooperation in defense, attended by General Cardenas, controls were placed on fishing activities in the Gulf of California and the Pacific Coast north of Mazatlan. Soldiers and volunteer militia were assigned to construct telephone and telegraph lines and roads in the peninsula.

Mexico's caution about entering the war vanished when two government-owned oil tankers were torpedoed in the Gulf of Mexico. On June 1, Mexico would join the United States in war against Germany, Italy and Japan.

Abelardo Rodriguez

The war seemed to erase all that was left of the troubled feelings that had existed along the United States border with Mexico as a result of the revolution which began in 1911. At one time 20,000 American soldiers patrolled the border from San Diego to Calexico and the Pacific Fleet stood by off Southern California. Tijuana was brought under attack by radicals, who were aided by United States citizens, but they were defeated by Mexican Army regulars. Later, United States forces directly intervened in Mexico by sea, to seize Vera Cruz, and by land from Texas. To Mexicans who never forgot that California and much of the Far West once belonged to them, the new actions were considered humiliating.

A National Guard regiment and artillery unit from Los Angeles were ordered to Calexico to guard the Colorado River water supply for Imperial Valley, which had to be diverted, at the time, through Mexican territory. What happened was recalled by a San Diegan, Lou Urquhart, then a lieutenant with the Guard. The governor of Baja California, Esteban Cantu, and Colonel Abelardo Rodriguez, later to become a governor and then a President of Mexico, posted crews with machine guns near Mexicali and opposite the Guard positions, presumably to resist any intervention. At a warning by Captain James G. Harbord, that he would use his artillery, Cantu and Rodriguez dismantled the gun emplacements and the chance of a direct clash was averted.

Juan Felipe Rico Islas

The era of cooperation between Mexico and the United States, initiated with Pearl Harbor, was extended into Baja California at the initiative of Commander Anderson, Public Information Officer of the Eleventh Naval District. General DeWitt, commanding the Western Frontier, would meet in Tijuana with his counterpart, General Juan Felipe Rico Islas, General de Division, Army of the Republic of Mexico. Mexican army officers would be treated at the Naval Hospital and Mexican fliers would train at the Naval Air Station. Contact would continue on an official and social basis, the latter through an organization known as "Mosqueteros de la Frontera" which attracted Army officers of Mexico and Navy and Marine Corps officers of the United States. Rodriguez later would maintain a second home in San Diego.

The Pacific Coast became one long defense line based in San Diego. In the City, factories engaged in war production were on 24-hour schedules and cafes and theaters never closed.

Streets were thronging with people coming and going at all hours of the night. Youths were drafted or volunteered, and disappeared into armed forces being distributed almost around the world. Other youths appeared in sailors' uniforms, serious and uncommunicative, survivors of the early losses in encounters at sea. Barrage balloons floated up on cables to entangle any invading aircraft.

In a ring of protection thrown around San Diego were barrage balloons designed to ensnare any invading airplanes in the earlier days of the war with Japan. They never met real action.

Forgotten were the old arguments of "geraniums vs. smokestacks," or whether the City should commit itself to seek industry at the expense of emphasizing its advantages for the attraction of tourists to enjoy the Winter climate and retired people who would buy the lands and homes which for generations had been a principal source of wealth. A staggering problem was rushing upon San Diego. The City might in the foreseeable future run out of water.

CHAPTER TWO

Water was life – and San Diego needed it. Under emergency efforts of the Navy, an aqueduct to bring Colorado River water was begun. It was a gravity flow line from the Metropolitan System and passed through a series of tunnels.

Water — the Real Key to a City's Survival

They continued to arrive by the thousands. And many of them would never forget a City bathed in the warm Southern California sun. Sailors and marines returning from battles at sea or from some fevered Pacific island could see, in the evening as their ships rounded Point Loma and headed for the inner harbor, the sun reflecting off the windows of buildings and homes on sloping hillsides. Above it all rose the friendly lights of El Cortez Hotel, a beacon high on the edge of the mesa and then the most dominant feature on the near horizon. Far behind it rose the mountains turning purple in the sunset.

To others away from home for the first time in their lives, and for the most part confined to military bases during training, the City they occasionally visited was merely a sea of busy people to whom a uniform was as common as a grain of sand. They would be glad to be away, to take their part in the great battles, or to endure lonely vigils at some distant place they had never heard of before. But they, too, would remember something, and many would return to make their homes.

San Diego was not a City locked up by severe Winters nor in Summer stilled by stifling heat. There were two bays, San Diego and Mission Bay, the latter undeveloped; miles of free beaches on wide ocean fronts; and Balboa Park, with its exquisite Spanish-Colonial buildings which had housed two expositions. The City's business, social and civic life still revolved around its tiny Horton Plaza on Broadway. On its streets one eventually met everyone else. The City's two largest department stores and chain department stores were in nearby blocks. Here were the theaters and the restaurants and the hotels. During the Great Depression financial institutions had largely drawn back to the center of the City. Most of its people lived on the broad mesa that rose a half mile back from the bay and stretched eastward from its great Balboa Park. Efforts to develop another section of the mesa, Kearny Mesa, cut off from the San Diego Mesa by the San Diego River and Mission Valley, had produced little results. Mission Valley itself was the location of dairies, some small farms and gravel and sand pits.

San Diego commanded a metropolitan area which included four smaller communities. To the east were La Mesa and National City. Before the war, the census of 1940 had given La Mesa a population of about 4,000 and El Cajon, a few miles further east, less than 1,500. To the south were National City and Chula Vista. National City had more than 10,300 and Chula Vista a little more than 5,000. Coronado, across the bay, had a population of 5,400. The only other incorporated communities in the County were Oceanside, with about 4,600, and Escondido, with about 4,500. The population in the unincorporated areas was less than 49,000. The total in the entire County was slightly less than 290,000.

By 1942, however, the civilian population of the City had grown to an estimated 276,000 and there were more than 390,000 residents in the County. San Diego had gone to war. Even the *National Geographic* magazine was impressed. An assistant editor, Frederick Simpich, wrote as follows, after a visit to the City:

> "Workers by thousands, and yet more thousands, swarm steadily in. More than four times as many are busy here now as there were soldiers in our regular Army when the Spanish-American war began. ... To shelter this ever-growing industrial army, Government scrapes down hills, lays miles of streets and water pipes, installs big sewage disposal plants, and builds not only rows and rows of houses, but whole new suburbs, complete with markets, movie houses, playgrounds, grassy lawns, and shrubbery. ... Old residents, pausing from golf or gardening, rub their eyes in sheer astonishment at all this colossal confusion."

The largest of the housing projects brought virtually a new town into being, Linda Vista, or "beautiful view," on Kearny Mesa. The name was bestowed on the project by the Works

Progress Administration at the suggestion of the San Diego Highway Association and several unmentioned individuals. There were to be 2,000 permanent homes, 1,000 temporary housing units, and 750 dormitories, over four square miles of the flat mesa. There were no garages or sidewalks. Linda Vista was dedicated by the wife of the President, Eleanor Roosevelt. The units were completed in 159 working days and the 14,000 persons who moved in protested that they had to go fourteen miles for a loaf of bread. A business section, schools and playgrounds followed quickly.

A virtual city was created when the Federal Government built Linda Vista as a wartime rush project. Much of it was permanent housing and became part of a northward expanding San Diego.

By 1944 there were all told twenty-three operating projects of more than 14,000 family units, and spaces for a thousand additional privately-owned trailers, which combined to provide shelter for 65,000 persons.

As far as many San Diegans were concerned, after the war the new arrivals could all go home, back to the cold Plains or the Deep South, or from wherever they came. There was a new saying in California, that "I'm here, now they can close the door."

But business men had other thoughts. There had come to

San Diego a civilian payroll which no one could have foreseen just barely ten years before. At a meeting called by the Chamber of Commerce and attended by all its directors and about a hundred other leading businessmen and industrialists, in December of 1941, a committee report was presented, which stated in part:

> "We have these industries and payrolls. Our business and economic life has been geared to them. Some say: 'Well, let them go, when the war is over.' We do not subscribe to that opinion. Do our merchants recall the 'business droughts' when the Fleet was away on maneuvers? The Fleet has now been away for more than a year. Who is it that lines our counters today? Who is going to occupy the thousands of homes, which were financed by local investors and financial institutions? Who will occupy the store buildings and offices and hotels – use the telephones, gas and electricity, ride the street cars, buses, trains and commercial planes – pay rentals – pay grocery, meat, milk and other bills? What of the City's water revenues?"

The Chamber committee answered its own questions and said it seemed "to us that we have no alternative than to bring about a retention of those payrolls and plan for the orderly development of a City and County to accommodate them." Hence, it recommended the naming of a new string of committees.

Chairman of the post-war committee itself was Philip L. Gildred and it included Donald E. Hanson, Albert G. Reader, Phil D. Swing, Walter B. Whitcomb, and with the Chamber's president, Hance H. Cleland, as ex officio member.

Think big, was the order of the day. One of the committee determinations was that San Diego should become a great air base as well as a great naval base:

> "The true possibilities and knowledge of the Pacific islands and China have been revealed by this war. Heretofore, except to a few individuals, they have been a mystery, and have hidden their secret. This war has revealed them as a storehouse – practically untouched. After the war there will result the opening of a vast development in these areas.
>
> "The China Clippers, or their modernized version, will operate on frequent schedules between the Pacific Coast ports and South and Central America, Mexico, Australia, China, and the Pacific islands. Large ocean-going planes with their freight-laden glider trains, will be a common sight... our geographical location makes us the natural United States port for trade with most of these areas."

At the top is the runway at Lindbergh Field and the adjoining plant of Consolidated Aircraft, taken before the war with Japan began. Below the runway and plant disappear in wartime camouflage efforts. The plant was covered with a netting while the runway was merely painted. Runway lights went on for monitored landings.

Who were the people coming to San Diego? In the language of the day, as reported from Washington, "the Joads and the Negroes are on the march. Abandoned shacks and half-empty villages along the main highways of the Deep South give mute evidence of the drift of population to northern and West Coast industrial areas."

The Census Bureau estimated that seventy-four percent of

San Diego's 165,000 wartime migrants came from outside the geographic region, the largest bloc coming from the west north central region and the west south central states. States in the first group included Minnesota, Iowa, Missouri, North Dakota,

Nebraska and Kansas. In the second group were Arkansas, Louisiana, Oklahoma and Texas.

The Census Bureau said that in the five congested areas of the West, San Diego, Portland-Vancouver, Puget Sound and San Francisco Bay, the Negro population grew from 107,000 in 1940 to about 228,000 in 1944. The President's Committee on Congested Production Areas estimated San Diego's Black population increased about forty-five percent, to about 7,500.

Big planes were rolling out of Consair, as Consolidated Aircraft was known, and the number produced and their departures were secret. The planes lifted off the City's municipal airport, Lindbergh Field, for England, Australia, Canada, the Netherlands Indies, or to American Army or Navy bases somewhere in the Western Hemisphere, or across the Pacific to Honolulu, Manila, Indochina or Singapore. Fear of a surprise raid on this huge plant, by a landing force from Japanese vessels, or from airplanes launched from carriers, resulted in the erection of a high concrete wall facing the plant along Pacific Highway and the spreading of a long camouflage netting across the highway and the plant. From the air, Consair disappeared from the scene.

The Marine Corps, which had been looking for some years for a West Coast training center, moved quickly to acquire the lands of the Santa Margarita y Flores Rancho which were situated in San Diego County. The ranch was an original Mexican land grant. A Federal Court condemnation order gave the Marines immediate possession, on July 9, 1942. The final judgment, ten months later, gave the Marines 121,387 acres for which they paid the estate and heirs the sum of $4,110,035. A number of acres was added in later years. It became known as Camp Pendleton. Here were trained the Marines who would make the landings on Pacific islands, and move bases for bombing planes ever closer to the heart of Japan.

The crews to land invading Marines were trained at a great new base on the Coronado Strand, the Naval Amphibious Training Base. Warbred landing ships could slip right onto shore. A field on Kearny Mesa, which the Navy had acquired long previously from the Army Air Corps, was put into service in 1943 for use by the Marines as an air supply and logistics center. It was called Miramar, which in Spanish means overlooking the sea. By 1945 it had two 6,000-foot runways and another of 3,000 feet. The Marines also acquired land in El Cajon Valley for training parachute jumpers and named it Gillespie Field in memory of Archibald M. Gillespie, a Marine captain who had participated in the United States seizure of San Diego from Mexico. The parachute training later was abandoned and the field became an auxiliary to the Marine Air Station at El Toro.

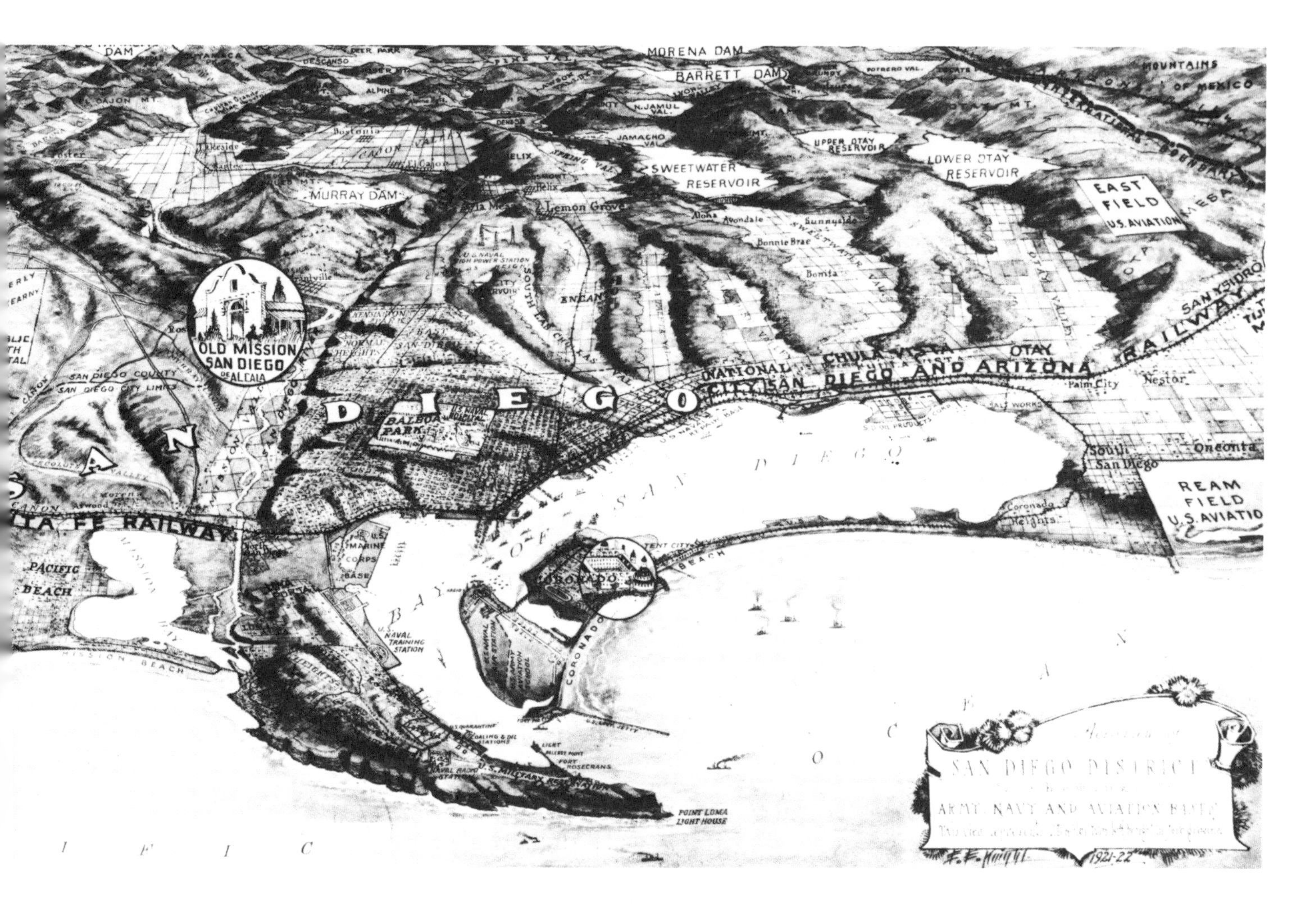

The Navy also moved onto a mesa to the south, creating an airport on Otay mesa named Brown Field after a Commander Melville S. Brown who had been killed in an air crash near Descanso. It had three runways and more than a hundred buildings. An auxiliary landing field for North Island at Del Mar, which had been owned by the Navy for many years, was converted into a field for lighter-than-air ships which patrolled the coast for submarines. The Navy's air arm also moved into active occupation of an old and virtually abandoned Army Air Corps auxiliary field in Imperial Beach which had been named in memory of Major William Roy Ream, the first flying surgeon to be killed in an aircraft accident. Other small and temporary fields and landing strips were in use throughout the County. The Navy also took over Camp Elliott, on Kearny Mesa, from the Marines, who were transferred to Camp Pendleton, and it became a personnel distribution center. Newly-filled land along the foot of Point Loma, created by dredging of the bay, was taken by the Navy for extension of the Naval Training Station.

This is the way it was, long before World War II. The San Diego River still emptied into Mission Bay and San Diego had not yet decided to build a major airport. When it did, it placed the airport on San Diego Bay. The Army Air Forces and the Navy still shared North Island; there was no Miramar airport; Brown Field was a practice landing strip on Otay Mesa and had not yet become a major field. The opportunity of the future was lost.

Fort Emory, an Army installation to supplement the guns of Fort Rosecrans in guarding the sea approaches to San Diego, rose north of Imperial Beach on the Silver Strand which closed in the port from the south and connected the mainland to Coronado and the Navy's air field on North Island.

The waterfront was being shaped by numerous wartime construction projects. The embarcadero was extended 3,000 feet to the vicinity of the Coast Guard Base; a $2,000,000 pier a thousand feet in length was constructed by the Navy near the foot of Broadway to serve the district Supply Depot, and almost $3,000,000 was being spent on a graving dock to accommodate cruisers as large as 10,000 tons, at what was then known as the Destroyer Base.

With so many new military establishments and thousands engaged in civilian war production, transportation in San Diego was chaotic for a time. Many street car lines had been abandoned during the Depression, the cars replaced with buses. It was too late to replace the power lines, to replace tracks or uncover those hidden under pavement, and the company scoured the nation for old buses and any street cars they could find to use on remaining tracks. Buses and cars were brought from Utah, Pennsylvania, and New York City, refurbished quickly, and put into service for the duration. They were crowded and often broke down, but to conserve rubber, with gasoline rationed only for necessary trips and pleasure driving a thing of the past, there was no other way to get around the City, its suburbs and adjoining communities. A report by the City Manager, Walter Cooper, said that street car and bus passengers increased from 2,306,518 in June of 1940 to 7,344,043 a year later.

Rationing boards were set up to control the distribution of food and some goods, as well as gasoline. Without a book of stamps a person was an alien in a controlled land. Manpower controls tied young workers eligible for the draft to vital war production. Zoning restrictions were eased to permit more than one family to occupy a home in single-family areas, or to take in boarders. Most of Balboa Park itself was still available for public use, including the expanding Zoo. The Zoo under its director, Belle Benchley, instituted emergency procedures to protect the 3,000 specimens and prevent their escape in advent of a bombing. Security guards were equipped with rifles and instructed to shoot if necessary. Gradually, as the first panic wore off, rules were relaxed and the Zoo became a place of pleasure for thousands of recruits and war plant workers. Permanent buildings, such as housed the Fine Arts Gallery, Natural History Museum and the Museum of Man in the California quadrangle, and

Belle Benchley

three other structures had been taken over by the Navy as auxiliary hospital units. Exhibits were removed or stored for the duration. The Naval Hospital, which before the war had been caring for about 1,200 patients, by the summer of 1945 was caring for an average of 8,000 patients a day. In December of 1944, the hospital and its auxiliaries had more than 12,000 ill or wounded men. Before the bombs fell Major Fleet had warned a civic group in San Diego that the nation already was in the war then – embracing so much of the world – and that "it will be a long war, and there are many of you here today whose sons will be killed before it is over."

Dimout regulations brought about the darkening of windows and the lowering of speed and dimming of headlights. One of the early victims of gasoline rationing was Major Fleet, the president of Consair, who lost his right to have gasoline for sixty days for exceeding the daytime speed limit of thirty-five miles an hour. The City's official rent control committee soon ordered that rents must be lowered to the level of January 1, 1941. Landlords were forced to refund $75,000 to tenants.

Though civilian flight operations at Lindbergh Field had become subordinate to the military, a City that once felt itself isolated by lack of adequate railroad passes through the mountains and the difficult highway crossings, now believed that once the war ended the City would be freed by the dynamics of the new air age. While it had lost the service of United Airlines, another major carrier, American Airlines began service to San Diego, linking it with the East, on the recommendation of the Secretary of the Navy, Frank Knox. At that time Western Airlines was operating two daily flights into Los Angeles for connections elsewhere. Within a year of its leaving San Diego, United had returned. But flying was on a priority basis. The hopes of those who had longed to see San Diego an important transportation and shipping terminal rose again. The Chamber of Commerce aviation committee said it was not too early to begin developing airline connections with the Orient, the South Pacific and South America. In fact, according to William Sample, Jr., San Diego representative for American Airlines, the only reason then that the City did not have direct service to Mexico City was that Army regulations prohibited night landings at San Diego.

Three decades before San Diego had staged the Panama-California Exposition, and built the grand array of Spanish-Colonial buildings in Balboa Park, in an effort to capitalize on completion of the Panama Canal. The supporters of the Exposition had expected San Diego to become the first port of call in expanded shipping from the East Coast. Instead, the opening of the canal had merely shortened the distance, and the ships had gone right on by to the larger commercial and metropolitan areas of Los Angeles and San Francisco. Rising air traffic due to the war gave new hope that San Diego could become, if not a shipping center by sea, an air terminus of international significance. But those high hopes had a temporary setback when the Civil Aeronautics Authority closed down the airport, shutting off all airline connections, on the grounds of airline complaints of a dangerously cluttered field and inadequate management by the Harbor Department. The airport remained closed for two weeks, until it was cleaned up and made safe for landings and takeoffs. The harbor director, Joseph Brennan, acknowledged the conditions but blamed the Army and its Air Corps.

During the latter stages of the war, the runway at Lindbergh Field was strengthened and lengthened, by the Federal Government, for a new generation of big planes coming off the assembly lines, and a news article hailed it as a wartime dagger pointed at the heart of Japan and a peacetime guarantee of San Diego's leadership in the air.

Rev. Dr. Howard B. Bard

A casualty of the times, in a long political struggle and then in the expending of energy in converting a City from peace to war, was Mayor Benbough, who died unexpectedly November 4, 1942, at the age of fifty-eight. He had surmounted all his enemies and had driven those who had opposed him from power. He had cleaned up the town and broken an alliance between a "blue-stocking" City Council and a City administration and Police Department which had contended that gambling and prostitution were natural and desirable in a City dependent so heavily on tourists and on a Navy enlisted personnel which at that time was composed largely of unmarried men.

A successor to finish out Benbough's unexpired term was selected by the Council. He was the Rev. Dr. Howard B. Bard, pastor of the First Unitarian Church and a spokesman for the City's more liberal forces. But the man who would succeed him and, too, gain power as a Mayor which was not defined in the City Charter, was sitting on the Council. He was Harley E. Knox, a dairy owner. In the election in the Spring of 1943 he was elected Mayor at the primary. Knox had been brought to San Diego by his parents in 1912, and after graduation from the old Normal Training School which had grown into San Diego State College, entered the dairy business in 1919 in Southeast San Diego. He had known the periods of drought and what they could do to San Diego. Short of stature, but determined in action almost to the point of pugnaciousness, he moved ahead in politics as in business, with singleness of purpose.

Harley E. Knox

Another who felt the weight of San Diego's wartime experience was the man who had done the most to make it a center of production for war, Major Fleet. Even before the attack on Pearl Harbor Fleet had become restless, even frustrated. War production experts were critical of his organizational setup and his management practices of making all decisions no matter how small or how large. They felt he stood in the way of faster assembly line operations. To a person of Fleet's individualism, the situation was an unhappy one, and furthermore, wartime taxes were eating up the returns of growth.

He was summoned to the White House, and, he later insisted, he presented his frustrations to President Roosevelt and agreed to sell out. He said he told the President that though he and his associates owned approximately eighty percent of the corporation when the wartime tax act was passed, and after more than eighteen years of successful efforts, their investment had turned into a "load of polls." Roosevelt decreed that the Army and Navy should select a buyer. Fleet agreed to remain as a consultant.

He sold a controlling interest to Vultee Aircraft, Inc., of Downey, California, which in turn was controlled by Aviation Corporation of America headed by Victor Emanuel, a director of Republic Steel. In 1942, Harry Woodhead, chairman of the board of Vultee, became president of Consair. The merger of the two companies into Consolidated Vultee, or Convair, was completed in 1943. Tom M. Girdler, chairman of Republic Steel Corporation, was the new chairman. I. M. Laddon, who had designed the B-24, had remained as had other executives.

Operations were expanded to thirteen divisions throughout the nation, and peak employment reached more than 100,000, far beyond the small operation which Fleet had moved to San Diego from Buffalo, N.Y., in 1935. For the "little" company which he had founded in 1924, and which had then a gross sale of $211,000, Fleet received almost $11,000,000 for his and family interests.

Between December 7, 1941, and the summer of 1945, Convair divisions delivered 28,000 completed aircraft and approximately 5,000 equivalent planes delivered as spares, for a total of 33,000. Included were B-24 Liberator bombers and C-87 Liberator Express transports, trainers, liaison planes, PBY Catalina and PB2Y Coronado flying boats and PBYA Privateer patrol bombers. The Convair plants at San Diego produced 6,724 B-24's; the plant at Fort Worth, 3,034. The total of B-24's produced, by Convair and other companies, including the Ford Motor Company's Willow Run plant, was 18,481.

War production reached a peak and in some cases was beginning to decline by mid-1944, with American successes in the Pacific and the Allied invasion of the European mainland. The great naval battle of the Leyte Gulf in the Philippines, fought and won by the American Third and Seventh Fleets, sealed the fate of Japan. The Allied invasion of Normandy began only about three and a half months later.

The defense of the West Coast had changed dramatically, from the first days of the attack on Pearl Harbor. Now there were seventy-five radar stations to alert defenses to any possible attack. The Fourth Air Force ranged far and wide. A million and a half civilians served as ground observers. And in the Pacific and European theaters, American air forces were winning control of the skies. Before the end of the year the defense system was slowly being dismantled. Before the end of the war,

More than 28,000 completed B-24 "Liberator" bombers were produced on assembly lines of Consolidated Aircraft. In San Diego plants, alone, 6,724 B-24's rolled off the lines and departed for fronts around the world.

not one radar station was in operation on the West Coast.

As their plight had become more desperate, the Japanese had taken to drifting large paper balloons across the Pacific and the wind currents took them mostly into northern areas of the West Coast where rain-dampened areas refused to burn when bombs carried by the balloons detonated. There were some civilian casualties, however. One balloon came down in San Diego County, near Scissors Crossing, in the desert area, but the bomb, though dragged over the ground and dislodged, did not explode.

The persistence of many Japanese in collective farms to prove their loyalty to the United States resulted in the creation of a special Army division, and former internees fought in Europe with distinction. But it was only in 1944 that the first internees were allowed to leave relocation centers for coastal areas.

Though it appeared that before long some rationing might be eased, newsprint was still tightly rationed and newspapers had suffered advertising and circulation reductions. Unexpectedly a Federal agency approved the transfer of newsprint from a free circulation newspaper for a new daily, and awarded it additional newsprint. Clinton D. McKinnon moved in 1944 to found the *San Diego Daily Journal* as a competitor for *The San Diego Union* and *The Tribune-Sun*, both owned by Ira C. Copley. The

The bleakness of life in internment centers is depicted in this painting by a Japanese artist and inmate of one of the camps. He was K. (Joe) Sugaya and he exhibited in La Jolla before the war.

reason advanced by the Democratic Administration was that San Diego was a hardship case because its two newspapers nominally spoke for Republicans, and the Democrats had no publication to speak for them.

In 1944 the population of the City was estimated to be more than 286,000, and that of the County, 609,000. The big year for building was 1941 when construction permits were valued at $51,000,000. Afterward they declined and by 1944 they amounted to about $8,000,000. But the pressure of the times merely shifted to another phase.

That San Diego might face a crisis in water became evident

as early as 1942. The rains were diminishing and a period of drought was unfolding. The net safe yield from the City's reservoirs and from pumping of underground supplies was considered to be 26,600,000 gallons a day. That is, San Diegans could use that much water every day without endangering the supplies which had to be maintained to last over an extended drought. But daily consumption on occasion rose to 47,000,000 gallons daily. In July of 1943, consumption reached 57,700,000 gallons a day. Reservoirs were now only a little more than sixty-four percent full, compared with more than eighty-two percent the year before. The rains failed to come in October and then the rains that did come later fell in the wrong places and much water was lost to the sea or to unreachable underground storage.

The experiences of almost a century had taught that enough water had to be stored to last perhaps seven years. The year 1939 had been a wet season and the City's reservoirs almost filled to capacity, and in some cases, at Hodges and El Capitan dams, planks and sandbags had been laid across the spillways to prevent unnecessary losses. Water had seemed to be so plentiful that the residents had forgotten history and had rejected proposals to build another storage reservoir, San Vicente, on a tributary of the San Diego River, and expand distribution facilities. However, voters did ratify a contract to acquire rights to have the City's share of Colorado River water to be delivered through the All-American Canal to the base of the mountains, from where in time it could be lifted up and dropped down to San Diego.

But the City had grown so fast since 1939 that distribution facilities, as had been warned, proved inadequate and daytime watering was banned in sections of the City, particularly in Mission Hills, Point Loma and La Jolla. Another year passed and then the voters quickly approved $3,000,000 to build San Vicente dam and $1,300,000 for additional distribution facilities.

However, Samuel B. Morris, dean of engineering at Stanford University, and the City's chief consultant on water problems, urged the immediate drawing of plans to bring Colorado River water to San Diego. The water report of 1937 had shown that if all of the possible sources of water available to San Diego were developed, with full conservation, the practical yield would only be 51,300,000 gallons a day. And more than that amount was being used already, on occasion, and a dry period was now in full swing, and there wouldn't be time enough to build the reservoirs even if it could be assured they would be adequate.

It was clear to almost everyone now that the land no longer could support the number of people who wanted to live there.

No matter how many dams were built to store the runoff of inconstant rivers, or how much could be pumped from the vanishing underground reservoirs, there still would not be enough water to support a life built on hopes of ease and opportunity. But the Colorado River itself was being called the "last water hole in the West."

The City could wait no longer. Without more water there would be no shining city. San Diego was like the pueblos of New Mexico shining in the desert sun and which had lured Spaniards northward on a search for fabled cities of gold. But the pueblos, on approaching them, proved not to be burnished with gold but made of adobe which did reflect a desert sun.

The drift of white-capped sailors up Broadway became a tide during World War II, and afterward, as this later photo suggests. Hundreds of thousands of young men passed through the City, and many of them returned.

Would San Diego also prove to be a mirage to those who had seen it shine so invitingly in the warm Southern California sun, and had vowed to return some day? Would it be a City limited in growth? It would be, without water from afar.

In California, growth had been accepted as a fact of life. Only the retired, who existed on limited incomes, had resisted the idea of ever-rising land values and the building of dams and roads to meet the continuing demands of new arrivals. A limit to growth had not been a part of the philosophy of the Americans who since the Civil War had joined a Westward movement which saw the quick founding of new towns, and the moving on again, until the shores of the Pacific at last turned the tide

Fred Heilbron

Phil D. Swing

back on itself.

Fred Heilbron, a plumbing contractor by trade; Phil D. Swing, an attorney specializing in water law; and Harley Knox, a Mayor who liked to say that he had arrived from across the tracks, had one thing in common: they knew that water was the key to San Diego's future. They had known San Diego in the drought. And they did not believe, as did so many late comers, that the riches of Southern California came naturally. The real estate promoters liked to speculate on what would have happened if the Pilgrims had landed in California instead of Massachusetts. Their answer, of course, was that civilization would have gone no farther, that the European migrants would have been content to stay and that the Indians would still hold Manhattan Island. But to picture the Southern California seacoast as it would have appeared to the Pilgrims and actually appeared to the Spanish settlers, one had to take the present landscape and make some erasures. The palm trees would have to go. So would the oranges, the lemons, and almost all of the trees and shrubs that stayed green in the summer. To be sure there were Golden Live Oaks and willows in the canyons, but the native inhabitants had done nothing to alter the land. They had lived in ecological innocence, killing small game, collecting clams and gathering seeds. They moved, prospered and died off according to natural fluctuations. It was the Spaniards who introduced the trees and plants which were to so mark Southern California. The Spaniards' greatest innovation was irrigation. When added to the California sun, water was the ingredient that eventually made it possible to support concentrated populations.

But Spaniards made no attempt to supply water for commercial agriculture; that remained for the Americans to do. Ever since, however, it had been a race to find enough water to keep pace with the demand. Swing, Heilbron, and then Knox, understood this. The future of San Diego was across the mountains. They knew also that the military services were using almost half of the water San Diego had managed to obtain through costly pumping and the acquiring of expensive reservoirs. The military services were paying for what they used; but money meant nothing when water was being used up faster than it could be replaced.

The Water Report of 1937 had stated that of the two ways San Diego could bring in its share of Colorado River water, the cheapest would be to take it from the All-American Canal, lift it by pumps over or through the mountains at 2,700 feet, and then deliver it to the City's reservoirs by gravity flow. This would have cost, by the estimates of the times, $8,650,000. To bring it through the Colorado Aqueduct of the Metropolitan Water District, controlled by Los Angeles, and then deliver it to San Diego by a separate gravity-flow aqueduct, would cost at least $17,000,000, and perhaps much more, when all costs of joining the Metropolitan District and sharing its prior expenses were considered. San Diegans preferred the All-American Canal route, but the City and County joined in asking the Federal Government for a new study on comparative costs.

In 1943 a legislation drafted by Swing and approved by the State Legislature provided for the creation of county water authorities, and the San Diego County Water Authority consisting of nine public agencies was organized in 1944. It included the Cities of San Diego, Chula Vista, Coronado, National City, Oceanside, and the Fallbrook, Helix, Lakeside, and Ramona irrigation districts. Heilbron, a City Councilman from San Diego, was elected its first chairman.

The U. S. Bureau of Reclamation warned publicly that it would be foolhardy for San Diego, or Washington for that matter, to rely on a continuation of the favorable conditions of the past four years. San Diego already was aware that the rains were decreasing. The Navy intervened. Rear Admiral W. L. Friedell, Commandant of the Eleventh Naval District, and Captain Alden K. Fogg, District Public Works Officer, asked for Federal assistance in bringing Colorado River water to San Diego in the shortest possible time. Secretary of the Navy James Forrestal concurred. As a result President Roosevelt appointed an interdepartmental committee to present recommendations. The committee included representatives of the Bureau of Reclamation, War Department, Navy Department, Federal Works Administration, and the San Diego County Water Authority. One of its members was Swing, then general counsel for the San Diego Water Authority. As a former Congressman for the San Diego-Imperial Counties district, he had been co-author of the Swing-Johnson bill which had brought about construction of Boulder Dam and the control of the Colorado River, and the digging of the All-American Canal which had assured the prosperity of the Imperial Valley. Walter W. Cooper, San Diego's City Manager, was named a consultant. Before becoming Manager, he had been a consultant on public utilities. Cooper's role in the struggle for water was to be a limited one, as he was killed in the crash of an airliner approaching the Burbank airport in the San Fernando Valley, while returning from Sacramento. Mayor Knox was injured but recovered. To succeed Cooper, the City Council selected Fred A. Rhodes, at the time Director of Public Works, who had served before as City Manager and also as Manager of Operations.

Fred A. Rhodes

In October of 1944 the President's committee issued its report. It stated that the Colorado River offered the only available source from which an adequate and dependable supplemental water supply could be obtained and that the route by way of the Metropolitan Water District was preferable to the All-American Canal route in that it would be a gravity system requiring a minimum of critical materials, and could be completed in two years.

This meant that San Diego would have to merge its rights to Colorado River water with those of the Metropolitan District, and tap its Colorado aqueduct on this side of the mountains. While this would bring 50,000,000 gallons daily to San Diego, the report stated, the necessary tunnels should be built to provide for eventual delivery of twice that amount. Best of all, the report recommended that the delivery system be financed entirely by the Federal Government as a safeguard to Federal activities in the area, with seventy percent of the estimated cost to come from the Navy Department, ten percent from the War Department, and twenty percent from the Federal Works Agency. The Navy would be the contracting agency.

On November 29, President Roosevelt sent a message to the Senate advising that he had recommended that construction begin immediately. But the matter was not yet settled. A representative of the War Production Board visited San Diego, studied the situation, and indicated to Mayor Knox that he thought in view of the progress of the war San Diego could survive through the final years by a system of water rationing. After that, it would not be Washington's problem. He departed for Washington by train. Knox got to Washington ahead of him by air, and began a round of arguments that the Federal Government could not afford to abandon the City to its fate. The Spring of 1945 came and the War Production Board, unmoved, formally interposed objections to construction of the aqueduct on grounds of material and manpower shortages. Under pressure, it later recommended a year's delay. But a series of conferences in Washington finally resulted in an agreement to begin construction in ninety days, instead of waiting a year. The Navy assumed the task and contracts for construction of the Poway, Fire Hill and San Vicente tunnels were let on May 18, 1945. Construction started on September 12.

For those who were required to look even farther into the future, the Colorado River might not be the "last waterhole" for California and particularly for vulnerable San Diego. This became evident in the long, drawn-out struggle over division of its water and the rights of Mexico.

After years of debate and argument, the water of the Colorado had been divided by compact between Upper and Lower Basin states. The division had assumed that the annual flow of the river would amount to 18,000,000 acre feet and therefore a total of 7,500,000 acre feet was awarded to each basin, with the Lower Basin having an eventual right to an additional million acre feet of the surplus or unapportioned flow. This took care of 16,000,000 of the anticipated annual flow of 18,000,000. Time was to prove that the flow had been seriously over-estimated.

With the construction of Boulder Dam, and the regulation of the river's flow, Mexico had moved to firm up its rights to water from the Colorado. Before the building of Boulder Dam, Mexico used only 750,000 acre feet a year. Under wartime secrecy a United States treaty was drawn which granted to Mexico a right to 1,500,000 acre feet a year, in exchange for water for Texas from the Rio Grande and an agreement to discuss division of the flow of the Tijuana River as it passed through San Diego County. The State Department, when the treaty finally was made public, hailed it as an important step in the Good Neighbor Policy with Latin America. California officially reacted with anger and dismay, charging that in view of an over-estimation of the flow, such a large diversion to Mexico would in the end have to come from water it had expected to use sometime in the future.

Mexico had increased its use since the construction of Boulder Dam to about 1,500,000 acre feet a year, but insisted this amount could have been used at any time if crops other than seasonal cotton had been planted in the past in the delta. California insisted that Mexico should be limited to the amount used before the building of the dam.

Sheridan Downey

In 1921, Fred Heilbron, as a member of the City Council, had successfully urged San Diego City to stake a claim on the river. A legal claim in a can was placed on the bank of the river and marked with a stick and flag. By this act San Diego acquired a right to use 113,000 acre feet a year. Though the amount seemed relatively small, it could prove vital to the future, but in the view of San Diegans it was placed in jeopardy by Mexico's own claim.

Secretary of State Dean Acheson defended the treaty as being in the interest of the comity of nations. California's two senators, Sheridan Downey and the aging Hiram Johnson, fought its ratification to the end.

Hiram Johnson

Proponents of the treaty were led by Sen. Tom Connolly, a Democrat of Texas, who wanted to trade off Colorado River to Mexico in exchange for additional water for Texas from the Rio Grande. But California felt betrayed by the opposition of Upper Basin states. Senator Eugene Millikin, a Republican of Colorado, charged that California had "gambled for water rights that do not now exist," and the State had doled out allocations of Colorado River water to which full rights had not been established and to which Mexico, under the Colorado River Compact, must have first claim.

Though conscious that he was fighting a losing battle, Senator Sheridan Downey, a Democrat of California, who had entered the Senate after bowing to political demands of a welfare scheme called "Ham & Eggs," became the champion of California and doggedly and persistently fought a Democratic State Department every step of the way. He accused the United States International Boundary Commissioner of not having made "a fair and decent" investigation of irrigated lands below the border on which Mexico based her claim and "deliberately tried to mislead the Senate Foreign Relations Committee."

Johnson, who had only a short time to live, rose in the Senate and insisted that there was no difference between taking of land and the taking of water. Referring to the pioneers of Imperial Valley, he cried out, "I implore the Senate, I beg the Senate, to give them a square deal, rather than reach over into Mexico and give Mexico a square deal."

The Senate vote for ratification was seventy-six to ten. The vote came on April 18, 1945, less than a week after the death of President Roosevelt and the succession of Harry S Truman. Truman obviously was anxious to see the treaty passed as quickly as possible. Another "last waterhole" would have to be found.

In the death of Roosevelt San Diego lost a President who since his early political days, as an Assistant Secretary of the Navy, had made himself aware of San Diego's problems and had made many of the decisions which converted the City into a great naval establishment. His death and the end of the war would pose another problem in water for San Diego.

CHAPTER THREE

WALKERS
AIRCRAFT
EMPLOYMENT
1023 4TH AVE. TAKE ELEVATOR
BOWLING
CUT RATE
DRUGS
FURN
LIP
HOT
DENT

This was the day when news came of the end of the war with Japan. It is VJ Day in San Diego, on Broadway, looking east. What little confetti, or stock ticker tape, San Diegans could muster flutters to the street, and crowds and autos make movement uncertain.

Peace — the Shock of a Transformation

The approach of the end of the war had turned the thoughts of many San Diegans back to the great plans of the past. Interest in them was revived by the possible necessity of undertaking civic improvements long delayed or still in the realm of visionary concepts.

But at the same time there was ferment in the community over the future as to whether it had been wise to place emphasis on "geraniums" as against "smokestacks," that is, on recreation and tourists as against commerce and industry, or even if progress, as defined by frontier standards, should be left to chance, or even whether growth should be discouraged as desired by so many retired persons who had sought out the little City by the bay for its natural beauty and serenity.

But those who had a larger economic stake in the community, its growth and subsequent commercial rewards, the attraction of tourists and conventions seemed to hold the solution to progress, especially if the end of the war brought about an anticipated drastic decline in aviation manufacturing and related industries which had expanded so dramatically since 1940.

San Diego had no basic resources, other than agriculture and fishing, on which to enter the consumer market. Not long after the turn of the Century, the city planner from New England, John Nolen, had described the kind of a city San Diego could be, if its people wanted it. By nature, he contended, San Diego was a play City:

> "The scenery is varied and exquisitely beautiful. The great, broad quiet mesas, the picturesque canyons, the bold line of the distant mountains, the wide hard ocean beaches, the great Bay, its beauty crowned by the islands of Coronado; the caves and coves of La Jolla, the unique Torrey Pines, the lovely Mission Valley – these are but some of the features of the landscape that should be looked upon as precious assets to be preserved and enhanced. ..."

He could see a "City Beautiful" centered on the bay and connected with Balboa Park by a Prado a block wide and beautified with trees, flowers, terraces and splashing fountains. Public buildings would be in the central City grouped around a plaza also connected with the bay by another tree-lined avenue.

Many San Diegans were never to forget, though nothing much came of it at the time. It was too much to expect of a struggling City with a population of about 33,000.

After the passage of about eighteen years, Nolen was summoned to San Diego again, under the urging of the merchant George W. Marston, and produced another plan for civic development, and with the City approaching a population of 150,000.

This time Nolen proposed grouping public buildings on the waterfront, instead of around a downtown central plaza; the completion of a broad avenue around the harbor to the tip of Point Loma, and the division of the waterfront and bay into commercial and recreational areas. While he abandoned the concept of a single broad Prado connecting the bay and Balboa Park, he suggested there could be several attractive and narrower connecting parkways.

While he did recommend historical restorations in Old Town, he did not envision possibilities in Mission Bay and believed that the San Diego metropolitan area should expand southward along the broad flat lands leading to the International border, rather than northward where he thought the topography was unsuitable. The coastal land was broken by deep cuts and valleys and La Jolla clung to an almost secluded shoreline area. But this was in the days before the great earth-moving machinery developed during World War II.

A City Council, appreciative but not necessarily enthusiastic, adopted the new plan in 1928, not as a program to which the City was committed, but as a guide for the future.

During the Great Depression of the 1930's, San Diego had

seized the opportunity to begin work on some aspects of the Nolen Plan, with Federal financing, and a City and County Administration building had risen on the waterfront, the first, it was anticipated, of a line of public buildings facing the bay and the sea, in the manner of a number of European and Latin American cities.

However, the positioning of other public buildings, and the opposition of interests on the bay more concerned over commerce than recreation, stirred controversies which left the City

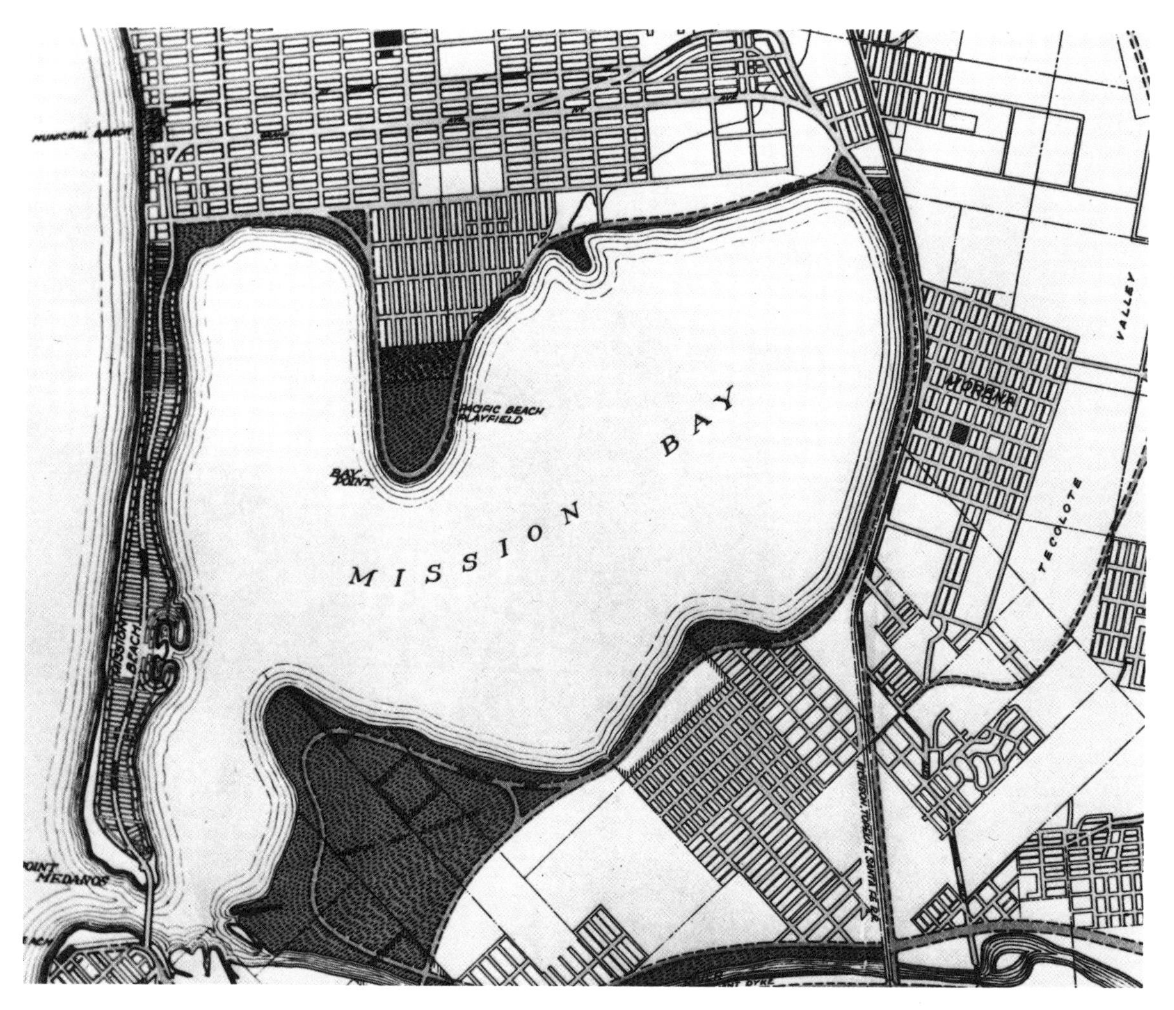

and County Administration building standing by itself, a lonely monument to public indecision.

Mission Bay looks attractive and orderly here. This is how it looked, on paper, to John Nolen, the city planner, who did not predict a future for the bay though he did urge a round-the-bay scenic road.

Though Nolen had not expressed any interest in Mission Bay, except for a view highway, a suggestion that it could be developed into an aquatic park had been made as far back as 1902, before Nolen ever arrived in San Diego, by the County's Horticultural Commissioner, George P. Hall, who had made a study for the Chamber of Commerce on the need for more public parks. Mission Bay had been neglected and even damaged by the concentration on the development of San Diego Bay as the commercial port of entry.

An estuary of the Pacific Ocean, Mission Bay in the early 1940's was a shallow, protected body of water of 2,600 acres, with a shoreline of approximately eleven miles. When the tide was low, only a small portion of the bay was usable even for small boats.

Historically, over great periods of time, silt carried by flood waters of the San Diego River had created two bays where one once had existed, by the filling in of the water area between Old Town and Point Loma. Then the river had changed its course alternately over the centuries, sometimes flowing into San Diego Bay, sometimes into Mission Bay.

Mission Bay really looked like this, before development took place. This photo was taken from the air in 1935 and the shoals and narrow waterways are clearly visible. An old causeway leads to a Crown Point not yet fully settled.

The depositing of silt into San Diego Bay became a threat to future development and in 1853 the Army Corps of Engineers under Lieutenant George Derby erected the first dike, to divert the flow of the river permanently into Mission Bay and thus save San Diego Bay. This effort failed within two years. In 1875 Congress appropriated funds to try again, and a long levee was completed two years later, and this time, it held. But the silting up of Mission Bay accelerated. In succeeding years the interest in doing something about saving Mission Bay, from being converted from a still partially usable body of water into a mud flat, persisted.

It wasn't until 1925, however, that the potential of the Mission Beach area as a resort area was beginning to be accepted.

The Spreckels interests had acquired much of the strip between Mission Bay and the ocean, and built a $4,000,000 amusement center. John D. Spreckels foresaw a "Venice of America," but with his death a year later his heirs and business associates began disposing of his properties. The Amusement Center was given to the City of San Diego.

Jurisdiction over the bay itself, however, rested with the State of California, and in 1929 the Legislature designated it as one of the State's seventy-two parks. In 1930 the City prepared a suggested master plan for development of the bay and though no immediate action was taken, interest persisted and the plan was modified from time to time.

The marshes of Mission Bay provided food for shorebirds and other aerial passersby. It was a somewhat lonely land, still, in 1951. The hills are vacant and the City can be glimpsed in the far distance, at the right.

The advisability of a definite development policy was stressed in 1935 by William H. Harper, a member of the State Planning Board. In 1940, Frank Seifert of San Diego, an Army Air Corps major, proposed that instead of thinking of all the mud flats area for recreational use, San Diego should consider the south side as the site for a new international airport.

Seifert was a former Councilman who had been recalled to military service, but he appeared before the City Council as a private citizen. He foresaw limitations on the use of Lindbergh Field, with the advent of larger and heavier passenger airplanes, and said an airport with mile-long runways could be developed by dredging the west side of Mission Bay and using the sand to

John D. Spreckels

Glenn C. Rick

fill in the southern marshes. The response was enthusiastic for a time but nothing came of the proposal, and the airport issue was to remain a City problem for at least another generation.

The principal figure in the future of Mission Bay, however, was Glenn C. Rick, the City's Planning Director, who had submitted the first suggested plan of development in 1935. With the advent of World War II, and with knowledge of the economic situation that might confront San Diego at its close, with the heavy loss of industrial payrolls, Rick, Mayor Knox and other San Diegans in official and civic life believed that recreation facilities and attraction of tourists could help assure a future of growth and prosperity. In April of 1945, with the winding down of the war, the State Legislature was induced to transfer 2,600 acres of Mission Bay tidelands to the City. In that same month, the voters of San Diego approved a $2,000,000 bond issue for Mission Bay, to begin work on a land and water recreational area. The City also pledged $1,500,000 from capital outlay funds.

Mayor Knox asked twenty civic organizations to designate representatives for an advisory board for Mission Bay, and sent Rick on a trip along both the Pacific and Atlantic coasts to inspect similar areas for ideas for development. Rick also conferred with the Army Corps of Engineers on assuming responsibility for changing the course of the San Diego River, to empty directly into the Pacific Ocean instead of into Mission Bay.

The concept of Mission Bay was different from that which would be held later. In a sketch prepared to introduce the voters to what Mission Bay could become in the years ahead, there were no hotels or motels shown but there was a small airplane landing strip and a ball park. The drawing also included a golf course, aquarium, nursery, a marine stadium, bathhouse and stables and bridle paths. There was room on shore and water for large and small yachts, rowing, sailing and power boat courses, and swimming and picnic areas. A research report to the Chamber of Commerce went even further and proposed Mission Bay as a site for professional football and baseball, for hotels and skating rinks, and perhaps even a Farmers' Market.

In his support of the Mission Bay project, Mayor Knox said its potential was superior to that of Newport Harbor, seventy miles to the north, which was serving Los Angeles:

> "This is a post-war project for which the groundwork should be started now. The sooner it is begun, the sooner San Diegans, and the unnumbered thousands of visitors attracted when peace comes, will be able to enjoy it. ..."

LET'S PUT IT TO WORK FOR US

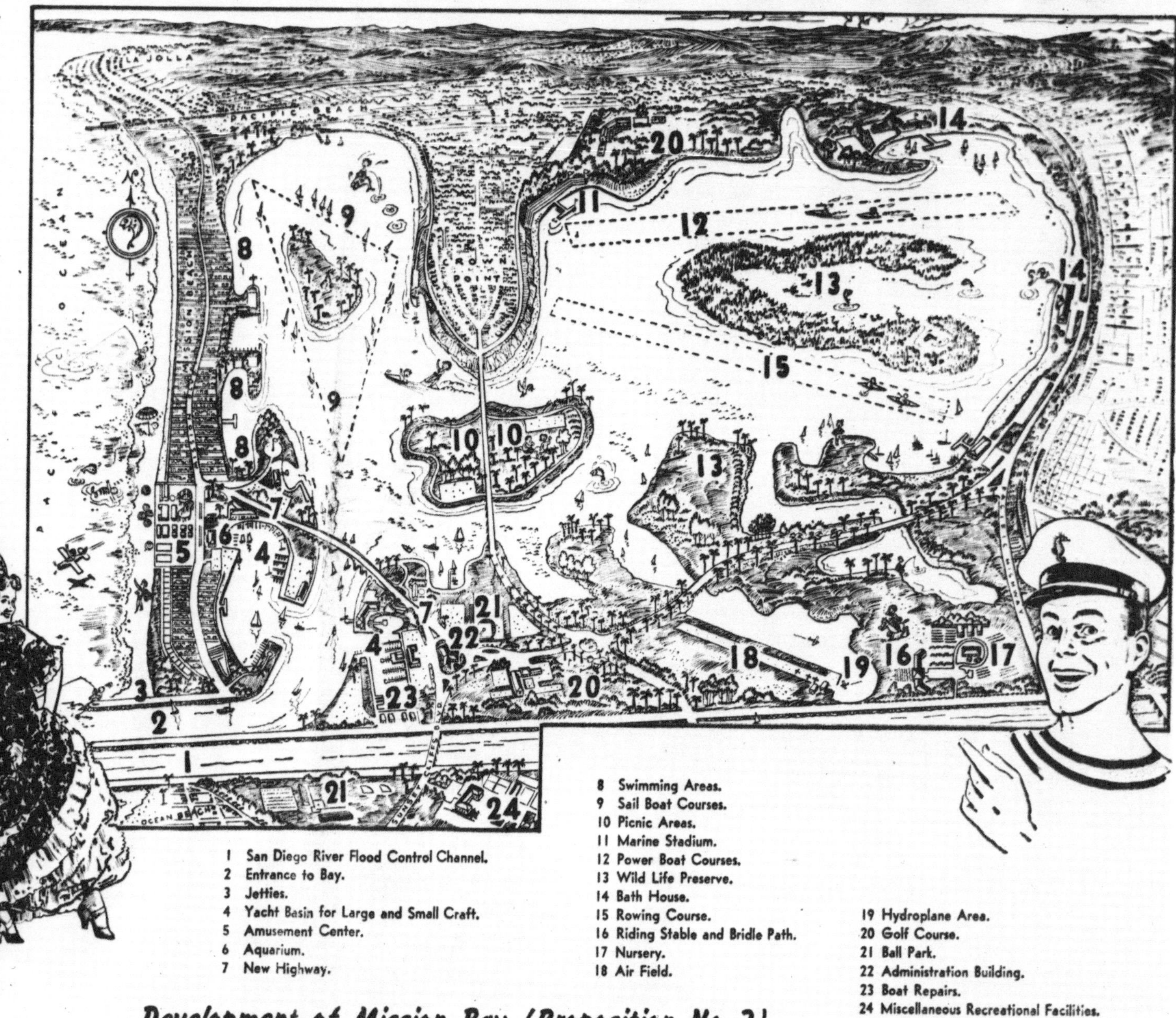

Development of Mission Bay (Proposition No. 2)

Even before the war ended, San Diego was looking to its future. This is the advertisement which helped to "sell" Mission Bay development as a post-war project, as a source of pleasure and a lure for tourists.

Roscoe E. Hazard

A large block of land in the southeast area of Mission Bay, on both sides of what became Midway Drive, was held by Roscoe E. Hazard, the highway building contractor, who with two partners had purchased 500 acres in the early 1920's. The founder of Grossmont, William G. Gross, had traveled the world and had assured Hazard he, too, believed that Mission Bay someday would become the "Venice of America." It was Mayor Knox who approached Hazard about selling the land to the City; it was done, at a price of $300 an acre, the same figure at which it had been purchased so long before. Though some pieces were selling for $6,000 an acre, most of the land was marsh land and tax delinquent, and acquired by the City through condemnation proceedings.

The enthusiasm for recreational development was not shared by all. Harry Woodhead, president of Convair, warned that it could be foolhardy for San Diego to revert to its pre-war dependence on the Navy and tourism, and compared its situation to that of Western "Ghost Towns" which had placed dependence on narrow groups and undependable resources.

"For San Diego," he told the Chamber of Commerce, "is in reality two communities – a haven of rest and a City of opportunity." He urged greater efforts on industrial programs and said as for Convair it was in the airplane business to stay and that it was producing for today and designing for tomorrow and San Diego owed also an obligation to provide opportunities for its youth. He was telling San Diegans, once again, that they could have it both ways, "geraniums" as well as "smokestacks," and learn to live with it in harmony. Industry was in San Diego to stay – and it represented the new technology, not the industrialism based on coal or ore or oil, or in close proximity to them.

But before the bay could be used it had to be saved. A program of development proposed the creation of a wide flood channel to divert the San Diego River directly into the ocean, near the mouth of Mission Bay, and thus avert further silting up of the bay. Subsequent steps called for dredging of the entrance, construction of protecting rock jetties, dredging of a harbor for ocean-going craft and further dredging to accommodate perhaps 6,000 small boats; to use sand from dredging to fill in 1,000 acres of marsh land to create new beaches and recreational areas.

Arguments of just how this was to be accomplished, and how to divide the bay between recreational-minded users and boating enthusiasts, was to continue for years. But the City went to Congress for endorsement of the recommendations of the United States Army Corps of Engineers for dredging operations based on flood control and navigational provisions of laws of the land.

For almost as many years as there had been interest in devel-

oping Mission Bay, Old Town had been the subject of concern, with its ancient and historic structures slowly crumbling away. George W. Marston had purchased the old site of the first settlement in California on Presidio Hill, and had converted it into a park which he presented to the City, along with a museum building. Nolen's interest in Old Town was echoed by Glenn Rick, the Planning Director, and the Planning Commission. Before the war had ended, a planning consultant, Charles H. Eliot, had been hired and he came up with a suggested program of preservation, and the merchant, George A. Scott, became chairman of a Chamber of Commerce committee which threw its support behind the Eliot plan, as it became known. The Eliot plan would have safeguarded historic sites as living museums; encouraged the construction of buildings in the style of Early California; developed crafts and home industries of that period in order to create a "colorful atmosphere of res-

The historical and tourist values of Old Town were recognized early, and the Eliot Plan was drawn up even before the end of the war. This is how the central plaza area would have been developed. But funds were lacking and landowners could not agree.

taurants, theaters, dance, fiestas, etc., which would attract tourists, and at the same time recognize the cultural contribution of Early California – Spanish-Mexican backgrounds to San Diego, to California, and to the nation." He suggested this could be accomplished through the cooperation of the City, the San Diego Historical Society, and private groups and church organizations.

The war in Europe came to an official end on May 8, 1945. President Truman ordered atomic bombs dropped on Japan in August, and San Diego turned to concern over its future as another V-Day, in the Pacific, approached. The end had been foreseen, economically, some time before by the National Administration. Convair's work force had been reduced to less than 14,000. By the end of the war, nearly forty percent of the workers at Convair were women. Two years before, when the bombing fleets were being rushed off the assembly lines, Convair had had 44,000 employees. Convair hoped to stabilize its work force at about 10,000, when readjustments were completed. Rohr Aircraft, specializing in aircraft components, had reduced its work force of 9,500 to less than 2,900, and thought through mergers it might manufacture refrigerators and washing machines as well as aircraft parts. Solar Aircraft was certain it had a future in aviation in continuing to build its heat-resistant exhaust manifold systems.

With the beginning of the war Ryan aircraft became a producer of parts for the Convair B-24 and the PYB, under military pressure, and it was not until 1942 that Ryan received a secret contract to develop the first Navy fighter with a jet engine. The Fireball came off the line in 1944, jet-pushed and propeller-driven, capable of flying on either engine. In December of 1943 came an order for one hundred Fireballs; 600 more were ordered subsequently. The end came before the new Ryan Fireball fighter for the Navy could get into action. Employment dropped drastically, from 8,500 to 1,200. Search for new business to keep the company alive led Ryan into a short-lived manufacturing of metal burial caskets.

The most hard-hit shipyard was considered to be the Concrete Ship Constructors, at National City, which had employed 1,700 persons in turning out landing craft which no longer would be needed. There were possibilities in the construction of new and larger tuna fishing boats, or reconverting those which had been on wartime duty.

In all, perhaps 30,000 more jobs were expected to evaporate with the end of hostilities. At the time, San Diego had no way of knowing the future of the many military establishments in the area, as to which ones might merely be reduced and which ones eliminated. One thing was certain, the sea of white caps which had flowed through the City's streets would remain for some time, as the Navy returned thousands of men to San Diego for demobilization.

Hance H. Cleland

The business leaders of San Diego considered that the stakes were high — a more stabilized and yet prosperous City for those who remained, or a City brought to a state of economic collapse. In the Chamber of Commerce offices, its president, Hance H. Cleland, and its general manager, Douglas Campbell, early in the war had poured over statistics and had come up with a publication that warned San Diego businessmen they were entering a game which had to be played with gold chips. If they wanted the new industrial capacity used in a beneficial way, and assure jobs for all who wanted them, San Diego would have to attract new industry and new commerce.

Japan signed the articles of surrender on September 12. The war was over. Only a few persons in the aviation industry could see the beginning of a new age of jet aircraft that could span the nation in a few hours. Almost nobody had any knowledge of a scientific team which in a corner of the huge Convair plant was working on a government contract to determine if the missiles which the Germans had introduced as buzz bombs or the rockets which had been developed in the United States, could be designed to travel 5,000 miles.

The end of the war, however, did not immediately bring about as great a depression locally as had been feared. Though by 1946 employment in aircraft and aircraft parts manufacturing had declined to less than 8,000, payrolls in industry as a whole dropped only about a third from the war-time high of $311,000,000. Population in the City actually rose by more than 42,000, to 362,000, though the total in the County declined almost 80,000 from the 1945 high of 635,000. The Chamber of Commerce estimated that some 50,000 war workers and their families were replaced by returning veterans and servicemen, and thousands of women who had been in mass production lines had returned to household duties.

Ships of war which had multiplied were being withdrawn toward the continent and San Diego was a natural home port of the future. Memories of the war were to linger in a reserve fleet which never went to sea. This was the so-called mothball fleet consisting of 175 warships tied up at the Naval Station, covered with preservatives against weather, a sleeping fleet awaiting another call to the defense of the nation. Air power had become dominant in war and here were the flying fields and the protected harbor and repair and training facilities.

Though thousands of wartime housing units had been con-

With the war's end, the ships – as did the men – came home. Large numbers of them were tied up, as at San Diego, in a reserve "mothball" fleet waiting for another call to the service of their country.

structed, many of them of a temporary nature, suitable housing was still in demand. Real estate sales and the value of building permits were higher than they were in any of the prior three years. The doubling up of families in cramped quarters was coming to an end. Thousands of unmarried workers who had been imported to work in defense plants simply left for their old homes. A high proportion of the families living in the permanent units of the Linda Vista housing project elected to buy their homes and remain. The big Camp Callan on Torrey Pines mesa was torn down and the lumber diverted to San Diego to build more homes. Almost 5,500 living units were reclassified from "temporary" to "permanent" by the Federal government so they could be moved and re-sited in County areas where building codes were not restrictive, or even into Mexico. Navy demountable housing was in time strengthened and much of it retained.

Controls were lifted gradually and often spasmodically, and with the scarcity of consumer goods that had marked the war years, the savings of years quickly found their way into the marketplace. San Diego train and airplane passenger totals did not decline though bus and street car traffic dropped twenty-seven percent. But by the late September of 1945 the number of unemployed rose to 17,600. By January of a new year it would reach nearly 25,000. The nature of the slow decline was evident in the statistics. Military payrolls were once as high as $288,000,000. By 1946 they were down to $105,000,000. In the aviation industry payrolls declined from almost $90,000,000 to $22,763,000 in one year. But they would start up again in 1947. Unemployment reached a high of 30,000 by May of 1946. Home construction was absorbing many former wartime workers but the full effects of the end of the great war would not be felt in some areas for several more years.

Vessels of the tuna fleet returned from wartime duty. Seven had been lost in the Pacific war. The use of clippers by the Navy had begun to ease up in 1944 and the construction of seven larger vessels, of either wood, or steel, was resumed in six San Diego shipyards and in a number of smaller ones. Many of the returning clippers were equipped with radar. Depth finder sounders and direction finders and refrigeration had been vastly improved.

The vessels that had stayed home had kept the tuna industry at a high capacity. Demand for tuna, as a substitute for meat, had risen under wartime pressures and the promotional efforts of the armed services. By 1951, five fish canneries in San Diego were employing 3,000 persons and an estimated 2,700 fishermen manned more than 700 vessels of varying sizes. Of these, 210 were big tuna clippers ranging in cost up to a half million dollars. Amphibious planes, based in southern waters, were added to scout for schools of tuna. In 1925 the earlier tuna boats could bring in a catch of 100 tons; twenty years later, a single boat could bring as much as 500 tons.

The impetus this gave to the economy of San Diego was important at a time of stress. But trouble for the fishing industry was rising in the same country which had drawn the tuna fleet into action — Japan.

The fear of a deep economic recession in San Diego was nothing compared to a situation which had not been anticipated, one which had been thought solved, and that was assurance of an adequate supply of water. The end of the war found the Navy cutting back on emergency projects which it had undertaken under the compulsion of war. On October 6, 1945, the Navy abandoned its financial support of the San Diego Aqueduct to bring Colorado River water to San Diego by way of the Metropolitan system. Rainfall had been above normal for several years but supplies in storage had continued to decline alarm-

Charles C. Dail

ingly, and there were indications by 1945 that the rains were letting up.

A delegation of officials from the City and the San Diego County Water Authority rushed to Washington by airplane and negotiated a contract with the Navy by which San Diego agreed to reimburse the Navy, if it continued the project, at the rate of $500,000 a year, without interest charges. In the delegation were Charles C. Dail, Vice Mayor; G. E. Arnold, Assistant City Manager; Fred D. Pyle, City Hydraulic Engineer; Fred A. Heilbron, Chairman, and J. L. Burkholder, General Manager and Chief Engineer of the San Diego County Water Authority.

In telephone conversations with Mayor Knox, who in turn conferred with City Councilmen and civic leaders, the agreement was reached to continue as suggested by the Navy. City Manager Fred A. Rhodes and City Attorney Jean F. DuPaul soon afterward went to Washington and a contract was signed by Rhodes on October 17, 1945. At every step San Diegans had the support of the Commandant of the Eleventh Naval District, Vice Admiral J. B. Oldendorf. The overall cost of the project was put at $14,180,000.

One of the recommendations of the President's committee had been that the San Diego County Water Authority press for membership in the Metropolitan Water District from which it had to receive water for the San Diego Aqueduct. On April 19, 1946, the Authority agreed to annexation terms stipulated by the Metropolitan District, which merged the water rights of San Diego City and County with those of the Metropolitan District, and for payment of $13,045,000 over a period of thirty years as the Authority's pro rata share of the original cost of the Metropolitan's aqueduct from the Colorado River. In turn, the District agreed to reimburse the Authority for half the cost of the San Diego Aqueduct and to operate and maintain its northern section. The terms of annexation were approved by City and County voters on November 5, 1946, and the San Diego County Water Authority became the fifteenth agency of the Metropolitan District.

At the same election voters approved a $2,000,000 bond issue to construct aqueduct extensions to various member communities or irrigation districts. However, the City of Coronado and the Ramona Irrigation District withdrew from the Authority. Coronado believed it had sufficient supplies already and the Ramona District feared excessive costs in lifting the water high enough for it to be used in its area.

A second threat to completion of the aqueduct came early in the following year, in 1947, when the Comptroller General of the United States questioned the legality of the project under the War Powers Act. The Navy supported Mayor Knox and Heilbron in taking the project to Congress for approval, with the aid of California's senators, Sheridan Downey and William F. Knowland. A Senate committee held hearings, then passed legislation authorizing the construction, confirming all steps that had been taken and ratifying the City-Navy contract.

The winding down of the vast operations in the Pacific was slow and many San Diegans in places of authority believed that the City had not yet felt the full impact of the end of the war. The San Diego of 1946 was a far different community from the one of 1940 which had been by-passed by the industrial revolution that had reached the West Coast. The Winters were still warm and the Summers cool, but the tempo of life had changed perceptibly. Its racial balance also had begun to shift. Its Black population more than doubled, from two percent to four and half percent; the number of residents with Mexican-Spanish surnames had risen from three and one-tenth percent to four and six-tenths percent.

The tourist trade, which had virtually disappeared during the war, had become a $30,000,000 annual industry in 1946, and there was a realization that San Diego should continue the efforts that had begun with the California Pacific International Exposition of 1935 and 1936. This time it could be Mission Bay. Mission Bay had popular support; Old Town did not. Mission Bay promised not merely a playground, or a monument, but a source of revenue in the promotion of a tourist industry, in the building of hotels and boating facilities, and the creation of many new jobs. The concept of a "City Beautiful" was another matter.

The virtual abandonment of the tidelands for expansion of a Civic Center came as the result of Harbor Department pressure which it insisted rested on the conditions under which the State granted jurisdiction of them to the City. The Harbor Commission had become more and more determined, especially seeing what happened to the port during the war, that waterfront lands should be reserved for improvements consistent with development of commerce, navigation and fishing.

"Commerce" was stretched to include recreation and tourist-oriented development and activities. At the time, available waterfront lands were limited and vanishing. The jurisdiction of the Harbor Department extended only to the City limits of San Diego, to the edge of National City. The Navy had laid claim to vast acreages below Market Street and on the shore-side of Point Loma. Then there was the airport and the industrial plants of Convair, Ryan and Solar; and, in addition, a baseball park had been built during the Great Depression, with Federal

Works Progress Administration help, at the foot of Broadway, and areas to its north, and south of the Civic Center were being used to stack lumber for San Diego's home-building expansion. The Harbor Department insisted new commercial piers were needed and the fishing fleet should have its own protected harbor area.

Old dreams die hard, and many San Diegans had not forgotten the future that might have been had the harbor lived up to the promises that had been forecast for it. A newspaperman who later was to become president of the American President Lines, George Killion, once wrote:

> "San Diego today stands on the edge of a new epoch that may result, if all the dreams and plans come true, in the creation of a magnificent 'City Beautiful,' and the permanent establishment of the Harbor of the Sun as a world port, which in time may surpass all other American ports, with the possible exception of New York. ..."

That had been many years before, and still the City waited for the ships to come, hopes based on the rise of industrialism in the West. However, the same conditions had brought about a reduced tonnage to the West Coast, and seen the erection of large warehouses in the Los Angeles harbor area which had begun to shape a distribution center for all of Southern California. If ships were to unload at San Diego, there had to be cargoes to pick up for other port delivery elsewhere. That this tonnage could be developed from throughout the Southwest had remained a constant expectation.

The Harbor Commission opposed the addition of a State Building to the originally-planned Civic Center, now consisting only of the City-County Administration building. The City Council had concurred and turned its attention to a search for a new site for public buildings.

Even the use of Balboa Park as a Civic Center was considered. After all, wouldn't it be in the spirit of the "White City" which had placed so much emphasis on the beauty of buildings and park-like settings? At the urging of the Park Commission, Frederick Law Olmsted, the noted landscape architect, whose Massachusetts firm had been involved in some of the early planning for the 1915 Exposition, was retained by the City Manager to examine the possibilities of using the park as a City center. His decision was entirely negative. The Commission wanted to retain him to draw a master plan for the future of the park, but funds were not made available.

This is a part of a San Diego that might have been. Development of a Mall along Cedar Street, anchored on the City-County Administration building on the waterfront, and lined with public buildings, was fought over a number of times – and always lost.

The City Planning Director came up with a Mall which, however, would be moved northward from the original street designed by John Nolen, to Cedar Street, so its base would be at

the City-County Administration building on the waterfront. Full blocks on each side of Cedar Street would have to be purchased out of tax revenues or out of proceeds of bond issues. The beginning, however, was to be a modest one, the purchase of blocks only for the placing of the four local public buildings deemed necessary at the time. The purchase of other sites up

Philip L. Gildred

Cedar Street would depend on the growth of the City and its needs.

The first of the proposed buildings were to be a new City Library, a School Administration Center, a Hall of Justice to replace the old Courthouse, a Convention Hall, and a hoped-for State Building. At first, only ten public buildings were foreseen; later, some supporters even talked of twenty structures.

Support for Cedar Street came from the Planning Commission headed by Philip L. Gildred who urged the City Council to take the issue to the voters. A vote in the Council came on May 14, 1946. The post-war period, after the immediate release of pent-up buying power, was indicating deep economic troubles ahead nationally. A Convention Hall had seemed to hold an answer in the search for new sources of local income.

The Mayor was full of doubts on proceeding with the Cedar Street plan at the time, contending that it was not an issue of City planning but of City financing. San Diego, he said, had the highest unemployment ratio in the United States and "was in for a blow," and a Convention Hall should not be delayed until a Mall was financially feasible.

"Were you ever in the position," the Mayor asked Gildred, "of hiring an architect and then not having enough money to build the building he designed? That is our position with the Planning Commission."

Councilman Charles B. Wincote did not believe the Mall buildings could be erected on land not already owned by the City, for twenty years. Councilman Ernest J. Boud moved that the Cedar Street plan be placed on the next ballot. Councilmen Gerald C. Crary and Paul Hartley voted with him. Councilmen Wincote, Charles C. Dail and Walter Austin voted "no." The Mayor did not vote, explaining he would not want to break a tie to put the issue on the ballot.

The issue went back to the Planning Commission, but the pressure for a Convention Hall kept the Cedar Street issue alive. Late one night, Mayor Knox changed his mind and announced he would put Cedar Street to a vote of the people. City Manager Rhodes presented a shortened version, to extend from the City-County building up Cedar only to Third Avenue, a matter of ten blocks, instead of all the way to connect with Balboa Park. Knox joined other Councilmen, some new to the City Council, in support of Cedar Street.

While the dispute over Cedar Street raged, and the fate of a "City Beautiful" was said to be hanging in the balance, George White Marston, who had been instrumental in bringing John Nolen to San Diego so many years before, and had continually fought for "carnations over smokestacks," died on May 31, 1946 at the age of ninety-five. A period of mourning was declared in a mayoral proclamation, and a moment of silence was observed in the City at the hour of the funeral in respect of the memory of San Diego's "first citizen."

Through the Winter and Spring mass meetings were held in many sections of the City. The Chamber of Commerce and the Central Labor Council endorsed Cedar Street. Charles T. Leigh, chairman of a Cedar Street Development Committee, said it was unlikely the Navy would ever buy the City and County Administration building, as had been suggested, and thus it could remain the anchor for placing of a public building.

The vote on Cedar Street did not come until April 15, 1947, though economic fears were still besetting the community. But at the same time the City Council placed a second issue on the ballot, and that called for a decision on whether the voters would prefer to have public buildings located in Balboa Park. While waterfront commercial interests and speculators in land contributed money to those opposed to Cedar Street, the times were uncertain and jobs were more important to many voters than grandiose plans for grouping of public buildings which most certainly would bring about an increase in taxes.

Laying aside any concern he might have had on the timing of the issue, Knox took to the radio to urge public acceptance of Cedar Street. "The grouping of public buildings on Cedar Street will cost you, the taxpayers, less than at any other location ever proposed by anybody at any time." He cited the support of City officials, the Library, Planning and Park Commissions, consulting engineers, the Senior and Junior Chambers of Commerce, organized labor, and the town's three newspapers.

In an oblique reference to the lack of enthusiasm for the plan by the County Board of Supervisors, Knox said the proposed Hall of Justice could be built near the existing Civic Center, as far as the City was concerned, as that was the prerogative of the Supervisors.

The vocal opposition was led by George W. Fisher, an attorney and National Guard officer, who said he was opposed to both the Cedar Street and Balboa Park locations. "There is only one issue to be decided ... and that is whether private property shall be needlessly condemned and removed from the tax rolls, thus permanently increasing our taxes." A "Save Balboa Park" campaign against locating the buildings in the park was described by Fisher as an elaborate and deceptive smokescreen to confuse the voter and conceal the real issue.

The people sent Cedar Street down to defeat with thousands of votes to spare, and also rejected the idea of using park land for public buildings. The latter vote was by a five-to-one margin.

The State of California subsequently said that had Cedar Street won the area would have been considered for a new million dollar State building in San Diego but now the best site available would be selected.

"We face a tremendous problem in location of public buildings as a result of this election," Councilman Ernest J. Boud said. As far as Knox was concerned, Cedar Street was a dead issue and there would be no further consideration of it as long as he remained in office. But Cedar Street would come up again.

The aqueduct, seventy-one miles in length, was placed in service in late November of 1947, and dedicated on December 11. The first drop of water for San Diego may have fallen as rain in the Green River Valley of Wyoming and have come down the mighty Colorado River, been impounded behind Boulder Dam, then let down to Parker Dam, and from there drawn off by the Metropolitan Water District and driven across the desert and pumped through the coastal mountains to Southern California. At the west end of the San Jacinto tunnel, San Diego drew the water of survival and delivered it by gravity flow to, first, San Vicente reservoir, from where it could be let down into the City's distribution system.

Transversing some of the most rugged country in Southern California, the aqueduct included seven tunnels, all in San Diego County, which totaled four and four-tenths miles and ranging in length from 500 feet to 5,850 feet. Except for one and three-quarters miles of steel forty-eight-inch pipe, the aqueduct was reinforced concrete pipe from forty-eight to ninety-six inches in diameter. The tunnels were concrete-lined to a diameter of six feet.

At a dinner meeting celebrating the completion, Ewart W. Goodwin, chairman of the San Diego-Colorado River Association, expressed the City's thanks to the Navy and Federal officials who had joined hands in what amounted to the "saving" of San Diego. Rear Admiral John J. Manning, Chief of the Navy's Bureau of Yards and Docks, said that while the Navy occupied ten percent of the area of San Diego it used more than forty percent of its water supply:

> "Of the many post-war jobs under the Bureau of Yards and Docks none had more potential hazards than this one. None had a tighter financial structure. Many times in the early days we despaired of making our finances cover the job to its completion."

The first water arrived just in time to avert rationing. But San Diego was a city still living on borrowed time. Goodwin warned that pending in Congress were projects proposed by other states which would drain off water from the Colorado

The City is saved. Water from the Colorado River, which may have dropped as rain in Wyoming, pours out of the San Vicente tunnel. The year was 1947. The City was required to contract for completion of the aqueduct.

which had been committed to Southern California. The San Diego-Colorado River Association had been formed to protect San Diego County's share of "the last waterhole of the West." And another period of drought was well advanced. In the six years, from 1945 to 1951, annual rainfall fell more than two and a half inches below normal.

CHAPTER FOUR

The domination of the auto was well under way by the beginning of the 1950's. A freeway creeps up Mission Valley and an interchange provides a flow of traffic from east to west and north to south.

The City — the End of One Civic Dream

Five years after the storm – what kind of a City was San Diego? Gone for a generation was the idea of a "City Beautiful" as represented by the grouping of public buildings. Those who had come to work during the war, and remained, and those who came later to the City they had remembered as servicemen, knew little of the civic exhortations of the past and were not concerned about monuments to progress. A shining city to them was a symbol of a way of life different from what they had known in the past. And these ways were not necessarily the ways of those who had pioneered the land and expected their returns to be more substantial.

For the development of Mission Bay there was both enthusiasm and financial support. A second great playground in the heart of a city was intriguing to those who wanted to be participants and not mere spectators in living. Balboa Park was devoted to the trees, shrubs and plants of the world, to living creatures from all the continents, and the arts and museums and hobbies. Mission Bay, even larger, would be devoted to water activities and resort living. And, too, an hour away by auto were the mountains often capped with snow in the Winter, and

By 1950 work was progressing rapidly on converting Mission Bay into a playland and tourist attraction. This is an air view in 1949, taken from above Ocean Beach, showing the new bridge on Ventura Boulevard.

beyond them the deserts. A new generation had learned to enjoy the deserts which the pioneers had crossed in haste and fear.

Attachment to a City was more casual than emotional. Twice more the Cedar Street Mall plan and proposals to erect new public buildings went down to defeat. In 1948 voters approved bonds for water mains and rejected bonds for a new Library, a Hall of Justice and a Juvenile Center. In 1949, Cedar Street was beaten again, and the Mayor and Councilmen denied pay raises. Efforts to modify the City Manager system of government, by expanding the authority of the Mayor and City Council and gradually reducing the power of the City Manager and City Commissions, had persisted through the years. But all such attempts had been turned back. The voters wanted Councilmen to serve, as it were, as members of a board of directors and leave operations and the appointments of such personnel as the Chief of Police to a professional manager. Efficiency, not politics, was the guiding thought.

O. W. Campbell

A Mayor and Council majority were concerned over the age of their City Manager, Fred Rhodes. Rhodes had been appointed Manager upon the death of Walter Cooper and had been expected to resign within a reasonable time. He did not. At a Council meeting on December 28, 1949, Mayor Knox swung around in his chair toward the Manager and told him the Council wanted his resignation and unless it was forthcoming he would be discharged. Rhodes puffed a moment on his pipe, and then remarked, "Then you have got it all fixed for Campbell." Knox replied that this was correct. Thus it became known that the Council had secretly agreed to hire O. W. Campbell, the City Manager of San Jose, as City Manager of San Diego, at $15,000 a year. Rhodes was sixty-nine years of age, and Campbell, forty-three. And thus passed from the official scene the man who had played a prominent role in establishing San Diego's rights to Colorado River water and in its delivery to the County. Campbell was the eighth Manager in the City's history.

The outcome of the 1949 election may have been influenced in part by the business recession then settling over the country. But, more likely, the role of cities was changing. And in the West change would come more swiftly than in the East, as so many cities of the West had no tradition of centralization. They had risen out of a Westward movement in which the pioneers had paused, created settlements and towns, then moved on, until the Pacific Coast had been reached. By the 1950's the auto had added a new mobility and there was no need to huddle together; no need to reside near places of employment. Modest shopping areas were following the people, out along the wide avenues leading from the City. Improvements of streets and highways hastened the process of shifting patterns of life.

San Diego as yet had no central core in an advanced stage of decay. People did shift around within the City and its suburbs, in a restless movement of a new age, leaving older sections for newer ones. Few remained long in their first homes. But surprisingly, civic, social and business life was still "downtown." Its principal stores and its restaurants were easily accessible by auto from the suburbs and the neighboring communities. Yet, no new major buildings had been erected since the start of the Great Depression. The suburbs had grown because that is where the newcomers settled, in the subdivisions being scraped out on the mesas or in the interior valleys.

The topography of San Diego averted much of the density of building so common to Eastern cities. Suburbs followed the fingers of mesas cut by attractive canyons which provided open spaces so lacking in most metropolitan areas. Even before the end of the war the electric street cars had been unable to follow the lines of development; the suburbs grew away from them.

After the war, R. E. McNally, assistant general manager of the San Diego Electric Railway Company, declared that street cars had to be replaced entirely by buses:

> "Buses are more flexible. In a City where population is growing and shifting as fast as it is in San Diego, we can shift our routes to meet changing needs faster than we can with street cars."

In the industrial cities of the East fixed transportation systems had delivered people from their homes to their jobs, and to the facilities which made cities areas of attraction — warehouses, offices, shops, theaters, libraries, universities, and railway stations. In the newer cities of the West transportation experts believed that flexible bus lines could follow growth and development but warning signs for public transportation were difficult to see. The attractions for people — their jobs or their recreation — were not to be centralized but diffused.

In 1948 the Spreckels interests sold the electric railway company and the San Diego and Coronado Ferry Company to a firm headed by Jesse L. Haugh, a former railroad executive who had entered local transportation on the West Coast. The sale followed that of Hotel del Coronado to Robert A. Nordblom and reduced the once-great empire of John D. Spreckels to holdings of about a hundred acres of land considered of little value.

At the time of the sale only three areas were being served by electric street cars. They were out to Adams Avenue, up Broadway to Thirtieth Street, and out University Avenue to East San Diego. On March 27, 1949, a "farewell to street cars" excursion was conducted by railroad boosters. On April 23, the street cars made their last runs on the three lines, and were replaced with buses. Some cars were sold; most of them were scrapped. San Diego thus became the first major City in the Southwest to abandon street cars for buses.

Anderson Borthwick

The Harbor Department had made a concession to the Nolen Plan, and to the lure of recreational attractions, by dividing the waterfront for three uses and thus assigned the lands south of Market Street to National City for industrial purposes. Lands from there north to a point just beyond the City-County Administration building were assigned to commerce, with commercial piers extending out from in front of the Administration building. Harbor Drive was to be moved inland, along Kettner Boulevard. Between the commercial piers and the Coast Guard Station was to be a small protected harbor for the commercial fishing fleet. Recreation was to be assigned to the lee side of Point Loma, behind the two sheltering arms of a narrow island-like area which had been built up with sand from dredging operations and connected to the mainland by a causeway. Between there and the end of the Naval Training Station was to be a bay for sports fishing boats.

Residents of Point Loma at first had opposed the raising of Shelter Island in the belief it would result in disturbing their quiet and in the cluttering of their bayfront. They were reassured by Anderson Borthwick, Commission chairman, who said the island would be a calm haven, the west side devoted to fine hotels and private facilities, and the east side to the public as a park.

The clouds were still friendly, and shading, as San Diegans also began converting some of San Diego Bay into a vacation attraction. In the central channel, Shelter Island has been created and the first palm trees have been planted.

In the matter of commerce, the port had been disappointing. While goods brought by ships into the harbor in 1950 amounted to more than $14,000,000, exports, that is, in goods shipped out through the harbor, amounted to less than a fourteenth of that figure. This explained the reluctance of port enthusiasts to devote more tidelands to public buildings, especially in an area where piers could be located without more bay dredging.

Port commerce had to be a two-way street. Mayor Knox had been successful in bringing about the retirement of Joseph Brennan as Port Director and a younger man, an engineer in the department, took over. He was John Bate. To him, the future was the waterfront. His task would not be an easy one. There were only seventy-one acres of land available on the reclaimed tidelands which totaled 1,727 acres. About twenty-eight percent had been ceded back or leased to the Federal Government for military uses. Aircraft companies had leased about nineteen percent, in the vicinity of Lindbergh Field. The airport itself accounted for eighteen percent. More than eight percent was leased to industrial organizations south of Market Street, where the larger boat-building companies and fish canneries were located. About sixteen percent of the waterfront was assigned to recreational facilities and civic and commercial purposes.

The giant airplanes were coming. In fact, had arrived by the late 1940's. This is the huge B-36, built by Convair, which, however, did not have a long life, even though four jet engines were added to its six propeller engines.

In the fiscal year of 1950-1951, the harbor earned nearly a million dollars in operating revenue, but only two percent came from shipping, which indicated that existing tideland uses were not contributing to the development of water-born commerce.

There was considerable agitation to move the municipal airport from the tidelands, to an area freer of fog and with more favorable surrounding terrain. The Navy, reducing its vast Pacific Fleet air operations, entered into a fifty-year lease allowing the City joint use of the wartime Miramar field on Kearny Mesa, which it would no longer need unless some emergency arose.

The giant of San Diego industries, Convair, was reviving. It again was under new management. The Aviation Corporation, which had brought assembly-line methods to the production of the B-24 bomber and the PBY, bowed out after the war. The Atlas Corporation took control on November 20, 1947. Floyd B. Odlum became chairman of the board and La Motte T. Cohu, previously president of Trans-World Airlines, replaced Woodhead as president.

Convair plants were producing early models of a new fleet of bombing planes. The mighty B-36 transport plane, with its six engines, made its maiden flight from Lindbergh Field late in 1947. It was estimated that a fourth of San Diego's population

The airplane that did give a great boost to aviation, and particularly commercial jet transportation, was Convair's 240 which became the Convair 440. It was a turbo propeller plane.

gathered on the streets and hilltops to watch the flight. Later, four jet engines were added. The company was experimenting with a "flying auto" and designing high-performance Delta-wing fighter planes. Most important to the prosperity of San Diego, however, was Convair's entry into commercial aviation fields that began with the two-engine Convair-Liner which, proceeding through design and mechanical changes, became a workhorse of airlines around the world. There was only a limited military interest now in a missile that could fly a single ordinary bomb 5,000 miles. It was an era of peace. The small unit in Convair working on what eventually became the Atlas missile lingered near death.

James S. Copley

Clinton D. McKinnon

San Diego's other aircraft-related industries had readjusted after the war. Ryan Aeronautical Company had begun production of the Ryan "Navion," a high-performance private plane. Solar Aircraft, with the swift expansion of commercial aviation, had found new customers for its heat-resistant metals. Rohr Aircraft, in Chula Vista, backing out of its mergers, was on the way to becoming the world's largest producer of power packages for airplanes.

The return to "normalcy" brought other changes to the City. Commercial television arrived in 1949. Television had gone from the laboratory to the living room in a generation. People who had witnessed the birth of the airplane, and then its conversion from wood, wire and fabric, to jet-power with the speed of sound, also had experienced the transformation of atomic physics from theory into bombs that could destroy a civilization.

Two years before Colonel Ira C. Copley, founder of the Copley Newspapers, had died at the age of eighty-three and his publishing empire, which included *The San Diego Union* and *Evening Tribune*, was to pass into the control of an adopted son, James S. Copley. He sent William F. Shea to San Diego. The *Daily Journal* which Clinton McKinnon founded during the war on newsprint allocated by a Democrat administration, was sold in 1947 to John W. Kennedy of West Virginia. The Union-Tribune Publishing Company, freed of wartime newsprint restrictions which had been imposed on *The San Diego Union* and *Evening Tribune*, moved vigorously against its new competitor. In 1950, the *Daily Journal* was sold to the Copley interests, suspended, and its name merged with that of the *Evening Tribune.* McKinnon entered the community newspaper field and in 1948 ran for Congress as a Democrat, defeating Charles K. Fletcher, the Republican son of Colonel Ed Fletcher, one of the land and water developers who had shaped San Diego City and County for half a century.

The tremendous post-war expansion, particularly in Los Angeles, and the rising dominance of the auto, brought state legislative approval of a three billion dollar, ten-year highway improvement program. The era of the freeway had arrived. And so had smog, as yet only casting a shadow of the problems ahead for Southern California.

A modern highway cutting through the heart of Balboa Park, to provide the first across-town freeway artery, had been proposed as early as 1941. But the park had its defenders who opposed, as they said, cutting the park in two or the slicing away any more of its land area for civic buildings, roads or parking areas as had been done for the Naval Hospital and schools. But to city planners such as John Nolen, a park so large

in the heart of a City had been a mistake, and it would have been better to have had a number of smaller parks strategically situated. Those interested in the growth of the City reasoned that the park, if allowed to remain inviolate, would stand as a block around which all traffic would have to be routed at the cost of time and money. A freeway running through the canyon in the park, along a winding road bordering a lagoon and underneath the handsome span of Cabrillo Bridge, seemed to be the answer to the problem. A divided freeway could follow an

The serenity of life in San Diego, before the Great War, is evident in this photo of Cabrillo Bridge and lagoon in Balboa Park. A narrow road wound along the eastern shore.

This is what happened to Cabrillo Canyon, with the arrival of the day of the auto. San Diego's first freeway passed through Balboa Park, under the bridge, and down the Eleventh Street Canyon.

existing route and absorb only a limited amount of additional land. The State Division of Highways needed the cooperation of the people of the City of San Diego to withdraw land from the park, and got it back in 1941. The old publicly-held lands were not sacred to new voters. They also later approved the withdrawal of eight hundred acres of pueblo lands, in the Torrey Pines and Kearny Mesa areas, to be disposed of as designated by the City Council. In 1953, a City Charter amendment was to give the City Council the authority to build or approve the construction of any roads in parks.

A seven-mile state highway through Cabrillo canyon was completed and opened to traffic in 1948, providing a crosstown artery from the City's center to Mission Valley and with access to Linda Vista, by way of Highway 395. To allay the fears of those who had opposed diverting traffic through the quiet of Balboa Park, and that the beauty of the parkway would be sacrificed for expediency, the State Division of Highways set out 500,000 plants of twenty-eight varieties and transplanted many large trees for the dividing zone.

Work was progressing on a highway through the valley, from Point Loma to La Mesa. The route of the transcontinental highway through San Diego would be moved from busy El Cajon Boulevard, a wide street of many shops and homes, to an almost lonely by-pass through a valley that would soon be the heart of a growing City and come under the eye of those who planned for the future. At first, resistance to highway by-passing smaller towns was frequent. Merchants in La Mesa would fear the collapse of business with the diversion of traffic from the center of the City.

The face of San Diego was changing swiftly under the impact of the auto. Construction work on interchanges as well as freeways was proceeding. By 1951 there were four interchanges, the magic circles by which traffic would flow without interruption from one freeway to another, from one area of the city or region to another.

In the same year the final link of a twelve-mile east-west freeway through Mission Valley was dedicated on August 8. The City's first modern interchange was at Pacific Highway and Mission Valley, where traffic could be exchanged between the main route into San Diego and the new freeway through the valley. The most elaborate interchange, however, was at the point where the Cabrillo Freeway joined the Mission Valley Freeway. Another interchange was under construction at the extension of Fairmount Avenue where it too reached Mission Valley. Work also was underway on an interchange where a section of the new Wabash Freeway would join Federal Boulevard, before proceeding toward Harbor Drive on the south. Several cross-overs moved traffic without the interruption of converging autos.

The times were serene, the problems civic ones. Only the fear of a shortage of water could be summoned to alarm the voters. But belated post-war effects, and the worsening state of the economy nationally, had contributed to a steadily rising level of unemployment in San Diego. There were 23,100 persons listed as looking for work in January of 1950. In March, San

Diego was described as a critical unemployment area. On June 25, 1950, Communist troops of North Korea crossed the line between North and South Korea which had been established after World War II. The United Nations had pledged its support of the territorial integrity of republican South Korea. President Truman ordered American soldiers into action, and they did so, on June 30, and the Seventh Fleet was ordered to protect the island of Formosa, or Free China, from a possible attack by Chinese Communists. The effect on San Diego was instant and spiraling. The Cold War had begun.

Though the war in Korea, labeled as a "police action," was largely a land and air war and no large Naval surface forces were in action, 16,000 Marines from San Diego and 34,000 tons of their equipment were shipped out in record time in August. The airplane industry spurted ahead. For San Diego, it was World War II all over again, though on a smaller scale.

By the end of 1950, 188,000 persons had jobs. More than 14,000 were once again employed in the aviation industry, with a production rising to almost $105,000,000 a year. Jet-powered fighters were weapons of a new type of warfare. The Korean war took Ryan back into manufacturing parts for other military aircraft, at the request of the military, though the Ryan Navion, originally produced as a private high-performance airplane, also saw duty in Korea.

The Navy had proved to be a constant source of local income and now with a distant war again clouding the horizon, personnel increased by 10,000 and the payroll jumped from $55,500,000 to more than $71,000,000. Civilian employment by the Navy and Marines added 14,000 more persons with an income of $117,000,000. Unemployment dropped to 6,000 in September of 1951, from the post-war high of 30,000.

The City had failed to act on its rights to use Miramar air field and the Navy took possession and began building one of the world's largest Naval air stations for the new jet planes operating from a new generation of carriers.

The secret program to design and build a missile which could fly 5,000 miles, which had been starved by government disinterest, was revived and money poured into the tight little group at work in Convair. On Kearny Mesa, on a new area known as Morena Mesa, high above Mission Bay, another city within a city was rising, Clairemont. It was begun as a private enterprise by Louis Burgener and Carlos Tavares, with 400 homes.

True to predictions, the number of tourists visiting San Diego in 1950 rose to 660,000 and they left $60,000,000 behind them. Agriculture was booming, with the total value of products — field crops, truck crops, livestock, fruits and nuts, and miscellaneous products – rising to almost $71,000,000. Farming, however, was still a small, or family operation. The average size of a farm was about 150 acres; those over 100 acres numbered less than 200.

Population was on the rise again, as workers flocked to San Diego for war-related jobs. The City's population had dropped by 1950 to 334,387 from a peak of 392,000 only two years before. The population in the County had both risen and fallen during the war years, once reaching a peak of 650,000 in 1949, and falling back to 556,808 in 1950. But this would change again, drastically.

Little towns had become small cities, and small cities big cities. Chula Vista had tripled its population in a decade. Coronado was twice the size it was in 1940. El Cajon had jumped from less than 1,500 to 5,600. La Mesa's population had more than doubled as had that of National City. Oceanside's population had tripled. The age of the average San Diegan was still falling, as it had done since the beginning of the arrival of industry in the form of airplane production. By 1950, with the persistent arrival as permanent residents of servicemen who had trained in San Diego during the war, the average age had dropped from just under thirty-two to about twenty-nine and a half, and was still going down. San Diego no longer could be considered a City of the retired.

The guess that San Diego would grow northward, with a rapidly expanding population, was right. In 1954 Clairemont was rising on the mesa north of Mission Valley. Land was being leveled and tracts laid out.

The Korean War was not a long one, compared to World War II. Peace talks began in the Summer of 1951. Two years later with a new President in office, Dwight D. Eisenhower, an armistice was signed. The "police action" initiated by President Truman had cost 33,629 lives in battle and 20,617 other deaths.

Growth and drought seemed to go hand in hand. By 1951 the drought had entered its sixth year and a "Save our Water Committee" was formed in April to conserve dwindling supplies in the realization that the San Diego Aqueduct was going to prove inadequate. In the period between July 1, 1948, and June 30, 1949, the San Diego County Water Authority had delivered 71,570 acre feet of Colorado River water to its member agencies, an amount equal to about eighty-five percent of the total water they had consumed. By June, 1951, member agencies were increased by three with the annexation of the San Dieguito Irrigation District, the Santa Fe Irrigation District and the City of Escondido. By then the Authority was serving a population of more than half a million people.

As far back as 1949 the Authority had begun to worry and had executed a contract with the Bureau of Reclamation for a report on the feasibility of completing the aqueduct to its full capacity. The report was favorable and early in 1951 legislation was introduced in Congress again to authorize the Navy to add a "second barrel" to the original pipeline. Construction began in December of 1952. The following year heavy rains broke the drought. But the respite was only temporary. The rains diminished again within the year.

No civic persuasion was needed in the case for water. San Diegans knew they lived on borrowed time, unless water could be laid upon the land. Not enough reservoirs could ever be built and not enough rain would ever fall to supply a City that certainly would someday approach a million in population. Even when the second barrel was completed in October of 1954, the County Water Authority knew that additional water might be needed as early as 1960.

CHAPTER FIVE

Harris
&
Frank
WALKER SCOTT
WALKER SCOTT
Harris & Frank
Seagram's
Seven Crown
AMERICAN AIRLINES

A new age, that of jet travel, was rising before Southern California in the middle 1950's. Jet trails of Navy planes drift over a downtown that has seen buses replace street cars. But, as yet, no new tall buildings had risen.

A Fiesta — Re-living the Days of the Dons

By the 1950's the breakup of the central City as a trading center was beginning, a trend already in evidence in other large cities across the nation. The auto was winning out in the shaping of the modern city. There were not enough curbside spaces to accommodate all the autos which were crowding into the central cities. Something had to give. More than 400 cities of 10,000 or more in population had tried to meet the challenge by providing off-street parking lots or garages. In Denver, $3,700,000 in revenue bonds had been sold to finance public parking. Memphis had adopted plans for a 500-car underground garage. Boston had accumulated a $500,000 reserve for similar facilities out of parking meter revenues. San Francisco and Los Angeles were reported taking the same direction.

The San Diego City Council, under the urging of its City Manager, O. W. Campbell, came up with a program of its own, a proposal permitting the City Council to issue revenue bonds to establish off-street parking, to be paid back out of parking meter revenues. Mayor Knox insisted that only marginal land on the edge of the business district would be used to relieve downtown congestion, and ridiculed suggestions that as many as sixty full blocks would be taken off the tax rolls.

Proponents, who included the great majority of San Diego's downtown business and professional leaders, called the program "as sound as the San Francisco Bay Bridge" which had been built with revenue bonds secured by bridge tolls, and that those who were opposed to it were profiting from the scarcity of available parking space. Elmer H. Blase was chairman of the City-Wide Committee for Off-Street Parking. But, again, it was Mayor Knox who carried the fight, accusing opponents of distorting facts to confuse the poor old voters and that such tactics were the same used by Communists and were the surest way to bring socialism to America.

In the view of the opposition, the diversion of parking meter revenue would reduce the general fund and bring about an increase in property taxes. Oscar W. Cotton, a realtor and chairman of the San Diego Committee for Free Enterprise, charged that if the plan was carried out on the basis suggested, it would destroy a major part of San Diego's downtown area for the benefit of a small congested center.

Allen J. Sutherland

The proposal was easily defeated, by a margin of better than two to one. In the same year, in 1950, Sears, Roebuck and Company announced it was moving its operations from downtown to a new twelve-acre site in the Hillcrest area.

In Los Angeles, financial and business interests turned their eyes toward San Diego, with its rising military and industrial payrolls, due to the action in Korea and the widening of the Cold War. In a year 6,000 new homes had been constructed, 12,000 in the County as a whole. And the advances of science and engineering arising from World War II were beginning to spawn new phases of industry.

The Security Trust & Savings Bank of San Diego was merged into the Security First National Bank of Los Angeles. Allen J. Sutherland, president of the local bank, said that larger financial resources would now be made available to finance the progress of San Diego. With the exception of the Bank of America, the financial institutions in San Diego had been all locally controlled; now power was shifting toward a new financial center 125 miles to the north. The Security Trust was sixty-four years old and had been founded in 1893 as the Blochman Banking Co.

Ewart W. Goodwin

By 1952, Ewart W. Goodwin, the old-line Percy H. Goodwin Company, a real estate and insurance firm, was able to claim:

"The familiar discussion of geraniums or factories is a dead issue here. Industrialization is here and here to stay and grow. Despite the fears of old-timers, who saw the ruination of San Diego as a pleasant place to live – and a great tourist attraction – with the coming of factories and workers, San Diego is a more attractive City than it was twenty years ago."

The year 1951 also saw the end of another civic ambition that had kept alive the hopes of many early promoters and developers. Passenger service was abandoned by the San Diego & Arizona Railway, which ran from San Diego to the Imperial Valley by a circuitous route through Baja California in order to avoid the numerous mountain crests. The line had been the project

The failure of the voters to approve centralization of public buildings resulted in a bond issue to replace the old Public Library. Here it is being torn down, with a new and larger one to rise on the same site.

of John D. Spreckels, who at the start had the secret cooperation of the Southern Pacific, and he had hoped it would end the City's geographical and economic isolation. The San Diego & Arizona connected with the Southern Pacific, whose main line still ran to Los Angeles by way of San Gorgonio Pass. No rush of passengers to San Diego arrived by this southern route; and rail shipments had not yet indicated that San Diego would become the port of entry for the goods in and out of the Southwest.

Major trials for San Diego still lay ahead when Harley Knox, tired and listening to warning signs in his own life, declined in 1951 to run for re-election. Thus the man who had guided the City through the war years and through the crisis of survival in the matter of a water supply, passed from the official scene. He was to die in 1956 of a heart attack at the age of fifty-seven. An attorney, John D. Butler, was elected Mayor over Councilman Gerald Crary. He was the first native son to assume the office in the City's history.

John D. Butler

But before Knox retired, he had witnessed an act of the people which wrote a formal end for the time to the grouping of public buildings. Advocates of a new Public Library, to replace the one built forty years before with funds from the Carnegie Foundation, were successful in winning voter approval to tear down the old structure and replace it with a new and larger building, on the same site on E Street between Ninth and Tenth Avenues, a long way from Cedar Street. The Library opened on June 27, 1954.

Watching the "downtown revolution" which was sweeping over larger American cities, George A. Scott had quietly retained research and design firms to study and recommend a future course for the Walker Scott department store. The Great Depression had not run its course when the Walker Scott Corporation moved into a deserted department store building and opened San Diego's second locally-held major downtown department store, at the very heart of the City, Fifth Avenue and Broadway.

The County Courthouse, too, a relic of the past, had to be replaced, and with no agreement on placing of public buildings generally, voters approved the removal of the historic building and the erection of a new one, on the same site.

This is a model of the new Courthouse as shown to the voters. It would be based on Broadway and cover two blocks northward, and would be described as the tallest building in San Diego lying on its side.

In September of 1954 he announced that he personally had acquired sixty-two acres of land in the eastern section of the metropolitan area, at the junction of Broadway and College Grove Avenue, not far from Lemon Grove. Scott in making his announcement, said:

> "... experience in other cities indicates clearly that San Diego is rapidly approaching the size and economic status that justify the development of an integrated shopping center. ..."

The selected site, though at the time outside the City limits, was near the center of San Diego's long-time growth pattern, on the mesa eastward to the foothills, and already construction was progressing rapidly on a new freeway that eventually would connect the downtown area, at Eighteenth and F Streets, with Grossmont summit and Highway 80, a distance of a little more than eleven miles, and designed to serve what then was the fastest-growing area in the County, La Mesa, Lemon Grove, Spring Valley and Grossmont.

Within a year the land had been sold to a Los Angeles real es-

tate developer and the Walker Scott Corporation signed the first lease for the building of a major department store in what would be known as the College Grove Center. There would be space for 5,000 autos at one time, 17,500 during a shopping day, and perhaps as many as forty stores. But the road ahead would be a long and troubled one, and six years would pass before the goal could be reached.

George A. Scott

There was no thought of abandoning downtown. Scott simultaneously announced that Walker Scott would expand its store as evidence "of our belief that the downtown shopping district will remain a major factor in serving the 750,000 persons who comprise the metropolitan area."

A year after the City voted in favor of a new Public Library, the County voters failed to return the necessary two-thirds majority on a proposal to build a new Hall of Justice, but the proposition came back two years later and was approved. The new Courthouse and Jail were to replace the old structure on Broadway, between Front Street and First Avenue.

Thirty years had gone by since the Community Auditorium, a building left over from the Exposition of 1915-16, had burned down the evening of the firemen's ball. In 1939, the San Diego Convention Bureau had unsuccessfully urged that the Federal Building in Balboa Park, built for the 1935-36 Exposition, be converted into a convention facility. In 1949, the grouping of public buildings, including a Civic Auditorium and Convention Hall along Cedar Street, had been defeated. Other proposals had been discussed and rejected, including the erection of a Convention Hall on Horton Plaza and the land immediately to the south, by private interests. Subsequently the City Council authorized a research institute to conduct a survey to study the economic and cultural value of a Civic Auditorium and Convention Hall to San Diego, and to recommend a site.

Since the end of World War II, the nature of the national economy had been changing. Higher pay, longer vacations, new highways and more autos, faster and larger airplanes, and the great expansion of business, industrial, professional and civic conventions, were sending people in all directions as never before in history.

In its earlier days San Diego had been looked upon as a Winter resort country, for the well-to-do who could afford extended vacations in the seasons of rough weather in the Midwest and East. Hotel del Coronado and the La Valencia Hotel in La Jolla and La Jolla Beach and Tennis Club had represented the type of resort living that attracted the Winter people. Now Summer travel and conventions were the attractions for new millions of people. And San Diego was convinced it had a year-around climate superior to any other city in the nation, and the vacation potentials of Mission Bay were just beginning to be fully appreciated.

The research report took the City back to Cedar Street, recommending as a site a four-block area bounded by Cedar and

Ash Streets on the north and south and First and Third Avenues on the west and east.

Several buildings were proposed to form what was considered an economically feasible public assembly facility for sports events, spectacles and conventions; a Concert Hall and Little Theater, and an Exhibit Hall for conventions and trade shows, and with adequate parking. Conventions, concerts and traveling dramatic productions were being accommodated in school auditoriums, principally the Russ Auditorium of San Diego High School at the southern edge of Balboa Park, or in scattered park buildings.

The arguments were persuasive. Only three cities with populations in excess of 250,000 were without public assembly facilities. A bond issue of $8,500,000 was placed on the ballot for the June election in 1956. *The San Diego Union* took a look at Miami Beach and told the voters what they could achieve if they so desired, as residents of the nineteenth largest metropolitan area in the country:

La Jolla also lingered in relative quiet until long after the war. It, too, attracted Winter visitors. Here is a scene looking south toward the La Jolla Beach & Tennis Club and the famed La Jolla Cove, at the extreme right.

> "Competition for tourists and conventions ... has grown more intense. ... While other cities have stepped ahead in providing attractions for visitors, San Diego has worked largely with pre-war tools. ... San Diego will move forward culturally and economically if the June 5 election ... is favorable. A yes vote will mean dollars and entertainment for the community."

The four blocks were considered to be depressed in value and therefore acceptable for public use and were accessible to downtown hotels and restaurants. Sites in Balboa Park and Mission Valley were considered too remote. Opponents, however, merely claimed it was "Cedar Street Mall Again."

But a new Mayor, Charles C. Dail, an insurance man and a former Councilman, who had been elected to succeed John Butler, insisted that a Cedar Street Mall was impossible because some public buildings already had been scattered about the downtown area.

The Convention Hall and Civic Theater complex received the approval of a majority of the voters who went to the polls, but

Hotel del Coronado was still a symbol of a Southern California of past years. It represented the days of Winter visitors. Its rich woods and vaulted ceilings suggested a time of leisure for those able to spend their Winters where they chose.

lacked the two-thirds margin required for a bond issue. But as the decision had been so close, petitions were circulated to put the issue back on the ballot in November, this time with a new name, the Hall of the Americas, with George Scott leading the campaign. It seemed certain that it would win the second time around. Such was not the case. There wasn't even a majority vote in favor of it. A City centered on Cedar Street, which had been with the City's leaders for so many years, was dead and buried for good.

Not all of the opposition was based on taxes or anti-Cedar Street sentiment. There were doubts as to how the City should proceed in regard to its future. Before the November voting, a committee representing the Downtown Association listened to what was being described as a "downtown revolution" sweeping other American cities and how 100 or 200 blocks in San Diego could be torn apart and re-assembled as a "city of the future." Piecemeal solutions were held to not be valid any longer, and the random placing of public buildings would only add to the problems arising with growth and increasing traffic. The committee was conscious of the planning then under way for a new crosstown freeway that would take traffic entering San Diego from the north, sweep it across the City on an elevated roadway, with off- and on-ramps serving the downtown area.

Morley H. Golden

A Los Angeles architect, Victor Gruen, who had presented a similar concept for downtown Fort Worth, described a plan which would create a downtown pedestrian preserve surrounded by freeways, with ramps leading to parking garages, and electric glide-cars serving all facilities. Accomplishment would be by stages, with new buildings and open green spaces replacing older structures as they could be torn down.

On the committee were Morley H. Golden, chairman, and Walter Ames, Chester Dorman, James Forward, Jr., Philip L. Gildred, George Henderson, Carleton Lichty, Hamilton Marston, Peter Peckham, Allen J. Sutherland and Charles K. Fletcher. It was heady stuff, and they were not ready to commit themselves, or all downtown interests. But the idea of a "City Beautiful" was taking a new form.

The citizens had no hesitancy in producing sufficient votes for schools, harbor improvements, water distribution, and Mission Bay development. But time and again they turned back suggestions that the salary of the Mayor and Councilmen be substantially increased. Under the City Charter, administrative and executive responsibilities rested with the City Manager with power partly diffused through commissions, and with the Mayor and Councilmen in the roles of policy makers. Over the years voters had refused to disturb the system by providing any remunerative excuses for City fathers to assume roles beyond those granted in the City Charter. They feared a return to politics by opening the door to full-time Mayors and Councilmen. Service to the City called for candidates who had substantial private incomes.

The voters did relent somewhat in June of 1956 by raising the pay of Councilmen from $2,000 to $5,000 a year but at the same time, and for the fifth time, rejecting an increase in the Mayor's $5,000 salary. Now the Mayor presumably was only one among equals. Politics being what they are, and leadership resting with persuasion, strong-willed men made strong mayors anyway. Percy Benbough had been one; Harley Knox was another.

They sought to bend events to their will, though not always successfully. But the voters relented again in November, at the time of rejecting the Convention Hall and Theater, and in view of the demands on the time of the Mayor as the City's ceremonial chief, and assured that he would not hereafter enjoy an expense account, raised his salary to $12,000.

But while enough voters were still reluctant to accept the idea of taxing themselves to make San Diego a convention and tourist center, a new San Diego was ready to emerge and events more than political decisions soon would determine the course of growth.

Charles H. Brown

In 1953 a developer by the name of Charles H. Brown had a study conducted as to where in the Southwest he should build a resort-type hotel. All factors pointed to San Diego, and after further study, to Mission Valley. The valley then was a quiet retreat in the geographical heart of the City, with riding stables and bridal paths. The site was at the junction of two freeways. One ran north and south, the other east and west. They connected the site with Mission Bay, waterfront commercial activities, downtown San Diego, the principal highway leading from San Diego eastward, and the mesa to the north which was beginning to fill with homes and businesses. There was room for a ranch-type hotel with swimming pools, tennis courts and other recreational facilities that could not be offered in the central City by the older hotels such as the U. S. Grant, San Diego and El Cortez Hotels. Brown declared Mission Valley to be the "perfect location." In a few years the decisions which had moved him to locate in Mission Valley would have explosive effects.

The fortunes of San Diego had so risen and fallen with war and aviation that any alteration in ownership and management of Convair was certain to have repercussions throughout the community. On March 30, 1953, it was announced that control of Convair would pass to a new corporation, General Dynamics, which had purchased 400,000 shares from the Atlas Corporation. On May 15, John Jay Hopkins, chairman and president of General Dynamics Corporation, succeeded Floyd Odlum as chairman of Convair. It was the third change in management since Convair's arrival in San Diego. It became formally the Convair division of General Dynamics.

Joseph T. McNarney

The new division president was General Joseph T. McNarney, who had retired from the Army after thirty-two years of distinguished service which included the command of United States Forces in the European Theater and Occupied Germany. On Convair's twentieth anniversary in San Diego, in 1955, he reported that slightly more than one in eight wage and salary earners in San Diego were employed at Convair and "During the next two decades they will face scientific and industrial challenges undreamed of in 1935 and only dimly discernible today. ..."

But the benign climate was still considered San Diego's greatest asset. Even Convair had come to San Diego because of it. In the past there had been two Expositions which had sought to spread far and wide the blessings of warm Winters and cool Summers. People could be induced to come to San Diego, to spend money; and perhaps to return, to buy land and build homes and even establish plants which might employ others who would surely come in time. Selling of land was still a principal business in Southern California. San Diegans wanted their share of the returns from the great Westward movement. The velocity of real estate sales per thousand of population in San Diego County was double that of Denver, Colorado, and more than four times those of Chicago and Washington, D.C.

As far back as 1950 the City's business leaders had envisioned still another exposition of international character, and even had agreed to subscribe $2,000,000 for it. But the Korean war postponed any such plan and by the time it was over, most of them were convinced an international exposition for a City the size of San Diego was now impossible. Wayne Dailard agreed.

On August 13, 1955, Ewart W. Goodwin, president of the Exposition Corporation, announced there would be a great annual Festival of the Pacific designed to draw thousands of tourists for a spectacle rivaling New Orleans' Mardi Gras.

Wayne Dailard, a polo playing showman of many years, had successfully rejuvenated the Santa Barbara Fiesta and then had turned his attention to San Diego. He also was convinced – and perhaps had convinced Goodwin – that the old world's fair idea was obsolete, and in the words of *San Diego Magazine*, he proposed, instead:

Wayne Dailard

"Threading a ribbon through La Jolla's caves and looping it over the back country and on along toward the border ... tying together the city's permanent summertime attractions and interlace them with a series of special events. Parade and pageant, tournament and aquashow, costumed street dance and formal ball."

He told his story to a hundred community leaders who formed the nucleus of an organization pledged to plan for San Diego's first annual Festival of the Pacific. *The San Diego Union* commented:

"It has long been evident that Los Angeles, once the tourist mecca of the West, has industrialized itself from that role. Vacationers don't like to grope around in smog, tears in their eyes ... the capital will shift. ... Santa Barbara's 'Old Spanish Days' draws 100,000 visitors."

An executive committee was named, to include Goodwin, George A. Scott, Allen J. Sutherland, Anderson Borthwick, Harry Callaway, G. H. Dillon, Robert M. Golden, E. Robert Anderson, Kenneth Nairne, Charles Brown, William Goetz, Carleton Lichty, John Quimby and Walter Ames, with G. Aubrey Davidson, president of the 1915 Exposition, and Guilford Whitney, a leading merchant, honorary chairmen. They represented a cross-section of banking, building, business, newspaper and television interests, the legal profession, and organized labor. Most of their names had appeared on the lists of all the things that a new leadership had tried to accomplish in what they were convinced was the spirit of civic ambitions as defined by the pioneers.

Expositions might have passed from the scene because of the attraction of television as a vehicle for introducing or exhibiting new products. But, if Alonzo Horton and a group of earlier residents in Old Town had been able to summon a City into being, and if a City of less than 40,000 in population could have conceived the Panama-Pacific Exposition, certainly a City now eleven times that in size, could invoke a similar unity and enthusiasm.

But enthusiasm at first came slowly and Goodwin told the San Diego Convention and Tourist Bureau members that they could have a "Frankenstein monster" on their hands if they did not contribute wholeheartedly toward the fiesta's success. A budget of $300,000 was set and Sutherland was designated to head the subscription campaign. The City and County governments gave $50,000 each.

The centerpiece of the celebration would be presentation of "The California Story." This was a state-owned historical pageant first presented in the Hollywood Bowl in 1950 for California's Centennial celebration, under the general direction of Dailard. Governor Goodwin J. Knight released "The California Story" to San Diego. "San Diego stands at the portal of this rich, moving saga," Dailard announced. "Here California History began."

Fiesta del Pacifico was a festive time – for a while. When the idea of a third Exposition was abandoned, a localized fiesta was substituted, as a tourist attraction. Spanish dress became the order of the day. At top left is civic enthusiast Harry Callaway

The Festival of the Pacific was translated into Spanish, and the fiesta became Fiesta del Pacifico. By the Summer of the following year, everything was in readiness. The money had been raised, the pageant rehearsed with 1,300 participants and thirty-five scenes which would require a stage in the Balboa Stadium as long as a city block. The fiesta was to run for thirty-three days; the pageant for fourteen days.

Production of the pageant was to be under the direction of Vladimir Rosing of the New York City Center Opera, with the symphony orchestra and 150-voice choir to be led by Meredith

Wilson, a musician and song writer of popular reputation.

Spanish-type costumes appeared in retail stores. The men's designated costume would have flat, rounded hat, a tie with sequins, a shirt milled for Mexican weddings, and spangled stripes down pant edges. Women were to don flowing skirts and mantillas, and wear large, high combs in their hair. The official fiesta colors were to be red and black. In June, thirty-two Navy jet fighters flew over the City streaming, red, green and yellow ribbons, the colors of Spain.

The centerpiece of Fiesta del Pacifico was the dramatic play "The California Story" which was presented in mammoth scenes in Balboa Stadium. This is a scene from the recreation of immigrant wagon train.

The fiesta opened with a grand parade of nearly 3,000 persons, with 200 richly-costumed men and women astride horses, 200 girls on floats tossing flowers at spectators, the massing of 500 American flags, twelve flags which had flown over California, and seventeen bands.

Everybody had a good time. The pageant was well attended, with the staging of California history from the explorer Juan Rodriguez Cabrillo to, eventually, the earthquake in San Francisco. Harry L. Foster received a special honor for his success in developing the parade. All agreed the fiesta should be presented annually. That is, perhaps all except members of the City Council. Councilmen refused to donate City funds for a 1957 fiesta, refused to rehabilitate the Ford Building of the 1935 Exposition for a fiesta headquarters and exhibit hall, and appeared reluctant to allow the Spanish Village to be diverted for such affairs. Cooperation would extend only in services.

There was some feeling in the community that the chief benefactor of the fiesta had not been the City and the tourist business but Dailard and his co-workers who had produced "The California Story" around which San Diegans had costumed, danced and paraded. It was agreed that the fiesta had run too long and next time it would be reduced from thirty-three days to eighteen. It had been difficult to sustain the interest of the citizens for that length of time and often visitors, arriving between events, had trouble finding what the fiesta was all about. There were more private parties than public events, and sales of Spanish-type costumes had not come up to expectations.

Fiesta del Pacifico ran for three more Summers, though its originator, Dailard, had been forced out, and then quietly passed from the scene. Vacationers who came to San Diego in the Summer were more interested in doing something themselves than in watching somebody else's performances. The tourist business, however, had seemed to be on the increase. In 1952 the money left behind by tourists was estimated at $75,000,000. In 1956, the figure was set at more than $130,000,000. Two years later, however, the rise had slowed somewhat and the revenue was estimated at $144,000,000. The fiesta, in a way, competed with the normal Summer attractions and hotels and motels wanted it presented in "off" seasons when rooms were more available.

San Diego also did not have the civic cohesiveness that could be found in a smaller city such as Santa Barbara or exhibited in the long tradition of the New Orleans' Mardi Gras. Of the 490,000 residents in the City in 1956, less than half of them might have been in San Diego in 1940. It was now a City of strangers.

CHAPTER SIX

The Hale telescope on Palomar Mountain was considered to symbolize a new era of science. San Diego County had been chosen as a site to avoid the lights of Los Angeles. But a new world was opening below it, as well as being revealed above it.

Cotton — the Promise of the Ships to Come

For a time in the 1950's it appeared that those who had envisioned the Port of San Diego as the trading heart of the Southwest, and sought to reserve waterfront lands for commerce instead of public buildings, might have been right after all.

Cotton was the promise. It had been shipped through the port ever since 1900. Cotton from Arizona and the Imperial Valley had trickled out to foreign ports, though never in amounts sufficient to bring about a balance between exports and imports.

That is, until the 1950's. Many circumstances effected a change in cotton production and shipment from the interior. Completion of Boulder Dam and the All-American Canal had stabilized a flow of water through an intricate system of irrigation canals throughout the Imperial Valley. Regulating reservoirs on the lower Colorado delivered water on a dependable basis to the Mexicali Valley, from where it also could be lifted to the Sonora plateau. Water and desert heat produced abundant crops; the cotton proved to be superior to much grown elsewhere; the world market demand, and price, were rising, and United States subsidies were available.

John Bate

The staff of the port under John Bate was quick to take advantage of an outpouring of "white gold." Here was a crop that could be moved from the Imperial Valley to the Port of San Diego by the little San Diego & Arizona Railroad. There were no Mexican ports available and the cotton from Mexicali Valley could be moved by truck to the first port of call, San Diego. True, the mountain barrier between Imperial Valley and the port had not yet been conquered by a new highway and there were four crests of more than 4,000 feet each which taxed the strength and maintenance of loaded trucks. But the route to San Diego was shorter than the one to Los Angeles, and there was less waiting for shipment, less warehouse costs, and faster loading.

In 1939 the first cotton from Calexico destined for shipment through the Panama Canal was delivered at the port by the San Diego & Arizona Railroad. In 1935, cotton was moving out for Liverpool. Three years later 6,000 bales went to Europe. In 1953, $1,540,000 worth of cotton went to Japan. A year later cotton was moving across the waterfront for England, Belgium, France and Germany, as well as for Japan, and the year's shipments exceeded 100,000 bales. Late in the year the first cotton from Mexicali arrived, for the 1955 season. In 1955 there were nearly 150,000 bales and San Diego was leading the port of Los Angeles in the shipment of cotton. Another year saw the first cotton arrive from Sonora.

In February of 1955 at one time there were 60,000 bales awaiting shipment, piled on vacant land next to the Civic Center and on the west side of the Lane Field baseball park. There were 140 more carloads waiting in South Bay freight yards. More thousands of bales were backed up on the highways or in the valleys.

The sheer immensity of the cotton flood inspired many San Diegans to foresee San Diego as becoming, not just a point of shipment, but a cotton processing center. A group of local businessmen was organized to look into the possibilities, and the chairman, Charles W. Blumenschein, asked:

> "A market for the product is right here on the West Coast. California fashions are setting the pace in industry. So why shouldn't we process the cotton in California and save the terrific transportation costs?"

The idea was exciting. Anderson Borthwick, the banker and chairman of the Harbor Commission, announced a port improvement program to double cotton handling facilities, including the replacing of the old shed on the B Street Pier and the development of the existing small pier at the foot of Tenth Avenue. In April of 1955 San Diegans by a vote of three to one approved a bond issue of $9,699,000 to finance construction of the first phase of a new earth-filled Tenth Avenue terminal which could load or unload eight ships simultaneously. There would have to be sheds and cranes and railroad connections.

There would be enough revenue from the port to satisfy the bond obligations. Revenues from the terminals alone had risen from about $31,000 in 1948 to more than $215,000 in 1956. The number of ships calling to unload or load cargoes had risen from eighty-six to 201 in the same period of time.

Hopes ran high. But San Diego had been through this once before. This time it was cotton, last time it was the opening of the Panama Canal. Port enthusiasts had been certain that the completion of the canal would vastly increase the amount of shipping between the East and West coasts, and that San Diego, with an almost landlock harbor and being the first port of call on the Pacific Coast of the United States, would at last come into its own and merchants and citizens would benefit immensely in an economic way.

But the canal had merely shortened the journey and the ships

Cotton was King for a long time in the Port of San Diego. Millions of bales moved across the waterfront – for a time – for ships from Europe and Asia. Cotton provided the impetus for port expansion.

It was the Tenth Avenue Terminal that raised the Port of San Diego to big league status in the middle 1950's. This is a construction scene. When it was completed, it could accommodate eight ships at a time.

had gone right on by, to the ports of Los Angeles and San Francisco, where railroads and much larger production areas, and industrialization, had made exchanges of cargoes more certain. But now San Diego, too, had huge shipments waiting to be picked up for the Far East and Europe, and ships did not have to leave with empty holds.

The possibilities of the bay were not limited to commerce. The scarcity of tidelands had brought about the end of an idea of a waterfront lined with beautiful buildings, but the conviction that San Diego's tourist and convention business had to be in a large measure water-oriented, persisted.

John Bate had a solution. Recreation and vacation activities could be assigned to new land which could be created through dredging. U.S. Government dredging of the harbor channel, for navigation purposes, already had created Shelter Island in the lee of Point Loma. By 1953 the Harbor Department itself had spent $700,000 in reclamation and improvements on the island and in additional dredging of yacht and commercial boat anchorages.

Motels and restaurants available to the public were begun, under leases to private individuals. Confronted, though with a proposed Harbor Department lease for a private club on the island, Mayor John D. Butler and City Councilmen displayed reluctance to be in a position of granting use of public lands for what Charles C. Dail, then a Councilman, described as a "class privilege."

Douglas R. Giddings, speaking for himself as an officer of the C. Arnholt Smith interests, assured Councilmen that the club to be known as the Kona Kai would not only be available to local yachtsmen and for recreational purposes, but would carry out the wishes of California and Arizona yachtsmen in providing a permanent home port as well as mooring facilities for some of the world's largest pleasure crafts. Mission Bay, at that time not anywhere near ready for large yachts, was looked upon more as a small boat and recreational park. Councilmen approved a twenty-five-year lease for Giddings and Smith.

Through the post-war years tuna fishing and canning had helped in a large way to sustain the economy of San Diego and assure the importance of the Port. It was estimated in 1950 that it would have taken a train of 1,500 boxcars twelve miles long to transport the tuna canned at San Diego. More than 200 white-hulled clippers ranged as far south as the Galapagos Islands off the coast of Peru, and for the choice albacore the going price was as high as $500 a ton. Clippers had a range of up to 15,000 miles which was equal to a round trip to Japan, and they could remain at sea as long as four or five months.

Though spotting of schools of tuna often was done with the aid of a small airplane or a helicopter, and while some boats were

Plans for Shelter Island in the bay were grand ones. One of them placed a circular restaurant at the tip, with glass walls, and doors leading to piers at which local or visiting yachtsmen could tie up for lunch or dinner.

Douglas R. Giddings

costing up to a half million dollars each, actual fishing was still being done in a time-honored way. Fishermen stood on the platform at the stern of the boat, with bamboo fishing poles and lines, hooking tuna attracted by live bait thrown from the boat by a crewman known as a "chummer." Strong arms were required to pull in the large struggling fish and a dexterous twist of the wrist and arm was necessary to cause the tuna to be unhooked while still sailing through the air and onto the deck.

While perhaps twenty percent of the annual catch was being taken by nets, purse seining was a laborious effort and considered risky in the fast-moving currents and sudden storms in the region of the Galapagos Islands. Nets up to forty to sixty feet in depth and perhaps 600 feet long were spread out around a school of tuna and then the weighted lower edges of the net, or seine, were gathered together by hand in the fashion of a purse. The tuna was slowly crowded into a small area, and then scooped out with other small basket-like nets. Porpoise which traveled with the schools were also trapped in the nets and caused great damage. They generally were taken, killed and tossed overboard. Hook-and-line fishermen contended that this practice broke up schools of tuna.

The growth of shipbuilding in San Diego almost paralleled that of the fishing industry. In 1951 there were six major shipyards and a number of smaller ones engaged in the construction of small naval vessels as well as steel and wooden-hulled tuna clippers. The principal yards were the Campbell Machine Company, headed by Dave and George Campbell; Harbor Boat and Yacht Company, owned by Arne Strom and Haldor Dahl; Martinolich Shipbuilding Company, founded and directed by Antony C. Martinolich; Rask Boatbuilding Company, in Coronado, operated by Peter Rask; the San Diego Marine Construction Company, a division of Oakley J. Hall's Star & Crescent Company, and the National Steel and Shipbuilding Corporation directed by C. Arnholt Smith. Smith already was becoming an important factor in the development of San Diego through control of the United States National Bank and other enterprises being put together with unusual secretiveness. In time he would create an empire that would rival that of the great John D. Spreckels, and change the face of the City.

C. Arnholt Smith

But the fishing boom was running into trouble. As early as 1948 about nine million pounds of tuna frozen or canned in Japan and other foreign countries entered the United States market. By 1950 imports rose to fifty-six million pounds; three years later, imports were 123 million pounds. The Japanese were undercutting the San Diego price by at least $20 a ton; the number of clippers began to decline, some being withdrawn and

In 1954 tuna was still caught with poles and hooks. Here a new tuna boat, the Dominator, slides down the ways. Only two years later the method of tuna fishing would be revolutionized with great effect on San Diego.

others lost at sea not replaced. Tuna fishermen demanded that Congress place a set quota on imports, and their wives paraded in protest.

In 1954 Americans consumed twelve million cases of tuna. Of this total, 1,600,000 cases came from Japan with the tuna packed in brine. Frozen tuna from Japan filled 2,600,000 other cases processed and canned in American canneries. Canneries insisted that if they did not accept and can frozen tuna from Japan, the Japanese would can all the tuna they could catch, ship it across the ocean and destroy the United States fish canning industry.

Competition was strong and growing, there were continuing losses of boats at sea due to poor navigation and lack of safety precautions. Heavy investments were required for larger and larger boats for longer and longer voyages. There were fears that the tuna was beginning to thin out along the coast of the Americas, necessitating the opening of even more far-distant fishing areas which would require the building of processing and canning plants nearer the sources of supply. For a good part of the decade the tuna industry was to labor in troubles. That is, until early in 1956, when the 120-foot Anthony M. was re-equipped with a power block and six nylon nets and proceeded to Latin American waters. She returned to San Pedro thirty-nine days later, with a successful catch. The magazine *Pacific Fisherman* described the power block and nylon nets as being the salvation of the industry.

While San Diegans pondered the future of the City, the curtain was beginning to lift on a new era, one which, as predicted by General McNarney, would reveal things as then undreamed of.

In 1956 Convair announced it would build a $40,000,000 plant, with a million square feet of space, to produce a ballistic missile named the Atlas, which could carry an atomic warhead and span the oceans in thirty minutes. The quiet work of James R. Dempsey, the project manager; William H. Patterson, an aerodynamist, and Karel J. Bossart had produced what was described as the "ultimate weapon." Development of the missile, according to Edgar V. Murphree, special assistant for missiles

The blessing of the tuna fleet was a ritual. Here Bishop Charles F. Buddy, of the San Diego Catholic Diocese, blesses a tied up fleet. The fleet needed it — Japanese competition would threaten its existence.

to Defense Secretary Charles E. Wilson, had moved faster than anticipated. The plant was to rise on Kearny Mesa east of Highway 395, on pueblo lands purchased from the City for $782,962. The City was moving north, or so it appeared.

James R. Dempsey

On Palomar Mountain, a peak of more than 6,000 feet in height, in northern San Diego County, man was peering through the Hale telescope deep into a billion light years of space. Way back in 1928 Dr. George Ellery Hale had written an article about the possibility of a 200-inch telescope, or one even larger. Soon afterward the Rockefeller Foundation in New York agreed to assume the $6,000,000 cost of a 200-inch telescope, and responsibility for its design and construction was placed with the California Institute of Technology.

The growing problem of a vast sea of lights in the Los Angeles area turned the search for a site for the new telescope to San Diego County and Palomar Mountain. The decision to locate there was made in 1934. The 200-inch reflecting mirror for the telescope was cast of pyrex glass in Corning, New York, and after a year of cooling, it was delivered across country to Pasadena, where grinding, accurate to a millionth of an inch, halted during the war, was completed in the Spring of 1947. Over a route where some roads had to be widened and bridges strengthened, the mirror was hauled up Palomar Mountain. It was placed in operation in a huge observatory complex in 1948.

Not long after the Most Reverend Charles F. Buddy had become the Bishop of the new Catholic Diocese of San Diego, which in actuality took in a large area of Southern California, he walked across the mesa overlooking Mission Valley and told himself that here could rise the great center of learning which he had dreamed of founding. That was in 1937. He described his plan to the Reverend Mother Hill of the Religious Order of the Sacred Heart, in San Francisco, which had a long record of achievement in the fields in schools and colleges on six continents. From there came his first financial encouragement. By 1949 the first buildings of Spanish Renaissance architecture began to rise on the mesa, to become the first privately-supported university in San Diego, and open to all students regardless of religious affiliation.

A private university was taking form on the grounds of the old Theosophical Society high on Point Loma. California Western University was an outgrowth of Balboa College, originally situated in the downtown area, and which in 1950 had been granted a zone variance to re-locate on Point Loma on land sweeping down to the sea and providing one of the world's finest views. Dwight E. Stanford was succeeded as president by Robert M. Griffin.

The Age of Science was opening up. John Jay Hopkins of General Dynamics pledged that if a high-level branch of the University of California would come to San Diego he would build a laboratory for the study of atomic power. This is the model.

In 1952 Balboa was reorganized to become California Western University, with Admiral Frederick C. Sherman, U.S.N., ret., as chairman of a Board of Trustees. Serving with him were George A. Scott, John Cranston, Ewart W. Goodwin, Kenneth S. Imel, Herbert Kunzel, Edmund G. Price, Hayden S. Sears, Donald E. Smith, Harold B. Starkey and Robert J. Sullivan.

In June of 1952, Dr. William Rust, formerly head of religious education and an associate professor of religion at the University of Denver, was named executive dean. In November, with the retirement of Griffin, Rust became president. Rust announced that the University would be formed into three colleges, Business, Liberal Arts and a Community College. Its future course as an institution was set in the path originally taken by the University of Southern California at Los Angeles. It was accepted as a Methodist-supported institution by the Southern California Methodist Conference.

There were expectations that many new buildings on the campus would bear the name of those who donated the money to build them.

In the 1950's the Board of Regents of the University of California was expanding the university system to accommodate sons and daughters of the millions of new residents who had settled in the Golden State. On December 16, 1955, John Jay Hopkins, the chairman of Convair and General Dynamics Corporation, came out from New York to appear before a meeting of the regents in Los Angeles.

In the university's expansion into San Diego, he urged the location there of a scientific and technical campus in the La Jolla area, and if this were done his company would provide a grant of a million dollars and also would build in the same area its own research center at a cost of perhaps $10,000,000.

His plea was supported by a committee from San Diego which included Captain Henry S. Bernstein, director of the Naval Electronics Laboratory on Point Loma; Dr. Edward C. Creutz, formerly of the Carnegie Technical Institute and then with General Dynamics; O. W. Campbell, San Diego's City Manager; James Archer and Robert H. Biron, a vice president of Convair, who were members of a Chamber of Commerce University of California Committee, and James S. Copley, publisher of *The San Diego Union* and *Evening Tribune.*

The suggested institution was described by Hopkins as "a practical ivory tower" which could team up with the activities of the world-famous Scripps Institution of Oceanography and be important to the state as well as internationally.

> "The success of the North Atlantic Treaty Organization may depend on moves of this type. It would not conflict with the present activities at San Diego State College as it would operate in the higher areas of science and technology. We feel a great new era of change is at hand, both social and economic. Maybe our project will help unlock secrets of knowledge as rapidly as possible."

The concept seemed to have been accepted. On July 10, 1956, Hopkins dedicated a site on Torrey Pines, a gift of pueblo land voted by the people for a new atomic research center and remarked afterward that "there will be discoveries here that will amaze the world."

San Diegans had envisioned something akin to the California or Massachusetts Institute of Technology. But there were repeated efforts to convert the proposed branch into a general campus. Resistance to the original idea had risen in the University system, especially at University of California at Los Angeles, but Dr. Roger Revelle, director of the University's Scripps Institution of Oceanography, advanced compelling arguments to retain the graduate school emphasis.

Dr. William Rust

John Jay Hopkins

Dr. Roger Revelle

It was not until August of 1957 that the Board of Regents reaffirmed the original concept, in part, that the La Jolla campus would emphasize science and technology, but at the same time would provide such undergraduate instruction as was considered essential to support the graduate program.

The new plan envisioned the need for at least a thousand acres and the necessity of perhaps serving as many as 10,000 students by 1970. As a result there would be, too, casual surveys of sites other than the Torrey Pines area.

With universities ranging from San Diego State College, the Catholic-financed University of San Diego, the assurance of a high-level branch of the University of California, and now with a private but church-supported university which, it was hoped, could grow into another University of Southern California, San Diego was being advertised by its ambitious promoters as the "Educational Center of the Southwest."

Though education of a high level was being offered to San Diegans, there was little general enthusiasm for cultural activities. This proposed Civic Theater in Balboa Park failed to win approval.

John Jay Hopkins did not live to see either his atomic laboratory completed or construction begun on the university. He had been a Wall Street lawyer who late in his career put together an atomic age industrial empire that had produced the world's first atomic-powered submarine and was producing the nation's first ballistic missile in a new plant at San Diego. He died on May 3, 1957, at the age of sixty-three. Frank Pace, Jr., former Secretary of the Army, assumed direction of General Dynamics. Bernard F.

"Sandy" Coggan was promoted to a vice president as well as general manager of Convair-San Diego in 1957, at the age of thirty-eight.

Bernard F. Coggan

The hope of a Civic Theater would not die. Russ auditorium was bleak and lacking in parking areas. Women leaders of the community took up the challenge and proposed a $3,500,000 bond issue to construct a theater in Balboa Park, just east of Park Boulevard, in the central park area. It would have 3,000 seats and provide for parking for 1,500 cars on two levels, with access from Park Boulevard, Laurel Street and the Florida Canyon road, and elevators would deliver people to proper seat levels. Though women civic leaders rallied their friends and supporters, the voting was light and they failed to win the necessary two-thirds majority. A Civic Theater for plays and concerts was not necessarily a great public enthusiasm.

In the Fall of the same year, the Soviet Union launched the first man-made satellite, Sputnik 1, and sent it spinning around the Globe in one and a half hours. That was on October 4, 1957. On November 3, the Russians launched another and much larger satellite which carried a live creature, a dog, into space. The United States had yet to successfully launch its first missile. Feverish reaction swept over the country and engulfed San Diego.

CHAPTER SEVEN

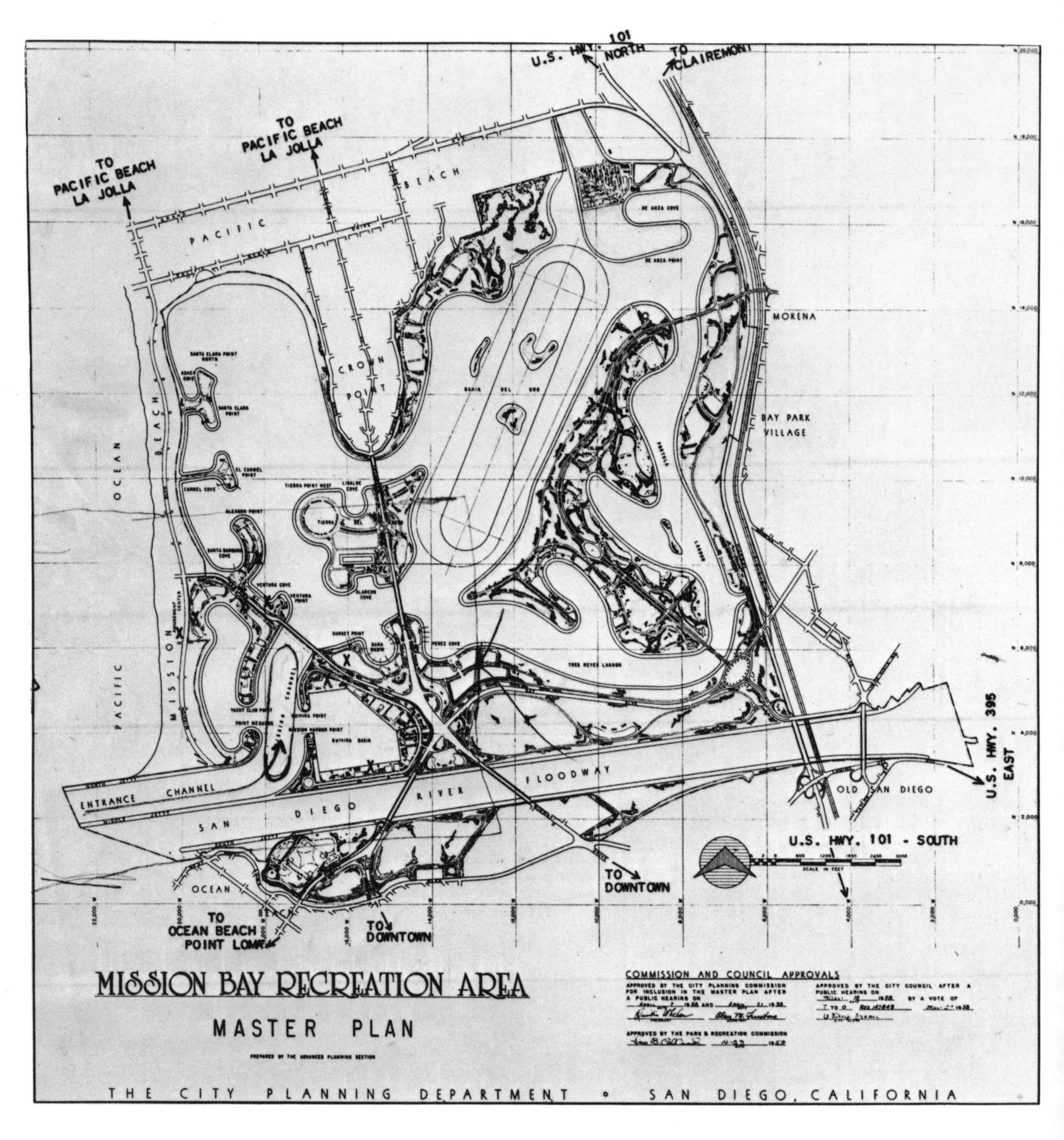

After the arguments had ended, as to what Mission Bay should be, this is the Master Plan adopted in 1958. There was considerable prior dispute first over the proper division between land and water uses, between picnickers and campers and boating and sailing enthusiasts, and how much land should be devoted to commercial purposes to help pay the costs.

The Price — Changes in the Land and the Sea

In the 1950's the word ecology was familiar only to a few people. Yet, the way of life in Southern California could be affected by seemingly minute changes in the environment. A change in the sea temperature of a few degrees could revolutionize the dynamics of the fish population; a drought could nearly abolish a whole grazing population.

The natural events which wrought ecological changes in Southern California were minor compared to another force that affected practically all life forms in the space of little more than a century. This force was the invasion of civilized man.

It is probable that no region on the face of the earth ever faced such a potential ecological force as this invasion. Certainly many other areas have felt the weight of man for millenia. There is a mid-East saying that when the Bedouin arrives, the sand must follow.

But the price — and effects — of this invasion were still only dimly recognized, even though local water sources had proved insufficient to meet the demands of growth, when in the 1950's a brown haze appeared over Los Angeles and would not go away. It soon spread across the basin and was even noticed over

A silent intruder on the self-satisfaction of Southern Californians was smog. It already had damaged Los Angeles when this picture was taken of a smog layer as it hovered over San Diego in 1956. This is a view looking southwest toward downtown and San Diego Bay.

San Diego. This was diagnosed with a new word: smog.

Other changes were occurring. Sea otters had long since vanished and as far as anyone knew, they were extinct along the coast. Whales had abandoned the San Diego Bay for Baja California. Sea lions and porpoises were no longer coming into the bay as they once had done. New signs warned swimmers of pollution. Some shore birds species were getting fewer in number. The California Brown Pelicans were hesitant to raise their young. The wide use of pesticides, too, soon would have an unforeseen serious effect on bird and animal life.

Evidence had existed for some time that there were cyclical changes in some of the kelp beds that covered a hundred square miles of ocean off California. But in the 1940's and early 1950's a widespread sickness of the kelp beds became noticeable. The kelp beds off Point Loma, the southern tip of San Diego, had permitted a harvest of 122,000 tons in 1917. By 1958, this had shrunk to almost nothing.

Only a few scientists were becoming aware of the price man had to pay for the dams he had built across the seasonal rivers and streams. The sand that had created the Silver Strand and the Mission Beach peninsula, and thus formed the two largest bays in Southern California, was no longer being carried down to the sea where currents could deposit it along the shores. Waves were slowly beginning to encroach on the beaches and wash them away.

Erosion, in the form of advancing waves, and wind and rain, was eating away at the cliffs on the ocean side of Point Loma. The restful structures which A. G. Spalding, the sporting goods manufacturer had left the City with his gift of Sunset Cliffs Park, were falling away.

Going north from San Diego Bay the lagoons are Mission Bay, San Dieguito, Los Batiquitos, San Elijo, Agua Hedionda and Buena Vista. In centuries past, and probably for thousands of years, native peoples had camped seasonally by the lagoons and lived off sea and bird life in a balance with nature.

In modern times, these natural environments would form probably the most controversial areas in San Diego County because they could be altered by man in many cases into recreational parks, or into green masses of stagnant water or even dry alkali beds. Developers would want to fill the sloughs and turn them into housing projects; the sportsman would want a waterfowl hunting area; conservationists would want a refuge for sea and bird life; the salt water enthusiast would want marine and water-skiing facilities.

As for Mission Bay, it long had been looked upon as an area of mud flats, with narrow winding channels and unnavigable marshes, a delight only to a relatively few people who lived along its shores, with small rickety piers for their boats, and who felt akin to nature and its wildlife. By 1877, when the Army

Jetties made of rock blasted out of the walls of Mission Gorge were forever changing the course of the San Diego River. Three jetties would divert runoff water directly into the ocean, provide a navigable channel into Mission Bay, and save both Mission Bay and San Diego Bay.

Corps of Engineers had again diverted the San Diego River from the main bay into False or Mission Bay, after the effort of the 1850's had failed, a Los Angeles reporter wrote that the confining of the river to a new channel sent the flood waters into False Bay, "which has no commercial value and can be filled up with impunity." In time the bay might have disappeared, because of silting, and the river could again have sought a new outlet to the sea.

State and Federal interest in the bay, however, either as a harbor or a park, had been manifested for years, though there were those in San Diego who argued in the late 1940's that the bay should be left to nature. But there was always the question of whether they also would have left the area of Balboa Park as unused open space covered with thick brush. Balboa Park had become a treasure.

Then, with the slow creation by dredging of small coves along the western shore, and the building of public beaches virtually up to the front doors of the homes of long-time bay residences, the value of privately-held lands adjoining the bay began to rise, and many property owners saw the possibilities of the future.

There was no general agreement, however, as to what a proper division of Mission Bay as a park should be, as between land and water uses for people and the requirements of any wildlife, and how much space would have to be devoted to the tourist industry and the creation of income to help make the park self-sustaining as had been promised.

Glenn Rick, the City's Planning Director who had originally set the plans in motion for development of the bay into a recreational area, had resisted a too rigid master plan which might jeopardize opportunities for income or uses as time moved on. He told the Mission Bay Park Commission that the prior commitments to the State on wild life requirements eliminated much of the possibility of change in the general plan for the northern half of the eastern bay area. In 1949 City planners had envisioned nine wildlife islands. But by 1955, the islands had been reduced to five, one of them to be heavily wooded.

Impatience at slow progress was expressed on many sides. There was wide dissatisfaction with the granting of a lease for a drive-in theater but Rick pointed out that the area of its location was landlocked and would not make a good camp site as had been suggested.

Edward Hall, president of the San Diego Taxpayers Association, argued before the Commission, and its chairman, George A. Scott, that the park had to be self-sustaining and not become a burden on taxpayer. In this he was supported by Elliott Cushman, chairman of a Chamber of Commerce Mission Bay committee, and Ray Blair, executive assistant to the Chamber's manager. Frank W. Seifert, the retired Army major and former City Councilman, was still urging that a major airport should be laid out in the southern area.

The San Diego Union brought the situation into focus:

> "Because the development of Mission Bay had been slow, there has been a temptation to grasp at whatever offers are made for the construction of park facilities. ... The idea of immediate revenue is alluring. And, unquestionably, revenue is important. But more to the point are questions regarding the best possible use of the land – uses of the most lasting good for the greatest majority. ... Pressures are being built up to set aside parts of the beach for varied private groups. Each group feels that the bay is large enough so its small request will do little damage. But all these add up to major proportions and do not serve the general public."

Frank Seifert

While everything from water skiing to gun clubs and playhouses was being suggested for a place in what had been conceived to be an aquatic park, and winning some commission favor, the principal pressure was to get on with the job. The Federal Government already had spent more than $7,000,000 of its estimated share of $10,000,000. The City had spent more than $8,000,000 of its anticipated share of $19,000,000. The State of California had reimbursed the City for river flood control work in the amount of $3,500,000.

Most of the City's work had been on the west side of the bay while the Federal Government had built the three great rock jetties which forever would carry the flood waters of the river out into the ocean and at the same time provide a deep water channel leading into Mission Bay. But so far only seven miles of beaches had been developed and only 565 acres of water had been made navigable for standard pleasure craft.

A bond issue of $5,000,000 was placed on the City ballot for June, 1956 and voters were warned that other Federal appropriations of about $3,000,000, to dredge the outer harbor to a depth of twenty feet in order to accommodate ocean-going craft, probably hinged on the outcome of the election.

The $5,000,000 would be spent for further dredging of the bay proper, to a low-tide depth of eight feet, and the creation of new beaches on the eastern shore, more recreational areas, camp grounds, landscaping, and general public facilities. City officials predicted a "whirlwind" courtship by commercial, hotel, motel and marine interests if the bond issue carried.

A comparison with Miami Beach could not be resisted by those concerned with the economic aspects of Mission Bay. *The San Diego Union* scouted Miami and found it had a well-developed package to sell to the East Coast and the Middle West and had parlayed year-round sunshine and salt water into a multi-million dollar annual business.

San Diego had the same potential, it was found, with Mission Bay, the weather, and its other vacation and recreational attractions, but its "tourist plant" – convention facilities, restaurants and hotels – was only beginning to take on aspects of importance.

The concern of most citizens, however, was for a Mission Bay as a playground, a water playground, for themselves. On one Summer afternoon it was estimated that 38,000 had enjoyed the beaches or the warm water. The bond issue was approved by the voters, but unhappiness over progress brought renewed de-

Quivira Basin was one of the great hopes for Mission Bay. This is the basin and its possible development as envisioned in 1959. Not all plans came to fruition, or were developed as had been originally hoped for.

bate on how best to administer such a large project so important to the City's future and its economic expectations.

An original Mission Bay Park Advisory Committee had evolved into a Commission but its role still was advisory and its authority vague. A Mayor's committee early in 1955 had recommended that a five-man board be designated to operate Mission Bay Park and that it be given the same autonomy as the Harbor Commission.

This would have required a City Charter amendment. The Council deadlocked on a decision whether to refer the issue to the voters. Mayor Dail soon afterward pressed again for such a Commission, and again to no avail. Instead, a study by a consulting firm was approved and it came up with a recommendation that the director of the park be an assistant to the City Manager and that he be made responsible both to the Manager and the City Council, and that a new seven-man Commission be constituted but only be advisory to the Council. This plan was adopted in 1956.

The fight for an autonomous Commission, however, was not over. It would come up again and again. In 1957, Councilman Justin Evenson took up the cudgels, while the new Commission itself sought clarification of its powers. *The San Diego Union* termed progress in the park as "faltering" and "lacking in strong, decisive leadership."

Feeling that it was unfairly receiving the brunt of public criticism for any delays in progress, or lapses in administration of the park, the Commission appealed to the Council to place the issue of an autonomous Commission up to the voters. The only change, however, was an ordinance re-defining the Commission's status, in that it would report to both the City Manager and the Council. An effort to have members of the Commission be appointed by the Mayor instead of by all members of the Council, failed in passage. More than a year after passage of the $5,000,000 bond issue, and eleven years of time and the expenditure of nineteen million dollars, plans for the park itself had not yet been made firm. A re-drawing of old informal plans produced a new one providing for central islands and a curving shoreline on the east side.

Scientists familiar with the bay expressed misgivings about the plan. Dr. Douglas Inman, of the Scripps Institution of Oceanography, said there was little reason to believe that the proposed shore lines would remain in the same shape they were built, because of tide, wave and wind action. A $25,000 oceanographic study was commissioned and it supported his contention.

A new Master Plan, and actually the first formal one, was prepared for public hearings in 1958, which were to be conducted, not by the Bay Commission, but by the Planning Commission.

There was a new cast of characters. Glenn Rick, who had brought the idea of an aquatic park into being, tired of political strife, had resigned as Planning Director to enter private business. Harry Haelsig was selected to succeed him and Lester Halcomb as an assistant to the City Manager was acting Mission Park Director.

Haelsig told a public hearing that dredging by the City had been too long delayed while plans were drawn and re-drawn, but now a fifty-fifty balance had been achieved between land

Harry Haelsig

and water uses, the configuration of the eastern shore had been modified, the central islands of the east bay, originally to be wildlife preserves, had been reformed into one large island of 418 acres which would provide camping and picnic areas.

Dr. Carl Hubbs, of the Scripps Institution of Oceanography, urged the retention of a wildlife preserve, and Haelsig replied that this had been done by setting aside seventy-seven acres of the northern shore, seven more acres than had been included in the 1956 plan with the islands.

The proposed central island was the principal dividing issue that seemed to remain, and water sports enthusiasts protested what they described as an over-emphasis on land uses. A yachtsman, Alonzo Jessop, called the island "downright ridiculous" and that picnic and camping areas were available at a dozen other parks throughout the County:

Gerald C. Crary

> "I don't know of any other place along the Pacific Coast where they are filling in water areas. In most places they are dredging out areas to make more harbors and canals."

The City's reply was a practical one: there had to be a place to put all the sand that had to be dredged up to convert mud flats into navigable water, and it was too costly to transport the sand out to the ocean. This had been done in a measure by the Army Corps of Engineers in dredging the channel entrance. The sand had been deposited to enlarge the swimming area at adjoining Ocean Beach, as well as in South Mission Beach, where beaches had been seriously eroded.

A former City Councilman, Gerald Crary, who had participated in planning for the aquatic park, and who at the time of the hearing was manager of the San Diego Tourist and Convention Bureau, described the new plan as the soundest he had seen, and he was supported by a former Mayor, John D. Butler. Both of them said the island could be removed later, if it were found advisable to do so. "Let's adopt this plan and get going on it," said O. W. Todd, Jr., active in sports and president of the Young Men's Christian Association.

O. W. Todd, Jr.

Ultimate uses in the new Master Plan would offer the public almost 2,000 acres of navigable water, more than 2,000 acres of park land and almost thirty-two miles of shoreline. Areas were designated in a general way for boat launchings, boat slip facilities, parks and picnics and beaches, hotels and motels and related facilities, for public activity and semi-public and public facilities. Of the available land, twenty-five percent was to be set aside for commercial purposes, principally hotels and motels, by which the park might become self-supporting.

The Master Plan, as drawn by the City Planning Department

and presented by the City Planning Commission, failed to win full support of the Mission Bay Commission, and its chairman, C. Harry Burnaugh, resigned. The City Council, however, adopted the controversial plan without a dissenting vote, in 1958, and it became the general guide for the aquatic park that Mission Bay was to become. But as Glenn Rick had foreseen, any plan could not be inflexible and there would be changes, particularly in the location of areas to be set aside for commercial enterprises.

Many were the schemes of promoters for Mission Bay. This was a suggested mobile "Fire Island" with an imitation volcano. A report on the future of the bay commended the City for resisting movie-set effects.

The dredging out of the mud and the filling in of marsh lands destroyed the normal feeding grounds of thousands of shore birds which were forced to adjust to new areas or leave the vicinity entirely. The Black Brant for which Mission Bay had been a principal wintering ground, and which was to be memorialized on sanctuary signs throughout the park, virtually disappeared.

While wildlife may have departed the City's waters, birds, animals and reptiles, including specimens of the survivors of

Charles R. Schroeder

man's rush to California, and others from around the world, were being assembled in ever-increasing numbers under the protection of the San Diego Zoological Society. A new director, Charles R. Schroeder, had succeeded Mrs. Belle Benchley in 1953. She retired with honors.

The Zoo in Balboa Park was becoming world famous. It was free of politics. While the exhibits were the legal property of the City, and thus the taxpayers, their care rested with the San Diego Zoological Society, a private organization.

Membership dues, some donations and gifts, and revenue from a two-cent tax return on each $100 of assessed valuation, enabled the society to free itself of political pressures and limitations. In 1947, Zoo attendance was 1,447,324 – for a total of more than 50,000,000 since its founding in 1922.

At one time, the City Manager, O. W. Campbell, had looked with some dismay on the Zoo's untouchability and suggested privately that its revenues were out of proportion to the money devoted to other social or civic institutions. He, in short, wanted to cut them down. He failed.

Again in 1959, some members of the City Council considered withdrawing support by eliminating the two cents tax. Councilman Chester C. Schneider claimed the Zoo no longer needed such financial assistance. Again, this move failed. The Board of Directors of the Zoo was almost self-perpetuating but it was becoming the most prestigious civic group in the community.

The loss of the early otter population, of course, had been felt economically as a loss of a source of valuable furs. Naturalists were disturbed by the loss of a species so numerous and so attractive. Their protests had finally led to the signing of a treaty between the United States, Japan, Great Britain and Russia to ban otter hunting. The signing was in 1911, long after anyone knew where there were any otters to protect.

It took much longer to discover and appreciate another effect of the otter destruction. This was the ecological effect that took a century to become of economic importance. It was discovered when, in the middle of the 1950's, the kelp beds started to disappear off San Diego and other parts of the coast. By this time the kelp beds were valuable for two things – they supplied shelter for sportfish and thus supported the lucrative sport fishing industry and the kelp was the raw material for the extraction of algin, an emulsifying agent used in making explosives, ice cream and many other products.

The grandeur of the kelp forests was not appreciated before the advent of scuba diving in the 1950's. For the first time men were able to penetrate among these great brown plants that provided a canopy as much as 200 feet above the ocean floor. Scientists and naturalists, equipped with air tanks and swim fins, cruised in the perpetual shadow of the kelp fronds and observed more kinds of wildlife per minute than the first explorers of terrestrial forests. They were in what seemed a fairy forest. The "trees" had neither roots or trunks, for the kelp can get its sustenance from sea water with the help of the sun shining on its uppermost layers and it obtains its support from the buoyancy supplied by the ocean. In place of trunks, the kelp plants have thin, waving stipes that connect with holdfasts which have the unique function of anchoring the plants to their positions on the seafloor.

A scientific inquiry made by Dr. Wheeler J. North of the California Institute of Technology resulted in the finding that sea urchins in great hordes were chewing away the kelp holdfasts and setting the great plants adrift. It was then recalled that in times past the urchins had furnished the principal item of diet for the sea otters. Thus destruction of the otters had removed the ecological brake on the urchin population, a brake which had protected the kelp. The fight to save the kelp was about to begin.

A fight to save the Bay of San Diego, however, was slow in getting started. This bay was not particularly envisioned by San Diegans as a place for swimming or water skiing, though they acknowledged its commercial importance. But throughout its history, its waters and tidal flats had been nursery feeding ground and a refuge for fish and wildlife.

Finally, and almost fatally, the bay was being used as a receptacle for most of the wastes from the communities developing and expanding on its shores.

Prior to 1943 the City had a primitive sewer system which discharged raw sewage into the bay and ocean through twenty outfalls. The pressure of population during the war forced the building of a primary treatment plant. It was enlarged in 1948 and was also handling sewage from National City, La Mesa, Lemon Grove and North Island. In the late years of the 1950's the bay had become so polluted that most of it had been quarantined. Bait and game fish virtually disappeared. Aquatic training by the military was seriously reduced and curtailed. Aesthetic uses were reduced.

A sludge bed 200 yards wide, leading from the treatment plant outfall, was reported in 1951. In a decade its depth would be increased to more than seven feet. In 1954, the City's voters had refused to approve a $16,000,000 bond issue to correct pollution of the bay by carrying sewage to Point Loma and disposing of it into the ocean through a long outfall. Opponents were led by the contractor, Roscoe E. Hazard, whose company was building the great freeways of the auto age. He deplored what he described as incomplete and incompetent engineering and said the costs of the system had been seriously underestimated. Those in favor of the project ascribed his warnings to his own fear of odors from the outfall drifting up to his home on Point Loma.

After the defeat of the sewer issue, a citizens' committee was named to find a solution on how to proceed in solving pollution of the bay. It recommended the employment of three engineers, who, in turn, recommended the location of a treatment plant and ocean outfall at Imperial Beach in preference to Point Loma. This would cost $26,000,000.

This is a restful and inviting scene. But already San Diego Bay was so polluted, by 1954, that swimming was considered unhealthy. Voters proved reluctant to do anything about it, in the turmoil of a civic dispute.

The original thinking had been for the City of San Diego to finance the cost of the system, and allowing other communities to tie into it through service charges. Some apparently would want to do so, as had been done in the past; others were hesitant. Now the thinking changed and San Diego contemplated asking all who wanted to tie in to participate in the total financing.

The obvious necessity of a metropolitan, or regional, system of sewage disposal emphasized the long-time contention of the City Manager, O. W. Campbell, that in time metropolitan government would have to be substituted for that of individual cities now inevitably merging into great urban areas.

George Bean

Too, Campbell perhaps was feeling the strains of the City Manager system which in San Diego had been modified to partially disperse governmental authority through a number of commissions, which, in turn, differed in the extent of their responsibilities. The Harbor Commission was virtually autonomous; the Mission Bay Commission, advisory only.

Mayors, too, were experiencing the frustration of office without power. A Mayor's vote was equal to that of any Councilman and his role as defined by the City Charter merely ceremonial. Both Percy Benbough and Harley Knox had sought, with some success, to override the limitations of office. Mayor Dail would try to bring about a change of importance; he wanted the power that in most cities went with the office of Mayor.

San Diegans, in adopting that City Manager system, with some modifications, and after experiencing years of police and political corruption, believed they had divorced the administration of City government from political interference. But, in the opinion of Mayor Dail and others, the voters also had tied the hands of political leaders, and that in some measure any surrender of political authority to a professional City Manager could mean, in fact, a disfranchisement of voters.

Suddenly, Campbell was gone. He resigned on July 22, 1957, to go to Miami to become Manager of Dade County. City Managers of the time knew their stay in one area must be limited; the effect of decisions would catch up with them and they had to go for political reasons. But in Dade County he would manage affairs of a number of political jurisdictions.

At first, Jerome Keithley, City Manager of Palo Alto, California, was selected by the City Council as the new City Manager, and then when he changed his mind about coming, the Council unanimously chose George Bean, who was City Manager of Peoria, Illinois. Bean was fifty-eight; Keithley, forty-two.

Bean, still in San Diego, was summoned to a special meeting of the City Council and he agreed to accept the position. First, however, he asked about the City's two major problems. He was told they were a new sewer system and a Convention Hall. "I'll get them for you," he said, "but by that time you'll fire me. I'll be around only about four years."

Man was creating an environmental revolution. Yet, in another sense, he was merely altering ecological systems by creating new ones. Sand did not necessarily follow man's appearance. It would have been difficult to return to a scene without palms, without oranges and eucalyptus trees, and without highways. Southern California had become a paradise in the view of those who sought a new way of life free from the rigors of climate and decay.

But there were so many people arriving now in San Diego that the inconsistencies of nature combined with population growth brought a new crisis. In the late 1950's Dr. Carl Hubbs of the Scripps Institution of Oceanography, told San Diegans:

"I have a number of reasons for thinking that the drought that started in about 1934 — this great drought — was perhaps the most severe of any which has occurred since the Ice Age, during the last 15,000 years ... the general trend seems to be in the direction of drier conditions. And if this is true, and I think it is highly probable that it is, it seems to me that man in and near the desert and semi-desert regions will need to think and act very boldly, or possibly suffer very severe consequences."

The second pipeline for the San Diego Aqueduct had been opened in 1954, the same year in which drought conditions returned after a slight interlude. The next year a report of the County Water Authority concluded that more water would be needed by 1960. However, the year 1956 saw rainfall drop to its lowest point, to four and half inches for the season.

An alarmed San Diego County responded with overwhelming approval of $35,000,000 in bonds to be issued by the Water Authority for construction of a second aqueduct. The Water Authority assumed responsibility for the ninety-seven miles of construction from Hemet, in Riverside County, to the Lower Otay Reservoir in San Diego County. The Metropolitan Water District assumed responsibility for thirty-eight miles of construction to the San Diego delivery point.

Construction could not begin until 1958 and meanwhile a "Don't Waste the Water Committee" was organized in the City to conserve supplies, as it was not certain that the little amount remaining in the reservoirs, and that which could be delivered from the Colorado River through two barrels of the first aqueduct, would be enough until the second aqueduct could be comcompleted.

The continuing growth in population and agriculture had broken down resistance of many County areas to joining the San Diego County Water Authority. By mid-1958 there were eighteen member agencies, the demand for water had been so persistent down the years. This included four cities, Escondido, National City, Oceanside and San Diego. The irrigation districts included Helix, San Dieguito, Santa Fe and South Bay, which also took in the city of Chula Vista. Municipal water districts were Buena Colorado, Carlsbad, Otay, Poway, Rainbow, Ramona, Rincon del Diablo and Rio San Diego, which also took in the Lakeside Irrigation District, and Valley Center. The eighteenth member was the Fallbrook Public Utility District.

Agriculture in the County as well as life in its cities and communities could no longer be sustained in a land where population had so outstripped an ecological balance.

New ecological systems – with their people and its trees – would survive. But the great changes were not over – an economic upheaval shaping all people's lives had reached San Diego. They would be related in a way to a dramatic re-defining of the authority of a City. In 1954 the United States Supreme Court ruled that it was within the power of a legislative body to determine that a community should be beautiful as well as healthy, spacificous as well as clean, well-balanced as well as carefully patrolled.

CHAPTER EIGHT

360

The missile that was to change the nature of war and open the Space Age was the Atlas. Here an Atlas is tested in its stand in Sycamore Canyon in San Diego. The Space Age spawned a new wave of technology of which few persons had forewarnings.

The Auto — the Rise of Shopping Centers

In 1957 it was learned that the United States Air Force had placed a huge, though secret, order for Atlas ballistic missiles even though one had not as yet been successfully test-fired. Thousands of personnel were preparing to move into the new Convair Astronautics plant being completed on Kearny Mesa. In its main plant at Lindbergh Field, General Dynamics was tooling up for production of the Convair 880, to challenge two major competitors in the field of jet-powered commercial airliners.

After two failures, an Atlas missile was successfully fired out over the Air Force's Atlantic range, in the last month of the year. The Convair plant rang with cheers.

In the same year it became known that the May Department Stores Company, with headquarters in Los Angeles, would, if zoning changes were approved, build a huge shopping complex in Mission Valley. A spokesman for the company, Albert C. Martin, of a Los Angeles engineering and architectural firm, told the City Council in a conference that the center, to be located near the intersection of Highways 80 and 395, had the top priority of all May Company projects in the nation. Ultimate cost estimates ranged as high as $35,000,000. Jobs would be provided for almost a thousand persons.

First, it would be necessary to re-zone about ninety acres of land from agricultural-residential to commercial. Martin assured Councilmen that in keeping with the beauty and history of the valley, the proposed buildings would "breathe the spirit of the Missions," with interwoven courtyards or patio areas, each with covered walks.

The decision on a site in Mission Valley came out of a research project predicting a northward growth for metropolitan San Diego which would place the center in the heart of the future. It also represented the first large invasion of out-of-town marketing interests other than the chain and variety stores common to most American communities and cities.

The nationally-known Jordan Marsh Company, of Boston prestige, which had occupied the former downtown home of Sears, Roebuck & Co., staggered into failure and closed its doors in March of 1958. There were various versions of its failure, ranging from a drift of shopping from downtown to a mistake of judgment in the quality of merchandise that had been offered. The store had not seemed to live up to the company's Boston reputation.

The grouping of stores in areas where parking could be made available had begun, in a small way. One of the larger ones was

The success of the Atlas, the nation's first ballistic missile capable of crossing the oceans in thirty minutes, is reflected in the huge plant built on Kearny Mesa for its production.

Mission Valley was still largely a farming area east of the Cabrillo Freeway interchange when the May Company of Los Angeles selected this site to open a shopping center and acknowledge the triumph of the auto.

the South Bay Plaza which opened in 1955 but it had not as yet had a significant impact on retail business in San Diego. The possible turn of a tide in shopping habits had prompted the San Diego Downtown Association to formulate a plan for pedestrian malls, the planting of trees, and the addition of scattered but accessible parking garages and freeway connections which would draw motorists into the central district.

In Mission Valley, hotels and motels already were rising rapidly and zoning regulations had been relaxed to allow C. Arnholt Smith to erect a new ball park for his minor league baseball team, the San Diego Padres. Other promoters were seeking to push through projects calling for a denser use of land than the Planning Department had thought wise, and Mayor Dail had responded by suggesting that "throwing out some of these red-tape ordinances" might improve the economy of San Diego.

The prolonged drought and the existence of dams on the San Diego River and its tributaries had lessened the fear of floods for many who saw commercial and recreational opportunities in the valley. The May Company gave the Council assurance that all structures in the center would rest on a nine-foot high fill which would bring ground level up to the grade of Highway 80 and provide protection against the highest flood ever recorded.

But the plan was not in the concept of Mission Valley as had been envisioned by the City Planning Department. And the department was concerned with possible flooding:

> "If the storm of January 1943, which centered in the San Gabriel Mountains northeast of Los Angeles were to occur over the San Diego River, Mission Valley would be subjected to the worst flood in its history."

Of course, this would mean that the upstream reservoirs would have been filled to overflowing by previous storms.

The department had been working on an elaborate zoning plan for the valley, to allow for a future flood control channel, but it was a general concept which mostly became an issue. Its own plan sought to provide "for the highest and best use of the property":

> "Mission Valley is the gateway to potentially the finest recreational area in the world. It will develop into an area complementing Mission Bay, offering accommodations and entertainment to visitors and residents. It would be possible for some future generation to tie Mission Valley, Old San Diego and Mission Bay Park together by a motor-boat canal, scenic roadways, bridle trails, and a scenic railway – further enhancing our position as a tourist center."

The May Company had made its own studies on possible floods in Mission Valley and would build its shopping center on a grade level with the new Valley freeway. This was the architects' plan for the center as originally conceived.

The May Company proposal, the City's Planning Director, Harry Haeslig, told the San Diego Downtown Association, would not be compatible with this concept.

In its conclusion, the Planning Department stated:

> "The lessons we can learn from our large Eastern cities should be obvious; they now wish they had not been so short-sighted when they traded the almighty dollar for their available open space. ... Once Mission Valley is

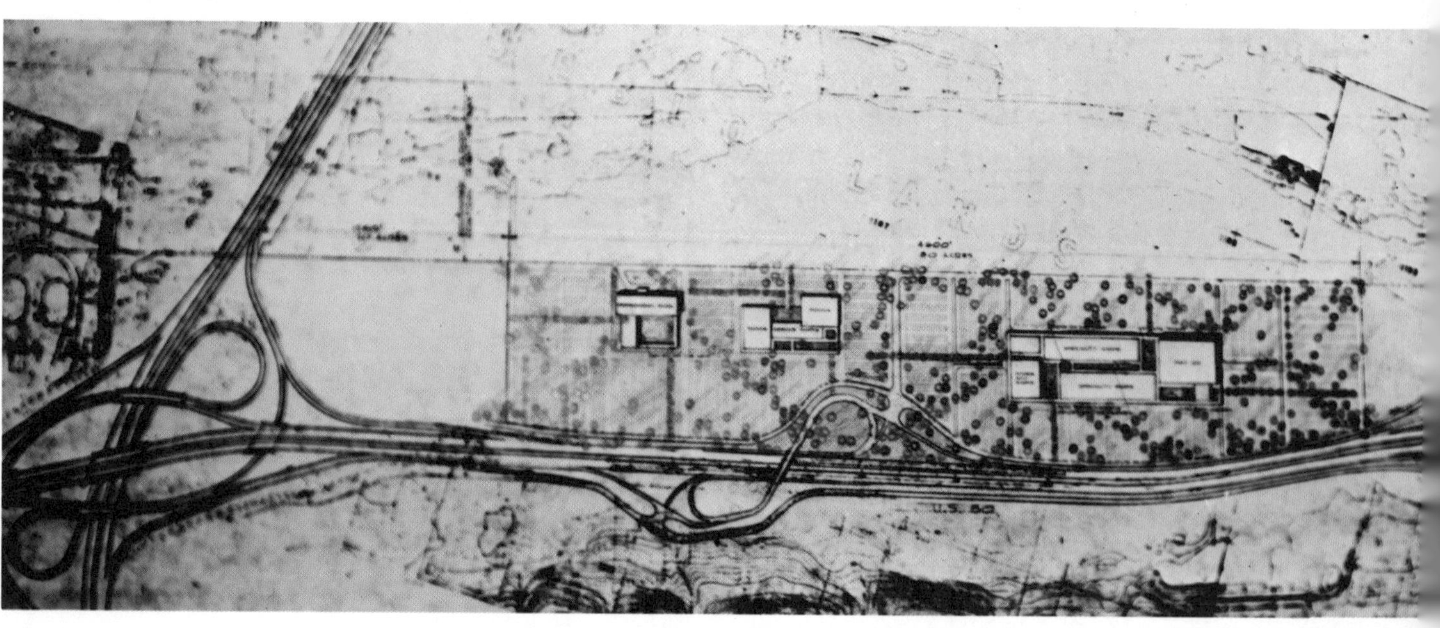

Some opposition to a shopping center in Mission Valley was based on resistance to a decentralization. Some opposition was based on the fear of floods, as suggested in this high water scene of 1952 at the Santa Fe railroad bridge, or who would pay for any flood protection.

paved with commercial enterprises it will be lost forever to the community as an open area within the City."

The Planning Commission voted three to two to overrule its planning staff and send the re-zoning request to the Council as a report and not a recommendation which would have required five affirmative votes. A formal hearing was set by the City Council for June of 1958.

The May Company was blunt. An executive, Walter Brunmark, declared:

"If we are not given the privilege and the right to come into your City and locate in Mission Valley, we will not come here. ... There isn't any other location suitable for the kind of a retail shopping center that we want to put in here, in San Diego."

The most prominent spokesmen against a center in Mission Valley were downtown merchants, but all of them insisted their opposition was not based on a matter of unwelcome competition but on other factors which they considered important to San Diego and San Diegans.

George A. Scott, who himself was interested in a shopping center in the eastern part of the metropolitan area, said:

"Business in this day and age should not unite to stop competition; we are not going to fight location of a competitor, whether in Mission Valley or some other place."

Hamilton Marston

Guilford Whitney

His concern, he said, was in the matter of flooding in the valley and who was to pay for the protection that might be necessary in the future.

Another view was presented by Hamilton Marston who said that the Council must know that a favorable decision would bring many more requests for the change of hundreds of acres in this central San Diego area. He asked the Council:

> "Do you know the consequences of what you are starting? What are the implications for Mission Valley and for all San Diego, our City and our metropolitan area? We know that shopping centers are a fact of mid-twentieth century American life. But how do they fit into the pattern of motor-age transportation and the pattern of residential, recreational, commercial, industrial and civic administrative land use of the modern American city, and especially San Diego?"

The possibility that the valley, if commercial building were permitted, might become the equal of the downtown area, or even surpass it, was raised by Arthur Jessop, of the pioneering jewelry merchandising family:

> "The valley is part of the Planning Department's future plan for ... tourists and we are considering throwing it down the drain. ... Should a decision be made before considering these consequences, we may as well tattoo on the Council walls right here: 'Thus died planning in San Diego.'"

The effect of outlying shopping centers on some other cities was recalled by another merchant, Guilford Whitney, who told the Councilmen:

> "You may know that in some of our California cities – and one of them is Fresno – the downtown area has gone backwards, very, very rapidly with the development of shopping centers. Our opposition is not to shopping centers. We feel that they are a normal growth. However, placing a shopping center of the magnitude of this one, with projected annual sales of fifty million dollars, almost half of what the small central business district now does, would be a blow to downtown San Diego. ... If we build another central city only four minutes away from downtown we may end by having a slum business district in what is now our central area."

While other fears were being expressed that Mission Valley was to be converted into a commercial alley, there was some evidence introduced that the people, or the voters, didn't look at a shopping center in the valley in an unhappy light. A locally conducted poll showed little opposition, even indifference.

The hand of conciliation was offered by the May Company. Frank Clark, an executive, pledged:

> "Not withstanding the differences between ourselves and our opponents. ... I would like to give this pledge on behalf of our company that if we are permitted to build our store and our center, we will extend the hand of

friendship and cooperation to one and all, including these opponents, and work with them to provide the City of San Diego with a new era of merchandising as to convenience and beauty of facilities. And we pledge to you, the City Council, that we will assume our fair share of each and every community service."

An ordinance granting the zone change was adopted unanimously by the City Council. Referendum petitions later were circulated for a public vote on the Council re-zoning action, but soon were withdrawn.

As the 1960's approached, it was obvious that the "downtown revolution" was in full swing in San Diego. The auto had won. The California Division of Highways had in its first construction stages a great curving freeway that would sweep across the top of the City, chopping off a corner of Balboa Park, as a part of the new coastal Highway 101.

Resistance to the location of freeways persisted, however, though their march across the State seemed to be relentless. The coastal communities between south Carlsbad and the Torrey Pines junction resented the highway which in spreading south and inland seemed to be cutting their communities in half. Angry property owners pulled up survey stakes and others burned in effigy the Highway Department's regional engineer, Jacob Dekema.

In San Diego, the City Council as early as 1955 had approved the route of the crosstown freeway which, while it would provide easy access in and out of the downtown area, also would make it possible for shoppers to cross easily from one metropolitan area to another, without ever passing through the central business district, by a system of traffic interchanges.

In face of this, however, the Marston Company had invested heavily in enlarging and improving its downtown department store. Now the May Company was beginning construction of its huge shopping center in Mission Valley and the Walker Scott Company at last had been successful in bringing into construction the College Grove center in the City's eastern section.

By late 1959, the shopping center race was on, and other Los Angeles merchandisers were driving to enter the competition for the San Diego market. After failing to entice Walker Scott stores into selling, or surrendering its shopping center advantage, the Broadway-Hale Department Store of Los Angeles looked southward and acquired a site in Chula Vista. The Marston Company finally joined the wave moving outward from downtown. It was instrumental in the development of another center in the eastern area to be known as the Grossmont Shopping Center, and accessible from Highway 80, by the Del Webb Construction Company of Phoenix, Arizona.

Thus the San Diego region soon would have in operation four regional shopping centers. And another was being formed to the east, outside the City, in El Cajon Valley, which would have a branch of Whitney's, an old-line San Diego store which was trying to expand into more department store status.

All of the leading downtown merchants who had questioned the advisability of the May Company creating a great merchandising center in Mission Valley were now themselves vigorously engaged in meeting the new form of competition spawned by the auto age.

Population was still soaring. In the twenty years since the start of World War II, the City had added more than 350,000 residents for a total of 554,000. The population of the County as a whole had passed the million mark. The annual rate of growth was approaching nine percent.

The economic figures for 1958 listed the value of agricultural products at more than 100 million dollars. Navy and Marine payrolls were more than $270,000,000. The total value of manufactured products was more than $1,266,000,000 and the revenue from the tourist business was estimated at $144,000,000.

The City's Old Guard, oriented as it was to the buying and selling of land, could take cheer in the fact that in 1958 almost 11,000 new homes had been built, or were about to be built, in the City, and more than 22,000 in the County as a whole.

By the early 1950's, Linda Vista had become a community almost unto itself. San Diego was spreading northward, following the curving mesa split by canyons. This was a future developers of shopping centers had foreseen.

If Linda Vista was almost a community unto itself, Clairemont was almost a City unto itself. This is how Clairemont appeared in 1956, and construction of more homes was still proceeding swiftly.

The City was moving northward, out on Kearny Mesa, as the May Company and others had foreseen, with huge tracts of homes rising in Clairemont as well as in Linda Vista.

A survey by the San Diego Unified School District indicated a continued expansion in home building in the north coastal areas of Soledad, University City, and the La Jolla Highlands, with 12,000 homes projected within the following five years, and perhaps as many as 3,000 more rising on Miramar Mesa, as yet untouched.

During the 1950's San Diego's Unified School District would complete more school buildings than in all of the preceding hundred years. In five years enrollments had risen from about 50,000 to nearly 85,000, and school bond issues had been readily approved by the voters.

In the County, outside the immediate City area, El Cajon, Santee, Fletcher Hills, Lakeside, La Mesa, Spring Valley and Lemon Grove, were experiencing building booms that seemed to assure the success of the new shopping centers to the east. To the south, National City and Chula Vista were also prospering and changing.

The growth, however, was no match for that of Los Angeles, which had spawned subdivision upon subdivision in a seeming endlessly expanding circle, and with the downtown district splitting into a half dozen centers with no dominating structures, an obvious object lesson in unrestrained building. The open spaces which had been provided by the many canyons which cut through the San Diego mesas were largely lacking in Los Angeles. It was a city in a basin which so persistently trapped the smog of the auto and industrial age. Only a relatively few people could escape to distant and more inviting hillsides.

In Los Angeles smog had become so bad by 1954 that in October of that year air traffic had to be diverted from the sprawling International Airport, on the seacoast, inland to Burbank, and ships were unable to penetrate into the inner harbor. Action was demanded and yet with all controls possible, based on the knowledge of the times, it was not certain that blue skies were ever to return to Los Angeles as in the days of the pioneers.

A survey in the late 1950's indicated that half of the residents would live elsewhere — in California, of course — if they could do so. San Diegans took a lot of comfort from that — but all of the story of building booms had not yet been written.

San Diegans didn't believe it could ever happen here. It was an isolated area open to the sea. It was blocked off to the north from a Los Angeles spill-over by a huge Marine base; to the east by mountains and to the south by Mexico; to the west by the ocean. Magnificent natural barriers — and much of the land in the City and surrounding country was still vacant. No one thought now of trying to slow it all down.

"Smokestacks or geraniums?" The old civic struggle seemed to have been long buried. The smokestacks which in the language of the times had represented heavy industry with belching clouds of smoke and fumes were not visible to any measure. The City had settled down with a new type of high technology industry. The new industries came to San Diego because in a measure here was access to the aviation industry and the Naval Electronics Laboratory, the atomic and high-energy research capabilities of General Dynamics and soon the higher scientific and educational opportunities of the University of California.

Not all business indicators were favorable, however. General Dynamics was running into trouble trying to sell its new Convair 880 airliner. The 880 had come on the scene late, and thus out of necessity to offer some sales advantages, the design had been modified in a number of ways to meet preferences and specifications of competing airlines, until the break-even point had receded, it seemed, almost beyond the point of recovery. Thousands of workers already had lost their jobs.

The value of airplane and related products declined in 1958, by $175,000,000, but it was still far ahead of the figure of 1956.

Though Convair was cutting back, only one sixth of San

The hopes of Consolidated Aircraft for the future rested on the 880, a jet transport plane designed originally with unique characteristics. These disappeared under pressure of competitive buyers who helped cause Convair heavy losses.

Diego's workers were now dependent directly on aircraft production, and 3,200 new jobs had been created in the County in one year through expansion of existing industries or the establishment of new ones.

Industrial parks were beginning to appear, to embrace electronic and related developments in industrial technology. Too, and with little attention, the floors of a number of the canyons which had provided so much open space for San Diegans were slowly filling with structures.

The commercial promise of the harbor, however, was diminishing somewhat. The flood of cotton had slowed down. Mexico had created a port of its own at Ensenada on the Baja California coast, and trucks were streaming across rough peninsula roads from Mexicali, loaded with Mexican-grown cotton which once had been shipped through the Port of San Diego.

The loss of some of the cotton trade was only a small cloud of distress, however. The City's Harbor Commission, with Harry L. Foster as chairman, in its 1959 report still insisted that the port was "the hub of the Great Southwest, and the gateway to the world."

The port was served by twenty-four trucking lines, two rail lines, five major air lines, and thirty-five steamship lines. The key to the fast movement of cargo, the port officials announced, was the proximity of sea, land and air transportation terminals, all within minutes of each other. And the dockside bunkering stations at the new Tenth Avenue marine terminal, where ships could load, discharge and take on fuel and water all at one time, were described as the most modern on the Pacific Coast, with fast turn-around service for all sea traffic.

The aggressive sales program of the Harbor Department still was reaching out to bring into fruition the old dream of the harbor as the port for all of the Southwest.

But in the opinion of many persons in coastal and world trade, and in developing waterfront-related businesses and industries, the Port of San Diego could not take its rightful place as a major port while split into a half dozen political jurisdictions.

As early as 1956 the Attorney General of California, Edmund G. "Pat" Brown, in a speech in San Diego urged the preparation of legislation for unification of the bay. But Mayor Dail instead argued that it would be easier to consolidate San Diego, National City and Chula Vista than it would be to create a new agency concerned only with bay unification.

Shipbuilding on waterfront land controlled by the City had become a major industry, too, whose production in 1958 was estimated to be worth $18,000,000. C. Arnholt Smith's National Steel and Shipbuilding Company was turning out cargo and cargo-passenger vessels, and he had taken as partners a group of large construction firms headed by the Henry J. Kaiser Steel Company with headquarters at Oakland, California. By the 1960's, however, Smith was out of the firm. But he was becoming a dominant factor in tuna fishing and canning.

Tuna was making a comeback, after the heavy setback due to Japanese imports, with the development of purse seining, the conversion of older boats, and the building of still larger and larger clippers. The value of tuna products was placed at almost $37,000,000 in 1958, up $4,000,000 from the preceding year, but still far below the high point of more than $58,000,000 in 1951.

By then, the United States Tariff Commission reported, Japanese tuna had taken forty-six percent of the American market, and it was reported the Soviet Union was preparing to enter the Pacific with a large fleet equipped for year-round fishing for tuna.

San Diego Portuguese and their boats had led the way to the great fishing grounds. It was in the Spring of 1929 that the Atlantic, the first of the real tuna clippers, led her sister ships across the Equator to fish off the Galapagos Islands, 300 miles off the coast of Ecuador and 3,000 miles from San Diego. Now their very existence as fishermen was being threatened.

A San Diego Representative in Congress, Bob Wilson, carried

the fight for the tuna industry to the floor of the House:

Bob Wilson

"We in San Diego have no intention of letting this industry go out of business if we can humanly avoid it. The 138 vessels we have left out of the fleet of 210 we had in 1951 still bring us about $25,000,000 in new wealth from the sea each year and this is a principal source of income to the port and the City."

Though United States foreign policy considerations were not supposed to be allowed to damage domestic industries, Wilson said that in 1951 a bill to provide a tax on frozen tuna imports, while a Federal study was undertaken for a long-range solution, passed the House and then was defeated in the Senate under a vigorous attack by the State Department:

"Time has gone forward and in the succeeding seven years our fleet has declined by twenty-four percent and while the Japanese share of the United States tuna market was increasing from twenty-one to forty-six percent."

The alternative of a subsidy was proposed by Wilson, as had been done with other industries threatened by low-cost importations.

In 1945, the Japanese agreed to talks concerning the tuna problem and Representative Wilson said he was "extremely hopeful" some kind of an agreement could be reached. Imported canned tuna was under tariff restrictions but there were no restrictions on fresh frozen tuna. The Japanese did eventually agree to limit imports but a suspicious tuna industry said that only time would tell how effectively it would be carried out.

As tuna was no longer present in abundance off the California coast, the California canneries had lost a locational advantage and larger companies set up a few receiving stations and processing plants closer to the sources of raw material. At one time there were six canneries in San Diego; now there was only one, C. Arnholt Smith's Westgate-California Corporation, which also maintained two freezing plants in Peru and operated two refrigerated freighters to ship frozen tuna to the San Diego cannery. The San Diego plant claimed twenty percent of American sales. Two other major tuna canneries were on Terminal Island, San Pedro, as were four smaller ones.

In the 1960's American tuna fishermen had met the competition of the Japanese and were holding their own, though by then they had lost half the American market.

The center of the City was becoming a commercial and financial district, but one from which the people could tend to desert at night. The continued failure of the voters to approve the grouping of public buildings had resulted in the erection of a new County Courthouse covering two City blocks and facing on Broadway. But even before its completion, it would be too small.

Impatient with the failure of the citizens to approve bonds for a Convention Hall, Harry Handlery was adding one to his El Cortez Hotel complex high on the hill overlooking the downtown district and which had been a prominent landmark for all those who came and went by the sea during the war.

No skyscrapers, in the eastern concept of tall office buildings, had been erected in the downtown area since the Great Depression. Building restrictions in California also had been influenced by the fear of earthquakes, but modern construction of steel and masonry was eliminating some of that.

It became publicly known in the late 1950's that Charles K. Fletcher's Home Federal Savings & Loan Association would erect a new office building, perhaps fifteen stories high, at Broadway and Seventh Avenue, as the first unit of a three-building complex. Not to be outdone, C. Arnholt Smith also had announced plans for a tower for his United States National Bank, at Broadway and Second Avenue, which, if necessary to be the most prominent structure in town, would soar to twenty stories. The business community breathed a collective sigh of relief. All had not been lost.

Downtown was changing, not dying, as had been feared by the merchants who had felt the City's future threatened by the intrusion of a giant shopping center into Mission Valley.

In 1958 San Diego was listed fifth in the nation in the volume of downtown building, ranking only behind New York, Los Angeles, Chicago and Houston. Downtown construction permits exceeded $35,000,000 in value.

Parking buildings became an accepted way of business life. As the taxpayers had refused to create a public parking district, and other attempts to induce property owners to form their own parking districts had failed because of the scattered ownership of downtown property, individual firms were erecting their own structures.

In the earlier days of aviation, and even during the war years when bigger and bigger airplanes were taking off and landing, the slogan-makers of San Diego, as they had done so many times in the past, adopted a new identification for the City. San Diego would be the "Air Capital of the West." Presumably the airport was strategically situated in the Southwest corner of the United States, the first landing field from the cities of the west coast of Mexico, Central and South America, and a logical termination for across-the-Pacific flights. All this had been said about the port — and weren't the ships now coming?

But the development of jet-powered aircraft by Convair and Ryan was creating a rising problem of noise at the airport, though commercial jets were not yet serving San Diego as they were at Los Angeles.

There were warnings, too, that the location of the field, with relatively high terrain to the east which forced a steep landing glide, and the presence of Point Loma and its crowded residential areas under the take-off pattern, meant that flying conditions might not be safe in a jet-air age and that a crash could sweep away many homes and cost many lives.

An opportunity to have eased onto Kearny Mesa by firming up rights to co-exist with the Navy on Miramar Field, had been

Jet transports were not yet serving San Diego, in 1957, when the City again saw itself as the "Air Capital of the West" because of the location of Lindbergh Field as the first airport for traffic from the other Americas.

neglected. The City had seen use of the field as limited to air freight, a business which had not developed as anticipated. The City's rights passed with the Korean war and the jet-age. But the City still had other plans. Its eyes had been fastened under on another area of Kearny Mesa.

Since 1943 Arnold H. Peik had operated a small airport on the southwestern shore of Mission Bay and by 1946 he had a 2,600-foot oiled runway and three hangars. The City bought him out and then in 1957 closed the airport down in connection with the development of Mission Bay Park. The City also purchased and closed down another small airport southwest of Peik's, or Pike's as it was known, and just north of Midway Drive.

On Kearny Mesa, William Gibbs, Jr. had operated another private flying field, since 1937, and by 1946 he had three dirt runways and several hangars.

In its move to provide a substitute location for the little air fields from the Mission Bay Area, and also to prepare for the future, the City acquired by condemnation 1,500 acres on Kearny Mesa which included Gibbs Field. Improvement of runways and facilities was made possible with Federal assistance. The new field was dedicated in 1950 and named Montgomery Field after the glider pioneer of early San Diego.

For a number of years the field was operated by Gibbs, until the City took over in 1954. By this time, however, it was too late. The Navy had so increased jet operations at Miramar that the two fields were not compatible as far as safety was concerned. The President's Air Coordinating Council flatly rejected Montgomery Field as a major jet-age passenger terminal. San Diego again was left with only Lindbergh Field and a soaring rash of complaints of noise and exhaust pollution. A decision had to be made on the future, as existing terminal facilities at Lindbergh were proving inadequate for the volume of passengers.

The City Council retained Leigh Fisher & Associates of South Bend, Indiana, to study the situation and suggest possible solutions.

In 1956, with the limited wisdom of a contemporary view, Fisher concluded:

> "With the advent of heavier turbo-prop and turbo-jet aircraft, which require flatter approaches, Lindbergh Field cannot be utilized in the future as a dependable air-carrier airport to serve San Diego's growing air trade."

The Fisher report recommended that the best solution would be for North Island to be shared by the Navy and the City:

> "Its clear over-water approaches, convenience and accessibility to the entire metropolitan area all indicate that this airport could be developed as a satisfactory air-carrier airport. However, the importance of the Navy to the San Diego area economy and the importance of the North Island mission as the primary aviation and supply point, including aeronautical outfitting and assembly as well as complete dock-side services to home-ported aviation ships, indicated that it would not be in the best interests of San Diego to ask the Navy to relocate these operations from North Island. It appears, therefore, that there is no area in which a suitable air-carrier airport can be located without substantial conflict with Naval Air installations and/or terrain, and therefore the problems of joint use of a Naval Air installation should be considered."

Charles C. Hartman

The Navy reacted quickly and angrily. Rear Admiral Charles C. Hartman, commandant of the Eleventh Naval District, in letters to Mayor Dail wrote:

"I regret to advise you that as far as the Navy is concerned the Fisher report recommendations are not acceptable, and are believed to be impractical and unworkable ... it seems incredible to me that Fisher would submit such an important matter ... without personally consulting with the senior responsible naval officers of this area."

An Air Use Panel, composed of representatives of the Armed Services and two other government bureaus, was assigned to look into the San Diego situation. Former Mayor Harley Knox in a letter to *The San Diego Union* and submitted to the panel commented:

"The City Administration apparently hopes that this panel will force down the neck of our Navy, the bitter dregs of witches' brew concocted for them by the people whom they benefit the most."

At Air Use Panel hearings, the Navy suggested two alternative solutions, one was civilian use of the southeastern area of Mission Bay and the other was Brown Field which it would be will-

The hopes for a future in air travel were dimmed because of terrain problems of Lindbergh Field, and protests of Point Loma residents. The Navy suggested San Diego move its airport to the southern marshlands of Mission Bay.

ing to consider surrendering. Mayor Dail and former Mayor John D. Butler both rejected the use of Mission Bay land as economically and politically unfeasible. Butler told the panel that "he didn't think there was a remote possibility that the electorate now would move to put a master airport in that recreational park."

The site at Mission Bay did have some terrain advantages over Lindbergh Field: the landing approach was more favorable, a longer east-west runway was possible, and takeoffs would be over the flat areas of the bay channel and south Mission Beach. But the land was unstable and would require filling and packing.

Brown Field was held to be too far from the City, though it was only sixteen miles from downtown, and subject to restrictions on operations by proximity to Mexico.

Brown Field on the Otay mesa had long been considered as a possible airport site for the City, and it was transferred to the City by the Navy. Here the Navy tests a vertical lift-off plane at Brown Field.

No solution emerged even though there would be many ideas and many bitter exchanges. Lindbergh Field was still a fact of life, and in need of improvements. In 1957 the Civil Aeronautics Administration rejected a multi-million dollar expansion into a jet-age airport. Mayor Dail assured the CAA that the City was not planning to permanently use Lindbergh Field as the City's master airport and as a result the CAA looked favorably on a request for Federal assistance in the interests of practicality and safety. It was considered that the terminal building eventually might be re-located to the Harbor Drive side of the airport.

In a letter released by Mayor Dail, William B. Davis, acting CAA administrator, said the CAA doubted that airlines would ever serve Lindbergh Field with jet airliners. In March of 1959 the first commercial jet liner in regular service landed at Lindbergh Field because of heavy fog at Los Angeles. Its 106 passengers were taken north by bus.

With no other place to which to turn, the City again took another look at Brown Field which the Navy said it would decommission in 1960. The City hired the firm of Charles Luckman and Associates of Los Angeles and its report found that the development of Brown Field as a municipal airport was feasible provided the runways were oriented in a north-south direction with landing approaches made over Mexico to avoid high terrain to the west, but that Brown Field and the Tijuana Airport could not be operated as separate fields because of air traffic conflicts, a problem so familiar to San Diego. The reaction of Federal aviation officials was not enthusiastic. But the development of a freeway south from San Diego would keep the issue of Brown Field alive.

But the civic dream of a jet airport which would open the door to the entire Pacific basin was fading, even though the annual number of passengers using the airport had climbed to almost 700,000. But very little air traffic could be originated along the west coast of Latin America; San Francisco was 200 miles nearer the Hawaiian Islands than was San Diego; and Los Angeles had the population, the industry, and the air line connections. San Diego, again, in an air age, was at the end of the line.

CHAPTER NINE

The Spanish-Colonial buildings of the first Exposition were showing their age and concern had risen as to whether they should all be torn down, or renovated. Some already had disappeared, victims of fire or destruction or for sites for new museum buildings.

The Hopes — Tourists, a Bay and the Park

There were still many people in San Diego who had been nurtured on the idea of the "City Beautiful" as had been so inspiringly described long before by the city planner from Boston, John Nolen. And hadn't the United States Supreme Court upheld this as a right?

They firmly believed that they somehow could control events, could summon form and beauty into the disorder of population shifts and municipal growth. They had envisioned a City rising on the bay which could provide, as no other American city, with the possible exception of San Francisco, a spirit of living.

But the breakup of the City by residential sprawl and the decentralization brought about by the auto and shopping centers threatened to leave the downtown section of San Diego only a limited commercial and financial center.

There still could be a shining City. Mission Bay was an aquatic park which in time could be unmatched anywhere. Balboa Park with its Zoo, the grandeur of trees and plantings, and grand museums, was also an unfinished business but it had more appeal, so San Diegans believed, than Central Park in New York City. Most of the people who had come to San Diego City after World

The protection of Balboa Park against any further highway or assorted non-civic uses was an issue of the late 1950's. The Zoo had become world famous. This is a scene of the Flamingo Lagoon at the entrance.

War II accepted most of this; but they did not accept any contention that the good life meant the preservation of downtown land values or an obligation to crowd into an urban center in the manner of the cities which so many of them had fled.

They came for the climate and the freedom of space. But the dream of Old San Diego had never died. The pioneer spirit of the West still flickered in San Diego and other towns and cities of the Pacific Coast region. It had been less than a hundred years since Alonzo Horton, from New York State by way of Wisconsin and San Francisco, had summoned the modern City of San Diego into being. A restlessness was still there and personal and civic achievements were often wrapped in high purposes or the drama of history. The pursuit of water, for example. In its booklet of 1962, titled "Water for People," the Metropolitan Water District stated:

> "Southern California is a section of the Earth where more people have come to live, and work and play, in a region far removed from adequate water supplies than has been true in any region at any time in recorded history. The Babylonians, the Carthaginians and the Romans built great aqueduct systems for the importation of water to their cities. In the light of engineering and construction developments as of their ages, the works they built and operated remain as wonders of the world. But these people traveled relatively short distances to their water sources. Here in Southern California we are bringing water from outside water sources through aqueducts 300 miles long. Even now we are looking to new water sources in Northern California more than 500 miles distant."

This meant, of course, transporting the excess waters of Northern California to Southern California, through an elaborate canal system running through the Central Valleys of California. The water would be collected near Sacramento, from, among other rivers, the Feather River, in what was described as the world's largest construction program, the California State Water Project. San Diego's share would be distributed through the Metropolitan system.

In this program, Councilman George Kerrigan was San Diego's representative with the Feather River Association. The voters of the State approved the issuance of $1,750,000,000 in bonds, to finance the project, and the voters in San Diego registered approval by a margin of better than four to one. The campaign for the bonds was led in San Diego by Councilman Frank Curran and Stacey Sullivan, a lawyer, and the margin in San Diego was enough to offset a loss in San Francisco and a poor showing in Los Angeles.

San Diegans were not to be allowed to forget that central Balboa Park had been summoned into being, as a reality, through an Exposition by which a City of less than 40,000 population had challenged the great metropolitan areas for the world's attention. While Mission Bay was on everybody's mind as it moved toward full development, Balboa Park to many San Diegans represented the beauty and heart of any shining City.

The grand sweep and beauty of Balboa Park are seen in this air view – and also of some of its still undeveloped areas. A report to the City recommended the removal of most of the buildings in the Palisades area in the center.

The languid beauty of this scene has changed. Buildings at the left and the right would go, in time. The one at the left would be replaced; the one at the right would have a substitute.

The movement to study Balboa Park and its future was initiated by the Chamber of Commerce in a letter to the City Council, in May of 1956. The City Council subsequently named a Citizens' Committee whose general chairman was Dr. Douglas McElfresh. Robert Frazee and Arthur F. Butler were vice chairmen. The chairman of its most important subcommittee, on buildings, was Samuel Wood Hamill, the architect. It was he who wrote the summary:

"The preservation for over forty years of many of the 1915 Exposition Buildings despite the fact that they were originally constructed of wood frame and stucco as 'temporary buildings' for a one-year life expectancy indicates the reverenced place these structures hold in the admiration and affection of San Diegans and visitors from all over the world. When one reviews the impermanent nature of certain of these structures and the fact that many of them have no known practical use for extended periods of their existence, we have proof beyond a doubt that their outstanding beauty has endowed them with a degree of permanence not inherent in their structure. ... The greatest tribute therefore which we can pay to this center of civic culture, will be to initiate and with perseverance carry on a continuing program of development in Balboa Park, which will insure that as each old structure passes into memory that it be replaced with buildings and/or gardens of commensurate beauty, blended into the inspired design concept of the original group of 1915 Exposition buildings and gardens ... it is our profound duty, therefore, that we pass intact to the future, Balboa Park, this transcendant work of the hands of men, some of whom have passed on and some of whom are still present in our day."

Samuel Wood Hamill

The committee listed only a limited number of buildings as permanent though it detailed the uses to which all were being put and which, in many cases, could be continued for some time into the future. In the Prado area only the structures of the California Quadrangle, the newer buildings of the Fine Arts Gallery and the Natural History Museum, and the Botanical building, were listed as permanent. In the Palisades area, only the Federal building was so considered.

The committee, acknowledging that its study was incomplete because of its limited resources, concluded that a detailed master plan was essential to preserve the present useful buildings and the architectural pattern.

The "capture" of Balboa Park for commercially-related interests was a possibility never far removed. In 1959 there was a new move to convert the unused Ford Building of the 1935 Exposition into a Convention Hall. Its primary virtue was that it would be half-way between the hotel interests downtown and those in Mission Valley. Support for a publicly-financed Convention Hall had been rejected by the voters time and again, and a reconsideration of the use of the Ford Building was proposed by Robert O. Peterson as president of the San Diego Convention and Tourist Bureau. A decision, however, was put aside pending a study of the uses and future of Balboa Park and its structures. The City Council commissioned a St. Louis planning firm, Harland Bartholomew & Associates to shape a master plan for the park.

There had been talk also of putting a Convention Hall in Mission Bay Park, but this would have required asking the taxpayers to finance construction of a building — an action they had so persistently refused, though there was general acceptance of the fact that tourist business was necessary to help pay for improvements in the park.

Development was proceeding slowly at Mission Bay. But, it

was true that Balboa Park, after ninety years, was still an unfinished business with a large area to the east lying in its native state. And Mission Bay Park was almost four times the size of Balboa Park.

Caution in granting leases arrived after De Anza Point was leased for a trailer camp. It had been envisioned that trailers would use the camp for short visits, as was desired. Failure to specify a time limitation resulted in the placing of mobile homes for "the duration."

The first to move into a prominent recreational-commercial position on the bay, in 1953, however, was William D. Evans, a young San Diegan, who began with the building of fifty rental

In Mission Bay, at long last, development of tourist accommodations began by 1953. The first into the bay was the Bahia Hotel shown under construction. Other hotels would follow, though perhaps not always as expected, or as many as had been hoped for.

units, a restaurant and cocktail lounge, which he named the Bahia. Additions were made in each of four years, from 1955 through 1958, when he proposed another 200-unit hotel on private leased land on the northern shoreline, in Pacific Beach, a plan approved by the City Planning Commission.

While the rush of investors into the park had not materialized as had been expected, at the time the taxpayers had been sold on approving additional funding for development, the City was concerned in going beyond the Master Plan for the bay itself and adopting some guidelines for the structures certain to arise eventually.

In 1959, City Manager Bean recommended to the City Council that the Community Facilities Planners of Pasadena be retained to study the park and make recommendations as to what should be done for the future. Their report found that the primary drawback of the park was its flatness. "The water is flat. The elevation of surrounding lands and islands is only five to twelve feet above water level." The major exception was Crown Point:

> "The fine, curving forms of islands and shorelines on the Master Plan lead one to expect comparable contoured curves in the skyline profiles of those land forms. What a disappointment to discover that such profiles are not planned and that the islands are merely flat shapes a few feet above the water."

What should be done regarding the bay was presented in some detail, and, they stated, that like many other large recreation facilities, Mission Bay Park would be a partnership between public and private enterprise. While the leased sites were only seven percent of the total land area, they were described as the key to the character, spirit, and quality of the entire park:

> "On these sites will be the park's largest buildings, its most bustling activity, the most people. If each of the many small parcels which comprise this critical acreage were subject to strictly independent private decisions as to physical development, the result would be chaos. Three hundred acres of uncontrolled whimsey in building styles, signs, parking and landscape patterns could produce in Mission Bay Park a visual disaster which would downgrade the entire park. Neighboring Mission Beach is a convenient example of the urban anarchy which could threaten Mission Bay Park."

They suggested landscaped walkways through Mission Beach, connecting the bay with the ocean; if highways were to be built through the park, and the report hoped they would not be built, they should be elevated, permitting local park roads, pedestrian and bicycle paths to flow underneath them. There should be continuity between land and water by a meandering promenade zone, paralleling the top of the riprap or edge of the beach, designed more for sitting and watching than for walking. All housing should be raised at least one-story above the ground, to improve the view of the water. Canals, basins, fountains, pools, lagoons should be developed throughout the land portion and leased areas; and the type of materials and color of all structures be rigidly controlled so that they "fit gracefully into the environment."

Though they believed the park should capture some of the flavor of the world's waterfronts, they agreed the City so far had resisted temptations to re-create Italian fishing villages, Paris quays and South Seas beaches which might lead to movie set designs or self-conscious quaintness.

A vision of the park, as it might appear in the future, was presented to staid members of the City Council. Mission Bay Aquatic Park was described as 4,000 acres of land and water, with thirty-one miles of shoreline dredged out from a marshy duck pond to offer recreation for three million people annually in the year 2000. The 12,000 boats which would call Mission Bay home port would provide a quiet panorama of sails. There would be a mighty spectacle of power boats and an impressive array of yachts, as well as a playful covey of paddleboats. Those millions of people would fish from piers for the afternoon or board a commercial vessel for a deep-sea fishing weekend. They would swim, hike, ride, picnic, play, explore, watch. They would stay in fancy and less fancy hotels, cottages, trailers, tents, and would eat at chowder bars or elegant restaurants. They could lie on the beach and watch sand castles under construction or wander about and watch fishing and boats and tides and the plants and animals who liked the edge of the water.

This all was very alluring, particularly for those who might still be imbued with some of the old pioneering spirit of summoning greatness, but might have been heavy going for those who were practical enough to believe they might be gone from the scene by the time this all could be accomplished in the year 2000. Their view of Mission Bay was of their time, and their use.

In 1960, on the recommendation of the Planning Director, Harry Haelsig, the City Council voted to make the report its "basic controlling guide" in the development of Mission Bay particularly in reference to the control, not necessarily of design, but of materials, textures and colors to assure a harmonious relationship.

Plans were the order of the day. Some of them, as has been suggested, came from the lingering pioneering spirit of personal achievement which had been able to influence the rising new cities of the West. Others perhaps were the result of a new professionalism in City Government and the characteristics of the City Manager system.

Though a professional study of Balboa Park had been suggested by a former City Manager, O. W. Campbell, he also had been held responsible for a neglect of the park. It remained for his successor, George Bean, to recommend the employment of Harland Bartholomew & Associates of St. Louis, Missouri, to make a thorough study in the spirit of the report of the Citizens' Committee and prepare a master plan for the future of the park.

In a preliminary report late in 1959, the St. Louis firm recommended the removal or replacement of thirteen buildings left

This is the famed Prado as it appeared in 1915. All of the buildings on the north, or right side, were to disappear, except for the permanent quadrangle with its California Tower, in the distance.

over from two Expositions, and this immediately built up a political and emotional resistance from those who had learned to love the park and its aging structures.

A final report, however, in 1960, somewhat tempered the resistance by describing the park more as people wanted to hear about it:

> "A park is first of all scenery and Balboa Park possesses some of the most majestic scenery of any municipal park in the United States. ... Buildings are incidental to a park, usually provided only to a minimum possible extent. ... Yet in the charming structures of the 1915 Exposition, San Diego has enjoyed a remarkable civic asset."

But, the Park "has become neglected — almost the orphan of San Diego." Ninety years before the State Legislature had pledged that "these lands are to be held in trust forever ... for the purposes of a free and public park ... and for no other or different purposes." The report lamented the loss of park lands for three freeways. New York, Chicago and San Francisco had successfully resisted the intrusion of freeways in their great civic parks and the National Municipal League cited Balboa Park as an example where a City had succumbed to nibbling encroachment. By 1960, almost a fourth of the park had been granted away for various uses, three schools, city streets, Naval Hospital, freeways, and for non-profit groups.

To preserve the park from further encroachments, Bartholomew & Associates said that the greatest financial return to the people would come only from using Balboa Park as a park, and prohibiting its uses for conventions, trade shows, schools, freeways and City offices.

Emphasis was to be placed on enhancing the museum, fine arts, theatrical, historical, scientific, zoological, garden and picnic complexes of the park. To set up these complexes, it was recommended that certain existing buildings be removed, some of them to be replaced.

Buildings to be removed and replaced would include all of the temporary Spanish-Colonial structures remaining from the 1915 Exposition but "the essential character of the Prado area ... should be maintained in perpetuity by the careful and sympathetic design of each new structure that is to replace one of the old temporary buildings."

This went to the heart of the worries of many San Diegans. Two of the main buildings from the 1915 Exposition had been long gone from the scene, and replaced by the newer Fine Arts Gallery and the Natural History Museum. Now, two other Spanish-Colonial style buildings, on the Prado and flanking the Fine Arts Gallery, were scheduled for demolition to make way for two new wings of the gallery.

These were known at the time as the Medical Arts Building and the American Legion Building, both in poor states of preservation and standing unused. The style for their replacements had now been suggested. How this would be carried out was another matter.

The Bartholomew report then would have the City proceed in removing the last four Spanish-Colonial buildings of the original Exposition. These included the House of Hospitality and the House of Charm on the opposite corners of the Prado plaza. Both were listed for early replacement. The two other Spanish-Colonial buildings to be removed, and later replaced, were the Electric Building on the south side of the Prado and the huge Food and Beverage Building on the north side of the Prado and

The arches and arcades of Balboa Park tied many of the buildings together. This is a scene from the 1915 Exposition. A report in 1960 urged the City to save them, or replace them, even in front of substitute structures. Resistance arose.

42

also facing on the east the Natural History Museum.

The permanent buildings in the California quadrangle would become a theatrical arts center and new quarters would be provided for the Museum of Man. A new Youth Cultural Center and a Museum of Science and Industry were recommended. The Spreckels Organ Pavilion would be retained, with repairs, as would the Spanish Village. The Old Globe Theater would be rebuilt in the same style.

Of particular interest to the future was the recommendation for replacement of the graceful arcades over the Prado walkways, and the addition of new ones along the front of the new wings of the Fine Arts Gallery, and another along the walk of the site of the Electric Building, while awaiting its replacement, which would connect with the new planetarium then being planned for the east end of the Prado area. It was stressed the arcades should be in the existing style.

In the newer Palisades area of the 1935 Exposition, to the south and below the Organ Pavilion, the report recommended that only the Balboa Park Bowl, the Federal Building and a complex of cottages for the House of Pacific Relations be retained. The site of the circular Ford Building would be converted into a park providing an overview of the City and an interchange for the new crosstown freeway. Its conversion to a Convention Hall seemed to be written off.

All of the buildings in the Palisades area, with the exception of the Ford Building, were in use at the time and the recommendations and protests against such a drastic action were many.

But, the report concluded that the temporary buildings in the Prado and most of those of the Palisades had outlived their usefulness as "evidence of termite infestation and dry rot was found in all the Palisades area buildings." Many of these buildings as well as those in the Prado area were held to seriously violate building code requirements and "can be maintained in a fair state of repair only at a very high cost."

Once before there had been a recommendation for removal of all the temporary Spanish-Colonial buildings, due to their general state of decay, with no replacements suggested, however, and this had raised a storm of civic protest. This occurred during the Great Depression, when money was scarce, but the newspapers, the Chamber of Commerce and hundreds of citizens joined together to raise enough money to assure Federal emergency financial assistance for preservation work. The buildings received another new lease on life during the second Exposition.

Carrying out of the Bartholomew plan over the suggested period of fifteen years, it was estimated, would cost more than

$21,000,000. There were other suggestions also, relating to the rerouting of traffic, separation of pedestrian and vehicle traffic, more areas for parking and picnic grounds, and more facilities for older persons.

The San Diego Union cautioned its readers:

> "The Bartholomew plan is not something that should be taken on an all-or-nothing basis. Rather it should be a guide. ... Adoption of the report as a whole, as a master plan, would mean ultimately the rejection of the entire program. The need of a guide, however, has been evident, if only because of the long neglect of the park and its development that has characterized City regimes over the past twenty years. Buildings have been allowed to deteriorate and changes made without long-range objectives."

Ivor de Kirby

Many public hearings were held by the Planning Commission, the Park and Recreation Commission, and the City Council, and with some access and traffic modifications presented by City Planning Director Harry Haelsig, the plan was adopted in September of 1961. Councilman Ivor de Kirby wanted the honor of making the motion for adoption as he had been a member of the original Citizens' Committee which had recommended that a master plan be prepared.

Not all San Diegans were pleased with the Master Plan, with its suggested traffic rerouting, and more particularly with the displacement of the Spanish-Colonial buildings with their ornate decorations. They feared the Prado as millions of people from around the world had come to know it, would be gone forever.

Balboa Park and Mission Bay were not isolated programs in the general planning for San Diego. The Park and Recreation Department staff had also worked out another master plan calling for four other metropolitan parks, five district parks, five scenic parks, nine shoreline areas, five parkways, thirty-eight community parks, ten plazas and a scenic drive.

Too, voters surrendered pueblo lands represented by the Torrey Pines park to the State of California, for preservation of the rare trees, and laid out two golf courses on public lands on the same mesa. Open space and recreation – a lure of San Diego.

The grandest challenge of all, it seemed, however, was in the port. The ambitions of the director, John Bate, had met frustrations in the matter of commercial expansion: there was only so much waterfront within the jurisdiction of the City. The shore from National City to Coronado was as tempting as an unclaimed gold field.

Various suggestions were being heard regarding the unifying of political and economic jurisdictions over the bay, when San Diego City made its first move toward additional waterfront land. San Diego had a stake in the unincorporated lands of the

South Bay by virtue of its purchase of the Otay River water system which had continued to supply residents of the area. During a shortage, San Diego had delivered water from the Colorado River and had been rebuked by the Metropolitan District for distributing it beyond the district borders.

And hadn't even Franklin D. Roosevelt, when he was President of the United States, suggested that a second opening be cut for the bay, across the Silver Strand, which would open the South Bay to maritime and industrial development?

A group of citizens of the South Bay petitioned for annexation to the City of San Diego, but as their land was not contiguous to San Diego's border, a way had to be found to form a direct land connection. Annexation of a corridor down the bay past National City and Chula Vista by the City Council was the answer.

As there were conflicting claims to land under the bay, a compromise was reached. Coronado agreed to let San Diego have a 600-foot wide corridor in exchange for Glorietta Bay, which was within the original line of San Diego's Spanish pueblo grant extending from the tip of Point Loma across the Silver Strand to National City. Later, San Diego surrendered half the corridor to National City, under a threat of legal action. Annexation was completed by City Council action in 1955.

In 1956 San Diego moved to annex a large area of the South Bay but met resistance from the population of Imperial Beach. When Imperial Beach was incorporated as a separate city, San Diego tried again, with the hope of annexing twenty-two and a half square miles of territory surrounding the City of Imperial Beach on three sides and reaching clear to the International Border.

Chula Vista was joined by Imperial Beach in seeking to prevent the annexation by challenging the legality of the corridor, but the filing of suits was not sanctioned in 1958 by the State's Attorney General, Edmund G. Brown, as required by court decision. South Bay voters approved annexation to San Diego on July 16, 1957. Thus the stage was set for the grand gesture.

Back when the port of Ensenada had begun cutting into San Diego shipments of cotton grown in Mexicali, there were uncomfortable accusations that public money had been wasted in building the Tenth Avenue Terminal. The *San Diego Magazine* asked the port director, John Bate, if the terminal would turn out to be a so-called "white elephant." Bate was ready:

> "Within one year after the Tenth Avenue Terminal is 100 percent operable, it will be completely inadequate to handle cargoes that will be forced through it. If that is what a white elephant is then I presume we need a whole herd of them."

In 1960, when the terminal had been in operation for a year and a half, it was estimated that 500 ships would call at the port compared to 259 only two years before. In one day there were eight ships alongside the Tenth Avenue Terminal and five of them flew foreign flags. That the port was becoming a gateway to the Southwest seemed to be evident in that sixty percent of the cargo moving across the quays came from 500 to 1,500 miles away. Revenues had multiplied more than a dozen times since 1948.

What was the future of the port, and what part would the rival communities on the bay, National City, Chula Vista, Imperial Beach, and Coronado play in it?

Under their new president, Chris A. Larsen, the Harbor Commissioners retained a New York consulting and research firm to look into the future, and in the Fall of 1962 they told the Commissioners, and Bate, what they wanted to hear.

A world-wide trade boom could send more than 2,500 ships a year to San Diego by 1980. They would stream down the bay in a growing parade of colorful commerce, their holds full of oil and gas, glass and steel, myriad products from the jute mills of India to the plywood plants of South Korea. More than $50,000,000 a year alone would be left at San Diego by vessels calling at the port.

In accomplishing this, however, there were some things San Diego had to do. It had to provide 100,000 more industrial jobs by 1980 and 370,000 altogether for a population that would increase by a million persons within eighteen years.

Thus it was spelled out that a community, in this case, San Diego, had a responsibility to provide employment for all those who wanted to come and live in its beneficent climate.

The report stated that to meet the challenge of population, jobs and income it had to look toward its port:

> "An expanded San Diego Bay port complex and adjacent industrial areas can eventually provide employment for 70,000 to 100,000 people. ... Only a small part of the port can be achieved without the development of the extensive tidelands areas yet outside the present port's jurisdiction. In brief ... a great port cannot be achieved without full utilization of the entire harbor. ..."

This not only depended on bringing the tidelands under a single jurisdiction, but upon the port getting a substantial share of goods already flowing through other West Coast ports, and sharing in the normal increases of the export and import trade. Upon unloading their cargoes at San Diego, ships could be leaving with their holds full of additional products resulting from the industrialization of the tidelands, from vegetable oil processing plants, coffee roasters, plywood finishing factories, furniture plants, steel fabricators and other industries whose raw material or finished products depended on seaborne trade.

Thus again San Diego – and its neighbors, National City and Chula Vista – heard that after all that "smokestacks" could be symbols of progress. Now there was a way to the future in the port, even as its business leaders had seen a way to the future in the City.

CHAPTER TEN

The City as perhaps envisioned by "Father" Alonzo Horton in 1867 was rising. The first new skyscrapers in thirty-five years were opened in 1963. Horton had said he had never seen a better site for building a City.

Downtown — the Tall Buildings Rise Again

As the year of 1963 began, a twenty-story building of glass and gold-sheen aluminum, the City's first skyscraper-type structure in thirty-five years, opened its doors on Broadway at Seventh Avenue.

The 278-foot high office building was to be the headquarters of the Home Federal Savings & Loan Association, and its president, Charles K. Fletcher, compared San Diego to "a sleeping giant just awakening to find the great potential that is here ... there is new blood in the community and it is amazing how much of it is second generation."

Charles Fletcher was a son of one of San Diego's pioneers who had arrived as a boy of sixteen from Massachusetts and had sold apples from a wagon, and became a builder of dams, a founder of communities and of roads and highways.

Soon to be completed on another downtown corner, on Broadway at Second Avenue, would be still another skyscraper, one twenty-five stories above the street level, to house the headquarters of the United States National Bank. This bank was the one controlled by C. Arnholt Smith. The twenty-four story First and C building, a project of downtown property owner and land

The first tall office building to rise in San Diego since the Great Depression was that of the savings and loan association headed by Charles K. Fletcher, son of a pioneer. This is a model as San Diegans first viewed the proposed building.

developer, Irvin Kahn, also was scheduled for completion early in 1963.

The towering structures were hailed as evidence of faith in the central business district. But they were scattered in location. There was as yet no center around which new buildings could be clustered; no dominating element to mark the beginning of a "City Beautiful."

The struggle to save downtown and create the "City Beautiful" was not over. San Diegans, Inc., was an outgrowth of the Downtown Association and it differed from its parent group by a concern over the future of downtown and not just the matter of maintaining retail sales. A committee from San Diegans, Inc., would meet on a regular basis with a team from the City Planning Department, year after year.

It had been Joseph Jessop, Sr., of the jewelry family, who had first suggested that downtown merchants should pay more attention to city planning, and through such an organization as San Diegans, Inc., Golden recalled later that downtown was fading and "a lot of people thought it would not come back." But San Diegans, Inc., believed that San Diego as a City had avoided the mistakes of larger cities such as Boston and Philadelphia which were described as typically European and laid out in the distant past with no provision for traffic patterns, and it was costing hundreds of millions of dollars to re-orient them. "One of these days," Golden told the businessmen, "capital will come in here, and find us waiting, and the outside will do what we don't do."

Golden had arrived in San Diego from Utah to work as a carpenter and remained to erect, as a general contractor, scores of the largest military and privately-owned structures in the area.

New and tall buildings rose swiftly early in the 1960's. The United States National Bank building was unique in that it had a small chapel, even as had the tuna boats of the Westgate-California enterprises.

Joseph Jessop, Sr.

Irvin Kahn

The San Diegans, Inc., commissioned a study by a real estate research corporation, at a cost of $65,000, which was undertaken with the cooperation of the City Planning Department. This was to be the first step toward a master plan.

The report presented by Joseph Jessop, Sr., president of the group, in April of 1960 recommended the attraction of regional offices of large companies; bringing about the building of a thousand new hotel and motel rooms downtown, together with construction of a large convention hall; inducing the addition of 6,000 new close-in apartment rooms, for downtown living, and the location of proposed and future government offices in the central area.

"We are concerned with the dangers of 'urban sprawl' as demonstrated in other cities," Ewart Goodwin told the City Council. "Central San Diego is the heart and nerve center of our metropolitan community." He predicted that with good planning a hundred million dollars in new private and government buildings could be built in the central area in eight to ten years. Guilford Whitney warned:

> "Construction of numerous shopping centers will have a tendency to divert shopping traffic now going to downtown stores. But we believe we have a reasonably bright retail future if we work together on putting the plan into effect."

The architect Hamill said the location of public buildings downtown would tremendously increase the stability of the central area.

The plan, however, did not present any large-scale beautification plans for downtown though some park-like atmosphere was considered possible in connection with some larger developments, and particularly with public buildings.

At a luncheon following the presentation, Graydon Hoffman, a vice president of the Bank of America and manager of its San Diego branches, said that the loss years before of buildings in the downtown district had been a "rather significant disaster" and that new programs were tremendously important to San Diego.

A week later the City Council authorized master planning for downtown as suggested by San Diegans, Inc., and recommended by the City Manager, George Bean, and the City's Planning Director, Harry Haelsig.

Over the decades Los Angeles had far outstripped San Diego in population, wealth and commerce, at a cost of urban sprawl, air pollution, and congested streets and freeways. Los Angeles had almost two million more residents than San Diego.

Where once *The San Diego Union* had noted that San Diegans

congratulated themselves that their City was not like Los Angeles, it now complained that there were those in Los Angeles who looked upon San Diego as being lethargic, and what they meant was that "it is a nice City, nice climate, but does San Diego as a City know, or care, where it is going?"

A contingent of twenty-five San Diegans representing San Diegans, Inc., the Chamber of Commerce, the Convention and Tourist Bureau and the City Government went to Los Angeles to see where it was going.

They visited the developing Civic Center where $350,000,000 in governmental buildings were being grouped in one central location, something that San Diego had never been able to accomplish in years of effort. They drove out along Wilshire Boulevard where twenty-five large buildings costing $172,000,000 had been under construction in a single year. Tall buildings were steadily marching westward in a line toward the sea. These buildings were farther removed from downtown than Mission Valley was from central San Diego.

Business conditions in San Diego were not good. The year 1959 had been a boom one, but now the value of building permits had dropped from more than $195,000,000 to $136,000,000. While there were 312,000 people employed in 1961, there were more than 26,000 out of work. A bond issue to revitalize downtown was out of the question. If there were to be a Convention Hall, and a Civic Theater, some other way had to be found to build them.

An answer on the feasibility of building a Community or Civic Center was needed and the City Planning Department asked San Diegans, Inc., to finance a study. It did, and the answer was an affirmative one.

Downtown was where the City made a profit. That is, downtown property paid in taxes one and a half times what the City spent there for services. City services in outlying areas cost more than the areas paid in taxes. More building downtown — and more tax revenue — supposedly was awaiting upon a Convention Hall and a resolution of San Diego's decisions on the future. In April of 1961 the City Council, with capital outlay funds, began purchasing portions of blocks in an area bounded by First and Third Avenues and by C and A Streets.

Before anything could be resolved, the City Council, to the consternation of business leaders, fired its manager, George Bean. Mayor Dail had been openly critical of the City Manager system, insisting that a strong Mayor was needed to guide the City through the turbulence of politics, and the existing system had tended to pit the Manager against the Mayor and the members of the Council.

Graydon Hoffman

Only two cities of the 1,600 with City Manager systems were larger than San Diego. Bean, often at odds with the Mayor, was quoted as saying:

> "The City Council is operating almost daily on the basis of expediency, with few members who understand basic principles. Responsible citizens must hold fast to long-range planning."

But Bean had opened the door by suggesting higher parking meter fees and the feasibility of combining of functions of the Police and Fire Deparments. These were politically unpopular both with the departments and a Council majority. Too, there had been political fumbling on the proposed metropolitan sewer system and gross errors in cost estimates. The Mayor also had been absent from his duties with an increasing frequency, leading once again to accusations that the City was leaderless and drifting, and to an incipient recall movement. The Vice Mayor, Frank Curran, was trying to keep things tied together.

While Bean was on a forced vacation, Councilmen argued his fate. Appearing on behalf of a large group of business leaders, Graydon Hoffman warned of the dangers of changing City Managers at such a time.

Though at least two Councilmen were opposed to discharging Bean, at a formal Council meeting the decision was made unanimous. Dail vowed that he would have a Citizens' Charter Review Committee look into whether a strong Mayor system might be better than the City Manager system for San Diego.

Thomas Fletcher

Waiting in the wings, as assistant City Manager, was Thomas Fletcher who had been hired originally by O. W. Campbell. He was thirty-seven years old. He was selected to be acting Manager and eventually received the formal appointment. "I realize that the future of the City Manager form of government may depend on my performance. I am walking on eggs."

The task of carrying out the revitalization of downtown, as worked out by the City and San Diegans, Inc., now rested with Fletcher. As a bond issue could not be considered, in view of past rejections of funds for a Convention Hall and Civic Theater, and because of the conditions of the times, another way had to be found. Also, a new City Hall had been long delayed. The City and County shared administrative offices in the isolated but handsome building on the waterfront which once had been considered the keystone of the "City Beautiful." It was no longer adequate for both of them.

In the beginning there was talk of somehow providing $45,000,000 for a Centre City. There was excitement in the air downtown: Besides the three skyscraper-type buildings already under way, the State of California was building its own new

State building; the United California Bank, one of the nation's largest, was entering San Diego and planned to erect an eighteen-story tower; the U.S. Grant Hotel was to have a twenty-one story addition; Ewart Goodwin, Hamilton Marston, Anderson Borthwick and Del Webb Construction Company were talking about a huge hotel-bank building project spanning B Street near Fifth Avenue, to be fifteen stories high on one side, twenty-two on the other; and there were rumors of another thirty-story bank and office building to cost $22,000,000.

Early in 1962 the City proposed to build a new City Hall, a Convention Center and Auditorium, a Civic Theater, and a parking garage, at a total cost of $15,000,000. A sum of $3,500,000 would come from the sale of its half of the Civic Center to the County. The City would borrow $8,400,000 from the City Em-

If the dreamers had their way, this is the way the downtown section of San Diego would have appeared in the 1960's. Many of the tall buildings in this architect's model were never built.

ployes Retirement Fund, as first suggested by the City Auditor-Controller, Frederick Lawrence, and divert $2,000,000 from its capital outlay fund for a total of $10,400,000. However, because of the shortage of money, the four buildings would have to be squeezed onto three blocks.

Still, more money was needed, a million and a half more to get the program under way to a point where there could be supportable income. Morley Golden suggested at a meeting of San Diegans, Inc., that public contributions be sought. Under the leadership of Guilford Whitney, more than $1,600,000 was raised in six weeks from 134 citizens.

The contributors were led by James S. Copley, publisher of *The San Diego Union* and *Evening Tribune*, with a gift of $200,000. Gifts of $100,000 came from Morley Golden, the First

As the people had refused to vote bonds for the grouping of public buildings, the City purchased three blocks downtown, shown behind the nearly completed United States National Bank building, and raised funds from other sources to build a Community Concourse.

National Trust and Savings Bank, Bank of America, Home Federal Savings & Loan Association, San Diego Federal Savings & Loan Association, U.S. Grant Hotel, and the San Diego Gas & Electric Co.

Hoffman acted as chairman of a Civic Center Advisory Board. Its vice chairman was Philip L. Gildred, who told the Council:

> "In the thirty-five years I have lived in San Diego, we have been in almost a constant squabble over a convention auditorium and a theater. This is the first time we have had a near unanimity of opinion."

Some of the pledges, however, would not be fulfilled.

The "City Beautiful" could begin with the graceful grouping of public buildings in the manner of the "White City." The old vision of a City fronting on the bay arose again. From the new City Hall which was to be placed across Second Avenue one could look south down the avenue to the bay – and why couldn't it be lined eventually with handsome new structures and small park-like open spaces? For a starter it was suggested that the block on Broadway bounded by the United States National Bank Building on the west and the U.S. Grant Hotel on the east be set aside for a plaza like the Rockefeller Plaza in New York. C. Arnholt Smith agreed to donate the share of the block which he owned. There was only one drawback at the moment – the plans for the new Civic Theater called for it to turn its back on any such plaza.

It began to look as if everything was falling into place. With a diversification in employment and income through the military, tourism, agriculture, shipbuilding, fishing and evidence of a growing representation in new technologies, the City and County appeared able to surmount the financial disaster shaping up at Convair.

The jet-age finally came to San Diego and to Lindbergh Field. There was no other municipal airport available on the immediate horizon and the Federal Government turned its face in the other direction. United Airlines and American Airlines began jet service to San Diego late in 1960. The Navy did surrender Brown Field to the City in 1962 but its conversion into a municipal field seemed to be far in the future, if ever.

Dail hoped to see Brown Field developed in cooperation with Mexico, at a time before Baja California began to expand and improve its own airport. He envisioned a north-south runway that would tie into one built by Mexico, with customs and immigration facilities of the two countries at either end. Frank Curran, however, campaigned for an off-shore airport with the argument that it was not a matter of ground location but of usable air space. The air space, as he saw it, lay beyond the Naval facilities.

Though in time the weak Mission Bay Advisory Commission would be abolished and its responsibilities placed with the Parks and Recreation Commission, hotels were coming to the Bay. Early in 1960 a lease was granted to Jack and William Skirball for a family-type Vacation Village to cost $1,600,000, in which Robert M. Golden, the son of Morley Golden, would become involved.

Less than six months later the Del Webb Construction Corporation, which had been developing the Grossmont Shopping Center, received a lease on the Highway 101 side of the bay for a resort which would cost $5,000,000 and include a fourteen-story round tower. The City Planning Commission and Council greeted this with satisfaction; high-rise is what they wanted, as suggested in the Community Facilities Report.

Within another six months a group of San Diego investors led by E. Garrick O'Bryan, Jr. unveiled a $2,000,000 resort hotel and restaurant for Quivira Basin. Though the buildings would be only two stories in height, they would be raised three feet above the ground to provide a view of the bay and ocean. Materials and shading would be in harmony with the recommendations of the Community Facilities Report.

There was considerable official disappointment, however,

The pledge of a branch of the University of California at San Diego was carried out, with upper-level schools coming first. The buildings are shown rising on the Torrey Pines mesa on former City pueblo land.

when the Del Webb firm returned to ask, and receive, a modification of its agreement, so it could build the proposed resort in phases. Low-level units would be built first and the tower later when occupancy rates justified it.

The Atlas missile produced in San Diego revitalized the nation when Lieutenant Colonel John H. Glenn, Jr., was lifted into orbit aboard a Mercury capsule Friendship, on February 20, 1962, and circled the earth three times.

The nuclear age had brought to San Diego, as had been anticipated, an expanding electronics industry. In 1962 there were fifty plants employing 11,000 persons, producing products valued at $280,000,000 annually, and sustaining a payroll of $72,000,000.

And already there was some substance to the boosters' new designation for San Diego as the "Education Center of the West." There were 12,000 students at San Diego State College, more than 2,000 at California Western, and more than 1,300 at the University of San Diego. Nearly $16,000,000 in buildings and ground improvements had been begun or authorized for the

University of California at San Diego. The Board of Regents had definitely settled on the Torrey Pines mesa campus. A master plan had been developed, with construction first of graduate schools, to be followed by undergraduate schools.

Nevertheless, as the Winter waned and Spring advanced into Summer, economic conditions in San Diego began to worsen. The missile business was being passed around among other astronautics firms.

The Astronautics plant had taken up the slack in employment when Convair declined from its post-war peak of 35,000 in 1957. New employment at Convair had dropped to 10,000 and soon would be down to 5,000. Convair Astronautics, the work of building launching sites for its Atlas missiles finished, was expected to drop more than 5,000 San Diegans from its rolls, and employment at the San Diego plant was expected to go down to 13,000.

Losses on production of the 880 jet-liner, and a companion airplane, the 990, had mounted to $425,000,000, the largest in the history of a single American industry.

Management of General Dynamics changed again. Control

San Diego, always a City where its boosters thought in slogans, saw the City as the "Educational Center of the Southwest." This photo shows San Diego State College in 1956. A few years later it had 12,000 students.

passed to a Harry Crown, a Chicago financier who merged his Material Services Corporation with General Dynamics. He assured stockholders that the giant corporation's financial troubles would be over soon. There was a new president, Roger Lewis, Jr., former Assistant Secretary of the Air Force. Executives tumbled from their offices in San Diego. A backlog of orders, mostly military, totaled more than two billion dollars for all its far-flung divisions.

Other airplane-oriented industries in San Diego were considered to be doing well. Ryan Aeronautical had diversified and now had more than 3,300 employes, with programs in electronics, sophisticated radar, jet drones and experimental aircraft. Rohr Aircraft had more than 5,000 employes, and though some reduction was anticipated, it was experimenting in electronics and prefabricated houses and bathrooms. Solar Aircraft, which had become part of Harvester International, had 1,800 employes and was working on a revolutionary new gas turbine engine.

Total employment in aircraft and parts manufacturing had declined by the Spring of 1962 from 51,000 to 40,700. The value of aircraft and missiles produced was higher in 1962 than in the year before, though still below that of 1960. The value of tuna was rising slowly and shipbuilding was on a rapid increase. In all, the total value of products manufactured was higher in 1962 than in 1961.

The number of workers in aircraft and missile production might be falling but there were almost as many people working as there were the year before, 312,000, and unemployment remained at about the same level. Sixty-two new industries, though small, had been established and 240 had expanded.

A decreasing reliance on manufacturing was indicated. The number employed in manufacturing had dropped from 73,750 in 1961 to 63,900 in 1962. But, those employed in the various service industries had increased by almost 3,000, and in government by about the same amount. Navy and Marine payrolls, both military and civilian, were soaring, as was the value of farm products.

The success of Shelter Island led to another one, Harbor Island, also created through a bay dredging project. Here Harbor Island begins to take a form that would lure hotels and restaurants, perhaps in competition to Mission Bay.

Tourist revenue was still climbing, to well over $165,000,000 a year – an income far more than the payrolls of all civilian workers in the military and about the same as received by all Navy and Marine personnel in the area.

Three of the new shopping centers, which had brought so much consternation to so many of the community's merchants, were open for business, though sales might have been less than expected. Retail sales downtown had declined only about thirty percent. George Scott's College Grove had opened first, in July of 1960, followed by the May Company's Mission Valley Center

in February of 1961 and Marston's Grossmont Center in the Fall of the same year.

The grandest name in San Diego merchandising, however, would soon be removed from the scene. Broadway-Hale Stores, Inc., already building in a shopping center in Chula Vista, bought control of Marston's early in 1961, primarily to position itself in the Grossmont Center. For the time being it was still Marston's. A third generation Marston, Arthur Hamilton Marston, Jr., remained with Broadway-Hale as president of the San Diego stores. Merchandising was changing into chain operations and there had been difficulties in management with third-generation holdings. George Scott had vowed not to surrender to the enticements of Los Angeles merchants and declared he would push northward with his own chain of department stores.

While the expansion of resort facilities was being welcomed for Mission Bay, the Federal Government was deepening and widening the San Diego Bay's main channel to accommodate the Forrestal class of aircraft carriers, and the dredged material was being used to create still another island which, like Shelter Island, would be devoted primarily to the tourists and conventions. This island was being created just off Harbor Drive. While Mission Bay had been envisioned as a small boat bay and a family recreational area, the development of resort facilities in San Diego Bay was following the dictates of a Legislative mandate for "the promotion of commerce, navigation and fisheries." "Commerce" had been officially broadened to include recreational purposes.

What Mission Bay could mean to the tourist industry was studied by the San Diego Convention and Tourist Bureau, early in 1962, and it presented a report to City officials, the Chamber of Commerce and the Mission Bay Park Commission:

> "While ninety percent of California's population lives within 100 miles of the ocean, only one-fourth of all the beaches are publicly-owned, and many are accessible only by crossing private property. Present beaches are getting smaller and more crowded, and it is increasingly difficult to find a place to fish, golf, go boating or spend a vacation."

All of this, the bureau concluded, pointed up Mission Beach's crucial future economic importance, particularly if it is acknowledged that within twenty years the population of the country would increase by twenty-one percent, and by the year 2000 San Diego would be a "metroport" sheltering some two million persons.

What the community should do, the bureau recommended, was to attract even more tourists to San Diego by providing year-around activities on Mission Bay:

> "The day of the inactive vacation is long past. People want to go where they can sightsee, swim, boat and fish. While a decade ago, most vacations were taken in Summer, today vacationing is a year-round activity."

There were still San Diegans, however, who wanted to "shut the door." For the first time, a bond issue, one of more than $12,600,000, to further the development of Mission Bay, while though it received a majority vote in 1962 failed to receive the necessary two-thirds approval. Also rejected was a $10,000,000 bond issue for general park and recreation programs. Perhaps it was all too much, at the time of some economic distress. Another round of bond issues, this time totaling $15,000,000 for various civic improvements, also went down to defeat in a special election in December of the same year.

There was still the port, and what it could mean in jobs and income. The Harbor Commission and the Director, John Bate, and the Industrial Development Council began a systematic wooing of community leaders, politicians and industry-minded people of the four other cities which bordered the bay.

When United States Senator Claire Engle, Democrat of California, asked for a unified voice on harbor development at San Diego, Norman Foster, president of the Chamber of Commerce, named a task force to study the creation of an agency that could surmount all political objections.

The reaction around the bay was encouraging. Unification might provide the funds to develop their tidelands without excessive tax expenditures.

City officials and community leaders of National City saw their City as the industrial hub of the metropolitan area. Chula Vista's officials favored unified bay development to provide industrial and port facilities and prevent the City from becoming only a "bedroom" community. Chula Vista had grown by 25,000 persons in ten years but the industrial payroll was no larger than before. Imperial Beach looked forward to the opening of a second entrance to the bay and it was proclaimed that "what was good for the South Bay was good for Imperial Beach." While the Mayor of Coronado, Robin Goodenough, saw his City's future as a residential and resort community, certainly development of the South Bay would increase the land values. "We favor development of San Diego Bay."

An enabling act creating a Unified Port District embracing the five cities was sponsored in the State Legislature by Senator Hugo Fisher and Assemblyman James R. Mills of San Diego. It called for a vote of the people in the five cities.

It was about at this time that a national news magazine published an article describing San Diego as a "bust" town with nowhere to go. Though San Diego business leaders declared that the article had been only casually researched and statistics misinterpreted, it had been widely circulated and the City would have to live it down. Assurances of San Diego's general economic stability and future prospects were sent to leading financial and business institutions.

San Diegans were worried, with the decline of aviation and missile production and the financial disaster at Convair, and with the tidelands as the site for a "City Beautiful" seemingly long abandoned, they were in a mood to accept what might perhaps be inevitable. Anyway, there wasn't any space left on the City's waterfront and if there had to be more industry it could go to the South Bay.

The port election was held on November 5, 1962. The voters of San Diego, National City, Chula Vista and Imperial Beach overwhelmingly approved a unification that would require them to turn their tidelands over to a new political entity. The voters in Coronado rejected unification by a margin of three to one.

Many of the residents of Coronado awoke to a realization that despite their vote Coronado was a part of the District. The decision rested with a majority in all five cities. Angry officials, differing with their Mayor's previous position, filed numerous legal actions seeking a way out. There was none, except beginning all over again with an entirely new legislative act.

The District was formally created upon verification of the vote by the Board of Supervisors, in December, and the difficult legal processes of transferring the tidelands to the new District began. The City of San Diego transferred assets with an estimated value of a hundred million dollars and a bonded indebtedness of eleven million.

Coronado's only relief could come from the stipulation that the majority of the members of the new Unified Port District Board would be from the four cities which might be induced to work together in each other's particular interests. The City of San Diego would have three on the board, and the other cities, one each. The first chairman, from San Diego, was Lorenz H. Ruehle, of National City.

By late 1963, a plan of development was ready. There were three main points: a huge marine terminal at National City, with a total cost of perhaps $20,000,000, and development there of an industrial area; a seventy-five acre backup industrial area and three additional cargo terminals, when needed, for Chula Vista, with preliminary work to cost $370,000, and a new passenger terminal at the port's Lindbergh Field, to cost $4,700,000. In all, the four proposed cargo terminals could cost $90,000,000 or more.

Cutting of a second bay entrance through the Silver Strand would not interfere with his bay program, Bate told San Diego's political and industrial leaders, but full development of the South Bay would indicate a bay opening through the Tia Juana River channel and then north to the south end of the bay.

Milton F. Fillius, Jr., president of the Chamber of Commerce, told Bate:

"We of the Chamber urge you to proceed with all possible dispatch, especially in regard to the new cargo facilities. We will need all you have planned if present indications of port growth are fulfilled."

In the new legislation creating the United Port District a word had been added to the uses of tidelands. That word was "recreation." Thus, with hundreds, even thousands of more acres available for industrial, shipping and commercial purposes, and with Shelter Island a going concern in recreation and tourism, and a new island of like nature being created, Bate could ask San Diego to turn its attention once again to the full possibilities of its waterfront. Where once he worked to exclude public buildings and public uses of the waterfront facing the downtown area on the west, he now planned the conversion of the old pier at the foot of Broadway into a tourist attraction. San Diego's principal avenue would now focus on the bay, a concept in the idea of the "City Beautiful" of two generations.

John Bate now seemed to be lord of all he surveyed. Now, too, all those ships would surely come.

Mayor Dail was not the lord of all he surveyed. His command of affairs was not all that he desired and the City was being rent again by a struggle over planning, a struggle that would last for several years.

After two years of work, the City Planning Department produced a General Plan Study for San Diego and submitted it to the City Council in June of 1962. It was described as the first suggested plan for development of the City in the 102 years since its incorporation and represented an effort to bring some order out of the disorder of growth, and to properly place responsibility for civic decisions.

Though still termed merely a study, it did project in general terms ways to achieve ideals in the fields of housing, industry, commerce, agriculture, schools, libraries, recreation, water supplies, sewage disposal facilities, police and fire facilities, and in government and transportation.

It did for the first time suggest civic pressures be brought to bear against "urban sprawl" and the establishment of residential areas as definable communities for which public and private services could be made available at reasonable costs. It was suggested that each residential area should contain different types of housing, varying in density. The primary function of the central area was held to be as an administrative center for all of the urbanized area.

And for the first time the metropolitan area was described as containing 710 square miles and bounded on the north by the Los Batiquitus lagoon between Leucadia and Carlsbad, El Cajon on the east, and the Mexican border on the south. It encompassed six cities, San Diego, Del Mar, Chula Vista, National City, La Mesa, El Cajon, and the communities of Lemon Grove, Spring Valley, Lakeside, Poway, Solana Beach, Cardiff, Rancho Santa Fe, Encinitas and Leucadia.

Before the end of the year, Mayor Dail appointed a 200-man Citizens' Advisory Committee for General Planning, as suggested by the City Planning Director, Harry Haelsig, to arrive at decisions. Dr. Don B. Leiffer, a San Diego State College professor of political science and former secretary to Governor Edmund G. Brown, was named chairman.

Haelsig told the Committee:

> "We can have the kind of a City we desire. In the last twenty years, better than sixty percent of the area that now constitutes the City has been developed. But we can't neglect the older areas ... we must revitalize and redevelop San Diego to its maximum potential."

Goals were to be set for the year 1985. Though San Diego exerted no direct influence on all of the described metropolitan area, its planners did not believe, in view of the decentralization of industry and the rapid appearance of new communities, that a City could exist in isolation. Mayors of the cities in the metropolitan area were invited to participate in year-long planning sessions, in the hope growth could be coordinated.

More than eighteen months would pass before a plan for the City of San Diego and its environs could be presented, and its course would be a rough one.

Mission Valley was up again. The City Planning Department had been successful in not allowing Mission Valley to become a commercial alley, such as along El Cajon Boulevard and University Avenue, though east of Highway 395 the character of the valley was changing from the original concept. Auto dealers and used car lots were beginning to appear.

West of Highway 395 the Planning Department and the Director, Harry Haelsig, hoped to hold the line. This is the end of the valley that opened up onto Mission Bay. Haelsig had no objection to office buildings but would impose setback and density restrictions, restrictions which in some cases met with resistance. The hotels in the valley so far represented what the planners had in mind, attractiveness and open land.

A plea for fewer restrictions was made by valley property owners, in particular Paul Borgerding:

> "Every building in Mission Valley was put there over the dead body of

the Planning Department. ... I think we will live to see the day when we will have tall buildings one after another — a second Miami Beach — in the valley. I think it would be the greatest thing San Diego ever had, because people like to come into a sensational city. What makes a sensational city? Bright lights and tall buildings."

This remark, though, recalled in a way Wilshire Boulevard in Los Angeles, which San Diego's official and business leaders had viewed, on which tall buildings were marching in a line toward the sea.

The line, such as it was now, generally held, however. The larger issue was the power of the Mayor to control affairs. The Citizens' Charter Review Committee appointed at his instigation went into the question of a strong Mayor vs. a City Manager system of government. The committee, headed by Howard Chernoff, once publisher of the *San Diego Daily Journal*, made many recommendations as to changes in the charter but abandonment of the City Manager type of government was not one of them. It did, however, recommend expanding the Mayor's authority and stature to the extent of granting him the power of all appointments to City Commissions, with Council concurrence. In the case of the Planning Commission, the Manager shared appointments with the Council acting as a body. As for himself, City Manager Fletcher responded by saying that "these Commissions advise the Council and I don't think the City Manager has any business appointing any of the Commissioners."

As a result of the Citizens' Committee review, the voters in September of 1963 approved of the Mayor appointing all seven Planning Commission members, as well as other Commissioners, though granting the Council the right to make the appointments if it twice failed to approve the Mayor's choices. But voters rejected a proposal to place the Planning Department under the Manager instead of the Planning Commission. The voters also approved expanding the Council from seven to nine members.

One of the civic achievements during Dail's time in office was the financing and construction of the metropolitan sewer system which cost $51,000,000, or almost $10,000,000 more than had been expected, and had finally surmounted a rain of criticisms and objections. Most of the City's civic groups had been brought together in support of a bond proposal, in 1960, and even Roscoe E. Hazard, the contractor who had opposed the earlier proposal, now, on the basis of new engineering studies and conclusions, fell into line and became chairman of the bond issue campaign. Dail said at the dedication in 1963:

"We have had more than our share of 'hell' from sidewalk engineers. There are some people who would complain if you sent them to heaven."

Frank Curran

Murray Goodrich

Allen Hitch

Ever since 1962 there had been increasing problems with sewerage all over the City, let alone pollution of the bay. Pipes had broken down, overflows had plagued Mission Valley and Mission Bay, and even La Jolla Cove had been closed to swimmers for a time. Housewives had been asked not to do their laundry on certain days of the week. Financing through sewer fees was approved by a wide margin.

There were twenty-seven miles of drains, designed for collecting and transporting sewage from eight cities, San Diego, Chula Vista, National City, Imperial Beach, Coronado, La Mesa and El Cajon, and from four sanitation districts, Lemon Grove, Montgomery, Rolando and Spring Valley. The sewage was to be carried under Point Loma and then 14,000 feet out to sea and deposited for dilution at a depth of 200 feet.

A connection with the sewer system of Tijuana was added by the Federal Government, to prevent, in cases of emergencies below the border, the emptying of its sewage into San Diego Bay through the Tia Juana River bed. The metropolitan nature of the sewer system, was to serve somewhat as regulator of population densities, or of development. Participating communities had to estimate their sewer system needs and any future annexations, which acted as factors in controlling growth.

In failing health, and loser in a bid for real power, Charles C. Dail declined to run for re-election and thus opened up another civic quarrel between those who wanted to maintain the City planning standards of the past and those who wanted to make it easier for property owners to use or sell their land for the highest possible return, and also to encourage more industry.

There were many candidates for Mayor, the principal ones, however, being Frank Curran, Helen Cobb and Allen Hitch, members of the Council; David Casey, an attorney, and Murray Goodrich, a dealer in surplus aircraft parts and owner of an aluminum smelter plant.

At various times, Hitch, Goodrich and Casey described San Diego a "slumbering giant with a village-type government," and a potential "ghost town with skyscrapers." Charles H. Brown, who opened Mission Valley to progress and now headed the Atlas Corporation controlling three hotels in the valley, was against what he called a cumbersome system that led to personal frustrations and abandonment of projects, and formed a Jobs and Growth Association which most importantly proposed that the Planning Commission be converted into a legislative body whose authority could be appealed only in the courts and not to the Council. It would abrogate State regulations in favor of local control and grant broad powers to establish and define all zoning regulations. Each Councilman would select a member of the Commission for his district and the Mayor one at-large. This, opponents contended, would lead only to narrow pressures with Commissioners trading decisions between them in a great "pork barrel" of politics. However, Goodrich and Casey as well as Curran opposed the Jobs and Growth proposal.

Dail, who had once remarked disparagingly of zoning restrictions, now charged that the measure was being forced upon the Council by members favoring other Mission Valley interests:

"There has been a lot of appeasement in this Council regarding Jobs and Growth. There has been a kowtowing to Mission Valley. ... The structure of our Planning Department has been under vicious attack for two years. ... The political maneuvering is all the more reason for us to retain independent planning as it exists in San Diego today."

An observer of trends nationally looked upon what was happening in San Diego. He was James C. Downs, Jr., of Chicago, who had been conducting seminars for real estate and financial dealers in San Diego for fourteen years:

"I have noticed with dismay the attack on City planning in San Diego. San Diego has a national tradition of fine planning, of high integrity and capability in its planning purpose. Prior to 1900 our society had no planning and zoning. Since then, we have made much progress and solved many problems with planning and zoning, and we certainly don't want to destroy that progress because of the advantage that comes to certain individuals who think that by beating planning or zoning, they can make a fortune."

What disturbed him equally as much, however, was that jobs and growth meant industry:

"The claim by anyone that San Diego's future lies in bringing in new industry here reflects inexperience. In the United States today, three-fourths of the people do not work in manufacturing. Cities like Buffalo, Pittsburgh and Detroit wish they didn't have to rely so much on heavy manufacturing.

"The idea that you can solve all your problems by bringing in a lot of industry here is in error in two respects – the assumption that you can get new industry, which I think is highly doubtful, and the assumption that you want industry, which I think is questionable."

The City's future, according to him, was in tourism, commerce and finance, in government activities, in research and education, in the professions, and in retirement living.

The Mayor and Council were accused of by-passing the people on the grouping of public buildings for what became known as the Centre City project, and that this was an example of the sinister influence that the downtown interests had on the City government. Property owners in Mission Valley had brought suit in a futile attempt to challenge the legality of the use of

Teams of architects went at it with a will in early designs for Civic Center, or Community Concourse, buildings. This is how the parking facility and related area might have appeared. Under the structure there were to be pools, flower shops and an outdoor eating area. Spaciousness gave way to practicality.

City retirement funds for public buildings, but nothing had come of it.

Curran insisted:

"The project led to a complete rejuvenation of our downtown core and won for us the All-American City award. In past elections the people voted for such a project but not by the two-thirds majority needed. Most of the people wanted it – we had to find another way to finance it."

The designation of San Diego as an All-American City had come from the National Municipal League for its work in development of the Community Concourse through the combined cooperation of government and its citizens. Congratulations had come from President Kennedy, while Mayor Dail accepted the award for the City at a civic luncheon.

Business and community leaders threw their support behind Curran and he easily defeated Goodrich in the run-off election and became Mayor at the age of fifty-one. An initiative petition to place the Jobs and Growth proposal regarding the Planning Commission did not make the ballot until the following year, and was defeated. Curran represented stability, a commitment to the way things were being done and the direction the City was going. Goodrich had promised to tour the country regularly to attract new industry to San Diego.

There was to be no final surrender to the auto. There was

brave talk of setting side eighteen blocks in the heart of the City which would be for pedestrians only. The stores and the people could come back.

A growing city, in order to become an important metropolitan area, would need two other things: culture and sports. Or, at least, so believed those who presumed to look into the future. The high-technology industries and educational and scientific institutions were attracting a new white-collar type of worker with leisure time and more-than-average income. The San Diego Symphony had existed since April 11, 1927, when Nino Marcelli conducted the first concert in the Spreckels theater but, as in all cities and communities, needed constant infusions of contributions to keep it going. William L. Dean had launched the Starlight Operas in 1946. In art, the Fine Arts Gallery had amassed what was believed to be a collection equal to larger metropolitan areas. The important collection of the Putnam sisters was now assured a permanent home in San Diego, in a gallery in Balboa Park.

A new attitude toward sports came with the arrival in San Diego of Jack Murphy as sports editor of *The San Diego Union.* Before him, local sports had been a matter of minor league professional teams, of high school competition, and the promise of things to come from San Diego State College. Limited horse racing had existed below the border, in Tijuana, then later at

This scene view of the Community Concourse looks south, to the City Administration building, with the Civic Theater to the left and the Convention Center and Parking Garage to the right. The graceful connecting overpasses and that center fountain did not survive.

William L. Dean

Barron Hilton

Dr. Albert Anderson

Agua Caliente, and then, too, at the Del Mar track of the County Fair. Attendance in large measure was from out of the immediate area. But sports were assuming a large stature throughout the country.

San Diego had experienced minor league baseball since 1936, when William H. Lane had moved his Hollywood Stars to San Diego and into a small ball park built on the waterfront largely by the Works Progress Administration during the Depression. In 1955 ownership passed to C. Arnholt Smith, through his Westgate-California Corporation, and he built the Pacific Coast League team a new park, Westgate, in Mission Valley, in 1958.

Less than three years later came the news that Barron Hilton, son of the Hilton hotel magnate, was interested in moving his professional football team, the Los Angeles Chargers of the new American Football League, to San Diego. The only difficulty was the seating capacity of Balboa Stadium which generally had been used for high school athletics. The City Council resolved that by agreeing to spend $700,000 to renovate the stadium and add a second tier to raise its capacity from 23,000 to 30,000. Two Councilmen, Ross Tharpe and William Hartley cast "no" votes only because the contractual agreement also gave the Chargers a year's free use of the stadium. Professional football games began in the Fall of 1961 with an attendance for the first game of only 20,000. The Chargers defeated the Oakland Raiders forty-four to zero.

The new football league was slow in prospering and at one time Hilton sought without success to sell the Chargers to C. Arnholt Smith for $750,000. There were many old-timers who insisted that large-scale professional sports would not do well financially in San Diego, because of competition with participator attractions available in a mild climate. There were no population concentrations of "blue collar" workers committed to spectator sports.

But as far back as 1960 there had been talk of big-time baseball for San Diego and in 1961 the owner of a Los Angeles team of the National League saw the City as the focal point of a struggle between his league and the American League for the most attractive new franchise on the West Coast.

Delegation after delegation of San Diegans, primarily under the leadership of Dr. Albert Anderson of a Chamber of Commerce sports committee, visited baseball league meetings and training camps. Two Mayors, Dail and Curran, gave their support. At one point, in 1963, Smith promised that he would convert his Westgate park into a major league stadium and meet an expected franchise price of $4,000,000. At times there were indications two teams might be available to make a move to San Diego, one from Milwaukee and another from Cincinnati. Nothing came of them, but the price for an existing baseball team had jumped to $7,000,000. And football in San Diego was taking hold.

CHAPTER ELEVEN

A helicopter takes Photographer Ed Neil almost up against the Community Concourse buildings. The City Administration Building is at the left and the parking garage at the top right, with the Convention Hall stretching from the garage and alongisde of the Administration Building. The Civic Theater is at the lower right. There were no broad boulevards nor placid lagoons. The best view was from above.

200 Years — What Kind of a City Was it Now?

The 200th anniversary of the founding of San Diego was approaching. By 1969 two centuries would have passed since the establishment on Presidio Hill of the first White settlement on the Pacific Coast.

For almost a hundred years of that time San Diego had lingered in isolation while great cities rose on the Pacific Coast. Now its day — if greatness is measured by size — was at hand. In population it was beginning to challenge San Francisco. The population figures were somewhat deceptive, however, as San Francisco, limiting itself in area to only forty-five square miles, was the Queen City of a Bay area which would exceed three million people.

Los Angeles seemed to be beyond reach, however. It had acquired the railroads and the shipping lines, and with untold wealth in oil, had become one of the most populous cities of the continent and dominated a metropolitan area of between six and seven million persons. The longing to be like Los Angeles had faded, though, even among the most ardent promoters. But they still wanted San Diego to be a City to be reckoned with.

By 1965, San Diego was the sixteenth largest City in the United States with a population approaching 640,000. Annexations were proceeding swiftly and regularly. The City now encompassed more than 305 square miles. A hundred years before it had contained only about seventy-four square miles; in 1960, 240 square miles.

Its residents were growing younger, in average age. The proportion of retired people was declining, and a newer generation of settlers represented families with children. The average age of the population in 1960 was about twenty-seven years compared to nearly thirty-three in 1930. It was even lower in the County.

The minority population, while rising, was not yet a significant political factor. Mexican-Americans in 1960 constituted only six and six-tenths percent of the total population; Blacks almost at the same at six percent. The percentage of Mexican-Americans in Los Angeles was ten and a half percent.

City government was convinced that growth could be guided in an acceptable and desired manner by annexing territory to the north and subject to subdividing and the founding of new communities. Control to the south and east was blocked by the existence of other incorporated cities. The "City Beautiful" was still the dream.

The use of urban renewal to rehabilitate a city intrigued San Diegans, Inc., and a group of them accompanied by City officials and other interested parties inspected work under way in San Francisco and Sacramento.

In San Francisco they viewed where private land was taken by a redevelopment agency, for developers, cleared of structures, and converted with private funds for apartment houses, buildings, town houses, and high-rise office buildings. People would reside near where they had to work.

In Sacramento, of particular interest, was the design and development of the Capitol Mall, with public and private buildings, and restoration of an historical zone known as Old Sacramento.

Not as ambitious as the projects of San Francisco and even Sacramento, the Community Concourse, as the new Civic Center became known, was dedicated on September 16, 1964. The Convention Hall, Exhibit Hall and parking garage were opened for business; the City Administration Building was to be ready in December and the 3,000-seat Civic Theater in January.

However, Guilford Whitney, chairman of the Community Concourse Advisory Board, called the center "the most conveniently located on the Pacific Coast and one of the most beautiful." Morley Golden, chairman for the celebration, said that now "the sky is the limit." Mayor Curran was a bit more restrained, asserting that while the buildings represented a lot of determination, they also represented a lot of consternation.

Compromise had limited the challenge of the Community Concourse. Its buildings were rather tightly assembled, with only a limited plaza for open space and there were no lagoons nor parkways. They did not rise spectacularly above downtown, nor could they be seen from a distance. But they represented a beginning – the assembling of public buildings considered necessary to the economic and cultural revival of downtown.

In the scheme of the "City Beautiful" public buildings were to dominate the City and skyline. Here, San Diego's new Community Concourse is almost hidden from view in a concentration of new structures. Only the parking garage stands out in the center left.

And the forty-year struggle to obtain a Convention Hall at least seemed to have ended.

The new Administration Building, however, faced southward, looking down Second Avenue toward an economic wasteland of old buildings, which while not representing decay in the same degree of the older cities of the East, were out of the mainstream of progress. No modern buildings now were rising in the area below Broadway. The City was steadily moving northward, as it had for a long time, retreating from the bay.

Conservatism dominated San Diego's political thinking and urban renewal was not the most welcome alternative to taxpayer financing of any downtown rehabilitation. There was a heavy

Richard M. Nixon

concentration of military personnel, both active and retired, as well as many pensioners from the Midwest. Conservative ideology was brought to bear on the voters by the quiet yet persuasive James S. Copley, through his *San Diego Union.* Republican Richard M. Nixon long had had a political base in San Diego County.

In 1960 San Diego County had cast a majority vote for Nixon for President, though he lost to Democrat Senator John F. Kennedy. Two years later San Diegans again backed Nixon, this time for Governor, though he lost to the incumbent, Edmund G. Brown. Kennedy was assassinated in 1963 and Vice President Lyndon B. Johnson succeeded to the Presidency. In 1964 Johnson was opposed by Republican Senator Barry Goldwater, a San Diego neighbor from Arizona and frequent visitor at William S. Kellogg's La Jolla Beach and Tennis Club. Johnson won in a nationwide landslide but in San Diego County it was Goldwater who led the ticket.

Though Senator Goldwater had been considered military-minded in international affairs, it was under President Johnson that the United States' commitment to South Vietnam began to expand into actual warfare. By 1963 there were more than 15,000 American servicemen in South Vietnam, as "advisors." Within a year major military commitments were being made and they would have a direct effect on the fortunes of San Diego.

In 1964 the Port District won approval of the voters of all the five communities on the bay for bond issues providing almost five and a half million dollars for a new passenger terminal for Lindbergh Field, along Harbor Drive. This time Federal Aviation Agency officials gave their blessings to Lindbergh Field. They said it could be used for all jet-type aircraft of the foreseeable future. There also was a million and a half for improvements for the new Harbor Island and almost four million for the first-phase construction of the Twenty-Fourth Street Marine Terminal. Taxpayers were promised that the bonds would be paid for out of port income and would not necessitate additional taxes. There could be only more jobs, more income, more tourists, more cargo, more industry and more prosperity, without cost.

Barry Goldwater

Again there was heard talk of another Exposition, as there had been when Fiesta del Pacifico had been abandoned in 1960. This time the idea was put forward by officials of the 1968 California World's Fair which originally had intended to place one in Long Beach, with the sanction of the Bureau of International Expositions. The centerpiece would be a 50,000-seat stadium on Fiesta Island in Mission Bay. Clyde Vandenberg, who had been involved in the Exposition of 1935-36, and Loren W. McCannon presented on behalf of the organization a research report forecasting 34,000,000 visitors for two Exposition sessions of 184 days each. But little public enthusiasm was evident. The growing problem of South Vietnam was disturbing in a City so dominated by military establishments.

The years of 1964 and 1965 witnessed a boom in the County arising in large part from the opening of vast new lands by the construction of modern highways and freeways. The auto provided access to one area and another with ease and swiftness. And now water was assured with the existence of the two aqueducts and the promise of the Feather River project.

George Scott had carried out his promise of meeting the challenge of the invasion of the County by Los Angeles mercantile interests and his Walker Scott store was the principal structure in the Escondido Village shopping center. Rancho Bernardo, one of the last of the old Mexican ranchos to be subdivided, was beginning its development along Highway 395 toward a goal of a community of 40,000 residents. Then there was Irvin Kahn's Los Penasquitos development along the same highway. Farther north, and facing the San Baquitas Lagoon, was Rancho La Costa being created with money primarily from interests in Las Vegas. Lake San Marcos was attracting retired people from around the nation.

The North County was becoming an invitingly shining country, attracting businesses and industries and homemakers who had few ties to San Diego's central city. While the City had a population of almost 640,000 in the 1964-65 period, the County as a whole had soared to more than 1,200,000.

In the North County, Escondido in twenty-five years had grown from about 4,500 to almost 25,000 population. Oceanside had increased from about 4,600 to 33,800. Carlsbad, which had become a city by 1950, had grown since that time from about 4,400 to 12,350. Vista had emerged as a community of nearly 20,000.

To the east of San Diego City, in just the same period of time, twenty-five years, La Mesa had grown from 4,000 to more than 35,000; El Cajon from about 1,500 to almost 43,000. To the south, National City was now 36,000 compared to 10,000 in 1940. Chula Vista had expanded from about 5,000 to almost 54,000. Though Coronado had remained somewhat isolated from the pressure of accessibility, still it had grown from 7,000 to about 20,000.

The unincorporated areas were absorbing a heavy influx of new residents. There were more than 250,000 persons now living in rural areas which had no central governments. Industries of the newer and higher technology were not dependent on the

Lionel Van Deerlin

John Alessio

Fred Kraft

inflow of heavy materials and had no need to locate near railroad tracks or waterfronts.

As the population of the County increased, San Diego was entitled to additional Congressional representation. First, it shared a Congressman with Orange County, even more politically conservative than was San Diego County. When it was entitled to a third Congressional representative, a politically-inspired redistricting created a new Congressional District in the southern part of the County, assuring the election of a Democrat in 1962. He was Lionel Van Deerlin, who had failed in a previous effort to replace Republican Bob Wilson. Van Deerlin was a radio and television broadcaster of an independent mind.

One of the programs advocated by Van Deerlin in his first campaign was the connecting of San Diego and Coronado with a bridge, as an economic benefit to the entire South Bay.

Venerable Hotel del Coronado had been purchased in 1960 by John Alessio who liked to recall that as a boy earning his own way he had shined the shoes of a banker, C. Arnholt Smith. From this acquaintance he had been enabled to enter the banking business in Tijuana and acquire control of the Agua Caliente race track. A fortune was spent on renovating the old hotel structure which once had attracted the Winter visitors of the luxury class and had been a pride of the late John D. Spreckels.

As far back as 1926 the Spreckels companies had prepared plans for a bridge across the bay, but nothing came of them. Time and again down the years similar efforts had been made by other companies, and in 1935 the City Council of Coronado even had initiated a plan for a bridge and then abandoned it because of objections by the Navy. The bay was shallow and it was feared that collapse or destruction of the bridge could block off the southern part of the harbor.

In the 1950's all over California ferry boats had given way to bridges, but the San Diego and Coronado Ferry Company, now nearing eighty years of age, still dominated the bay and was carrying more than 3,000,000 vehicles a year. Feasibility studies by the State had been initiated as early as 1955 through legislative action of State Senator Fred Kraft of San Diego. In 1962, the State Department of Public Works insisted that "progress will sooner or later require that the existing facility for crossing San Diego Bay be replaced by a more modern highway structure."

Alessio approached the City Council of Coronado in the belief that his plan for a bridge to bring Hotel del Coronado into the world of conventions was not only feasible but desirable, and that Coronado should prepare with a set of stringent zoning laws to control its future as a community of quality. A community plebiscite, which was not binding on any state action, had gone against the proposal for a bridge in 1958. Four years later the City Council rejected the idea by a three-to-two vote.

Alessio said he gave up, sold the hotel to Larry Lawrence and his associates, and the sale included lands on which it had been proposed to erect a high-rise addition to the hotel as well as a group of apartment buildings. Lawrence would carry on the struggle for the bridge.

The issue came to a head in 1964. A State feasibility study had concluded a four-lane bridge could be erected at less cost than a two-lane tube could be laid under the bay. It perhaps was politically fortunate that a member of the California Toll Bridge

The Old San Diego passed away with the end of the ferries that crossed the bay to Coronado. A bay bridge in 1968 was slowly closing a gap and becoming a reality. It rose 200 feet above the water.

Authority was the governor, Edmund G. Brown, a Democrat, who had received support from both Alessio and Lawrence. The San Diego City Council maintained a neutral position.

While Coronado was a quiet community, there were more than 5,000 civilian workers at the Naval Air Station who required daily transportation by ferry and could be considered supporters of a bridge crossing.

The opposition was led by a retired Rear Admiral, Dwight Johnson, who told a Toll Bridge Authority hearing that "we want to develop without excessive interference. Geographically we stand in the way of no one ... why try to induce traffic through

Edmund G. Brown

here?" A rebuttal was offered by another retired Navy officer who said that "living in the past may be a soothing pill to deny us the benefits that lie before us. ... We did retire the Pony Express despite its romantic heritage."

The question whether the Navy would accept a bridge revolved around interpretations of what high Navy officers had actually said about a bridge. The Toll Bridge Authority accepted the explanation that the Navy would not object to a bridge as long as design and location did not interfere with ship and aircraft operations in the bay. Representative Wilson warned, however, that "if a bridge is built I can say flatly San Diego will live to regret it to the tune of hundreds of millions of dollars" in presumed losses of Naval installations.

The Army Corps of Engineers approved a bridge. The California Toll Bridge Authority voted to build it, with revenue bonds, which meant that the ferry company would have to be purchased and put out of business. So Coronado, which had found itself bound to a Port District it did not want to join, now was to be tied to San Diego City, and many residents feared it would be swept up into a flood of growth with its burdens of congestion and high taxes.

After two years of study by the City Planning Department, and after a year and a half of review and revision by a Citizens' Committee, the City of San Diego's new General Plan was ready for printing and distribution. Times had changed, and, too, there was a new Mayor in the City Hall. The Plan faced an uncertain and unhappy future, chiefly over one issue: urban renewal. The Citizens' Committee report stated:

> "The spread of deterioration and blight in our cities is so enormous a problem that it appears to yield to successful solution only upon total mobilization of the resources available to the community and a concerted pressing of the attack. The program for conducting such an unremitting, comprehensive battle ... is known as urban renewal."

That was like touching a match to the dynamite of San Diego conservatism. Though the *Evening Tribune* was a sister newspaper to *The San Diego Union,* with the same ownership, it largely avoided partisan politics. The issue this time was not a partisan one and the *Evening Tribune* thundered in an editorial:

> "Mayor Frank Curran could never have been more right than when he observed the Citizens' Advisory Committee on the General Plan had handed the City Council an awful big package of problems. ... People who believe in freedom, who believe in property rights, who believe that government is the servant and not the master of citizens, will be instantly alert ... if you do not want City Hall to rule every condition under which you live and work in San Diego, you must protest now."

The Plan was generally considered to be the handiwork of the Planning Department more than that of the Citizens' Committee and it left to City officials determination of the "public interest" in the application of urban renewal programs which could take property from one owner and transfer it to another for the public's "beneficial use" as defined by the United States Supreme Court.

The Chamber of Commerce, though not taking any position on the question of urban renewal, had some second thoughts about the Plan as written. Its president, William E. Quirk, a utility company executive, suggested to the Council that the responsibility for determining the "public interest" should not be an arbitrary decision of City officials but be shared with responsible citizens. The *Evening Tribune* also suggested the Plan would be more palatable to voters if the reference to urban renewal were removed.

The statement on the "public interest" was altered to accommodate the Chamber's suggestion as to public participation. The recommendation on urban renewal was weakened from "utilization" of appropriate private, municipal, state and federal resources, to the "exploration" of "all appropriated means, both public and private, for this purpose."

Acting on the theory that the Plan was merely a guide and not a mandate, the City Council, on the favorable recommendation of the Planning Commission, adopted the Plan in 1965. Describing it as "socialism," a Citizens' Protective League, led by an insuranceman, M. J. Montroy, immediately began circulating referendum petitions to force a public vote on the Council's action.

The Citizens' Committee, through Dr. Leiffer, fought back:

> "A small band of willful citizens ... intend to grind to a halt the development of the City ... they are seeking to turn us back to the 19th Century."

Sufficient signatures were obtained for a referendum, and the Plan went before the voters in September of 1965 and was defeated, 66,223 to 39,516. The voters evidently weren't happy with events transpiring at City Hall and again denied pay raises to the City Council members and the Mayor. A General Plan was dead for a year, when it could legally be brought up again.

In reality San Diego had little control over the events which were now shaping its future. The rush to Southern California was on again. Many of those arriving in San Diego were better educated than those who had flooded in for wartime work. There were not many now alive who recalled the prophecies of the 1930's when so many had seen the United States as conquering its last Frontier, and the future would have to be one of turning inward and of reduced hopes. Science and knowledge had opened the door to a Frontier few had foreseen in its full splendor.

The Economic Development Corporation, which had been organized to encourage the location of industry in San Diego, reported that in 1966 there were 6,000 scientists and 70,000 semi-professional and skilled workers who existed in San Diego because of its expanding educational system. Education employed almost 30,000 persons, almost as many as when the aircraft industry was at its peace-time height and the dominant economic factor in the community.

The Chamber of Commerce could count sixty-three firms engaged in business related to maritime activities, other than shipbuilding, and they employed 3,000 people, twice the number of 1960. The National Steel & Shipbuilding Company had become the largest Western shipbuilder with a backlog of $315,000,000.

Fifty or more firms had moved to San Diego to be near the coast, the Naval Electronics Laboratory and the Scripps Institution of Oceanography. The electronics industry accounted for 12,500 jobs. Convair divisions, too, were on the rise once again, with 12,350 employes. Its missile divisions had perfected the Centaur to add to the Atlas missile, the workhorse of the space program. Rohr Aircraft had almost 10,000 employes; General Atomic had nearly 2,000 working primarily on advanced nuclear power systems and Ryan aircraft had a backlog of $110,000,000.

There was no dependence on a mass-consumer type of industry as in Detroit and similar cities. Smokestacks? Whatever had become of the old argument of "smokestacks vs. geraniums?"

Malcolm H. Love

Though businesses were expanding into larger ones, ninety percent of the companies in the County still had less than a hundred employees. But in five years, according to Dallas J. Clark, president of the Economic Development Corporation, 750 companies had added about 17,000 jobs.

The Veterans Administration was building a huge hospital in proximity to the University of California Medical School at San Diego, The National Cash Register Company in the Spring would begin clearing 114 acres at Rancho Bernardo's industrial park for a large data processing systems production plant.

There were now eleven universities and senior and junior colleges in the County, where ten decades before only three of them had existed in any semblance to their 1965 form. San Diego State College, under the leadership of its president, Malcolm H. Love, was granting masters' degrees across the board. It had 18,000 students, a building program of $25,000,000 and an expected enrollment of 28,000 by 1975. It was a university almost in fact, if not in name, and far removed from the little school for the training of teachers. The University of California branch at Torrey Pines now had 2,258 students and was assembling a faculty and scientists few institutions could match. On the same Torrey Pines mesa, on twelve acres of pueblo land originally owned by the City, soon would rise the Salk Institute for Biological Studies sponsored by a National Foundation formed originally to combat infantile paralysis. It expected to attract scores of scientists dedicated to the study of life. California Western had 1,300 students and the University of San Diego, 1,541.

Albert Harutunian, Jr.

Robert H. Biron, vice president for business and finance for the University of California at San Diego, and before that an executive of Convair, said that in time the university was certain to have the same dollar impact on the community as Convair once had.

The lowering age level and the arrival since the war of a new wave of settlers from the East as well as the Midwest fired an enthusiasm for professional sports so common to older cities.

With a professional football team, the San Diego Chargers, already playing in San Diego, and the prospects of a major league baseball team rising with the growth in population, a multi-purpose sports stadium was proposed and quickly accepted.

In 1963 the City Council had authorized City Manager Fletcher to study all City-owned properties on which a stadium might be erected, and named Paul Carter, president of the Greater San Diego Sports Association, to lead a feasibility study of a 45,000- to 50,000-seat stadium, costing, it was hoped, between fifteen and twenty millions.

The Mayor, however, was disappointed in the association's slow progress. The architectural and engineering firm of Frank L. Hope & Associates was ultimately named to select a site and present a plan. Though Barron Hilton, owner of the Chargers, had been enthusiastic about a "floating" stadium in Mission Bay, the architectural firm selected a site in Mission Valley for a stadium that would have to cost $27,600,000. Fletcher was ordered to buy the site.

Voters were assured by the City and Albert Harutunian, Jr., who was to become chairman of a Stadium Authority, that there would be no cost to the taxpayers if, as anticipated, major league baseball came to San Diego. The vote in November of 1965 was overwhelmingly in favor of a public stadium.

In 1967 C. Arnholt Smith, owner of the Pacific Coast League baseball team, the Padres, formally moved to acquire a National

League franchise and invited E. J. "Buzzie" Bavasi, a Los Angeles baseball executive, to become a partner and president of the San Diego club. The National League owners voted in 1968 to expand into San Diego, and the cost for a franchise, for a team to be started from scratch, was to be $10,000,000. In a few years the price had risen from $4,000,000 to $10,000,000. Smith hesitated, then agreed.

In the same year, Barron Hilton sold the control of the Chargers to Eugene Klein and Samuel Schulman, of Los Angeles, engaged in the theatrical business, for $10,000,000, but they would remain in San Diego with the new stadium as their "home."

The almost unprecedented wave of professional sports

There was one bond issue which certainly met with widespread public approval, and that was to build a stadium for professional football and baseball. Here the San Diego Stadium rises in Mission Valley. It was ready for play on August 20, 1967. Despite all that was promised, it would lose money.

brought San Diego another sports center, the International Sports Arena, in November of 1966. It was designed for seating 13,500 for hockey and 16,000 for other sporting and public events. The cost was $6,500,000, but this time, though erected on City-owned land in the Midway-Frontier area, the money came from private venture capital through a non-profit Stadium Lease Co., which, in turn, granted operating rights. The first rights went to a company formed by Robert Breitbard, one of the original arena promoters, who already had a franchise for a professional hockey team and within a year would add a professional basketball team.

Evidently not daunted by the prospective cost to him of bringing major league baseball to San Diego, though his financial entanglements would take him deeper and deeper into troubled waters, Smith in 1966 announced he would build the first new major downtown hotel in San Diego in thirty-nine years. Plans were changed and re-changed, and in 1967 it was announced there would be two hotels, the Westgate Plaza, to become a luxury hotel and the other the Executive Hotel, to serve the Convention Center. Further changes were made and progress was slow. The twenty-five story Westgate Plaza would open four and a half years after the first plans had been drawn. Furnishings and art from around the world went into the Westgate Plaza, and though it was to win acclaim as one of the world's finest hotels, the price that could be asked for rooms could never produce the income to pay the costs.

Leslie Gerhres

Political power in a conservative-minded San Diego was being exercised in a significant way by Smith, one of the largest California contributors to the Republican Party, who, however, did not neglect "deserving" Democrats. The Westgate Plaza Hotel had been allowed to intrude onto a public street for an entrance to its lower parking area, but those who complained of political influence were answered by pointing to a cross-street overpass walk for the El Cortez Hotel complex; the City Hall itself, which straddled the same street on which appeared the Smith hotel's main entrance; and the entrances for the City's own Concourse parking garage.

The chairman of the Republican Party in San Diego, and an executive of various Smith enterprises, Leslie Gerhres, a retired rear admiral and a hero of World War II, said that evident animosity toward "men at the top" in the belief they were in politics only for personal gain, and to control office holders, was incomprehensible to him.

MacArthur Gorton

Downtown, as an attraction for shoppers and visitors, however, was suffering. The end of the San Diego Athletic Club founded in 1928 signified the urbanization of San Diego. Housed in a handsome multi-storied building at Sixth Avenue and A Street, it had been experiencing a decline in night-time uses for many years, even under the promotional efforts of its manager, MacArthur Gorton, who had originally built the Valencia Hotel in La Jolla. But a club of its size could not exist on a luncheon business. In 1964 the corporate members sold the building to California Western University of Point Loma, for a downtown campus. In a few years it would be re-sold for an office building.

The Cuyamaca Club, the oldest incorporated club in California, had experienced similar difficulties and its charter was transferred to C. Arnholt Smith. He would sustain it as a club centered in his new office building. The University Club, totally supported by its members, sought to turn the tide of events and succeeded in financing a new home at Seventh Avenue and A Street, but it, too, would find the path a stormy one.

The spirit of downtown was sustained by tall buildings in which people would work in the daytime and abandon at night. The final end of the old Marston store came as hundreds of citizens in 1969 watched the destruction of the building which once had marked the splendor of downtown shopping. The site had been sold and the store closed by the Broadway-Hale Company. The Marston building would suffer a final humiliation of being replaced by a parking garage for another skyscraper rising just behind it. The new building would house the Union Bank of California and San Diego offices of the Pacific Telephone Company.

Another site for a Broadway-Hale store would be in a $50,000,000 shopping center being built in Mission Valley, encompassing, in part, the site of the old Westgate ball park. Fashion Valley would be called the largest single building project in the history of the City, a joint venture of the Westgate-California Realty Company and the Ernest W. Hahn Company.

The City Council had quickly granted a commercial zone variance. The center would open in 1969. Already San Diego was one of the bright spots in the nation in shopping center sales. Before 1960, the County had had three regional shopping centers; by the end of 1969 it would have nine.

Also gone from the scene was the ornate Commonwealth

Office buildings too had invaded Mission Valley, along with the hotels, motels and shopping centers. It was a new way of life for office workers and executives. But the rains and high San Diego River water always seemed to carry some warning.

Shopping centers, after a slow start, were now a way of life in an auto age. A second one, Fashion Valley, is shown under construction in Mission Valley, west of the May Company center. This view looks south.

building with its Orpheum Theater, at C Street and Fifth Avenue. It was replaced with a new home for San Diego's oldest bank, the First National, which was dedicated in January of 1966. The bone-white building rose twenty-five stories, an imposing home far removed from the days when the First National was the principal bank for the Spreckels' interests in San Diego. But it was still a local bank, largely locally-owned and locally controlled. Its chairman and chief executive officer was Anderson Borthwick, who had begun his career as a bank messenger at $10 a month.

Mergers with out-of-town banks had been resisted; but the invasion of northern financial power continued. The Union Bank arrived in 1965; the Bank of California in 1968. The power of decision as to San Diego's future would be diffused. San Diego's other important local bank, the San Diego Trust & Savings Bank, led by Thomas W. Sefton, passed its seventy-fifth anniversary in 1964 and proudly advertised that "all our decisions are made in San Diego County."

San Diego now was among the "have" cities. Public enthusiasm was high. A whole series of bond issues, to improve and expand parks, for public service facilities, for flood control and new sewers, won easy approval in November of 1966. Bonds in huge amounts were voted for water storage and distribution by the San Diego County Water Authority and the Metropolitan Water

Thomas W. Sefton

District. Public schools received $22,500,000 for new construction.

The widening circle of new communities and subdivisions, however, had created problems not foreseen at the end of the war, when the last of the electric street cars were retired and buses substituted in order to reach flexibility in transportation. Buses, it was reasoned, could follow growth. Such had not been the case. The San Diego Transit System had met with increasing financial problems and had been gradually reducing service. Crosstown bus service was impractical in many cases because of the broken nature of the terrain of San Diego County. Workers would rather drive their own autos than go by circuitous routes between their homes and places of work.

It became a question of public ownership or no bus service at all. In 1966 the voters approved a charter amending permitting public operation of the bus system. A year later a Federal grant was obtained to pay half the cost of establishing the service. San Diego voters provided the balance of the approximate $8,000,000 cost and the City began operating the transit system through a non-profit agency on July 1, 1967.

San Diego's bus situation, however, was not unique. All over the country local, private transportation was giving way to public service. Workers no longer were concentrated in central areas and industries had followed them to the surburbs.

Meeting for the first time in the First National's new tower, January of 1966, San Diegans, Inc. looked back over the years of its existence since 1959, and raised the question of where the City now found itself. Hamilton Marston, its president, said they had found the core of the City good, what with the new Community Concourse and the new office buildings. But the rest of the downtown district, embraced by what was known as Horton's Addition, with its small blocks, with no alleys, and with many small absentee ownerships, had imposed almost impossible problems of assembling land for commercial, industrial, residential and institutional developments. Single improvements were threatened with becoming lonely outposts in a desert of obsolescence. Marston said:

> "Our climate, location, site and scenery are more precious now than in Horton's Day, for there is less space in the world and more people wanting it. We have hundreds of acres, gone to seed and lying fallow, beside a great harbor and in the heart of a growing community, surrounded by the densest and most diverse population, backed by hills with splendid views and ringed by Point Loma and Coronado, the hub of private and public transport and centered by the vital core of governmental, commercial and cultural life of the City and our new convention activities. ... Must this area, except the core, continue to decline in value and utility? ... Ours is a common problem of cities."

His solution lay with urban renewal.

In the absence of any General Plan, communities and neighborhoods within the City had been encouraged to form their own councils by which they could contribute to planning for the future. The City's General Plan, after the required lapse of time, was brought up again. Before it was presented to the voters once more, however, references to urban renewal were restricted by a new City Ordinance to its uses for public facilities.

The San Diego Union now embraced the Plan:

> "The Plan is not a product of a concealed band of social plotters but of your neighbors — good neighbors. The General Plan merely sets down new guidelines by which business and industry and residents can continue to live together in a well-ordered and beautifully developed community.
>
> "Do we want to abandon all that? Are we now by our vote going to say we are willing to turn the community over to the promoters, the speculators and the exploiters?"

"No," said *The San Diego Union.* At the suggestion of Mayor Curran, however, the name of the General Plan was changed to "Progress Guide and General Plan, to avoid any inferences of inflexibility. Both Federal and State regulations required General Plans in order to qualify for some categories of financial assistance.

A saturation advertising and promotion campaign was waged on behalf of a Plan, now reduced in scope and promise, and it won a voter approval by a four-to-three margin, in November of 1967.

Events were moving swiftly in the late 1960's. The San Diego Zoo was fifty years old in 1966 and insisted it now maintained the world's largest collection of wild animals, with a total of 5,011 specimens of 1,664 species and subspecies. This included 879 mammals, 3,022 birds, and 1,110 reptiles.

In the early 1960's there came a realization that if the Zoo continued its acquisitions, more space would be needed. In 1962 Clayburn LaForce, Farm Manager for San Diego City, suggested the use of City-owned land in San Pasqual Valley. The land had been acquired at the time when the City considered the impounding of additional runoff water in the San Dieguito River, a move later abandoned.

While the Zoological Society originally had envisioned only a small addition, the philosophy of maintaining zoos was changing. A San Pasqual Study Committee with Norman Roberts as chairman was named in 1966 and the final concept of a Wild Animal Park as the "zoo of the future" was brought to head under the leadership of Anderson Borthwick as Zoo president. The first animals arrived in San Pasqual Valley in 1969.

T. Claude Ryan

Frederick H. Rohr

Edmund T. Price

Frank Curran was re-elected Mayor, by a two-to-one margin over Allen Hitch in 1967, and Councilmen again were denied pay raises, for the fourth time in four years. The new passenger terminal was dedicated at Lindbergh Field, and the Navy's last seaplane made its final flight from San Diego Bay. Devastating brush fires swept over vast areas of San Diego's backcountry.

In 1968, Richard M. Nixon was elected President of the United States. More funds were voted for additional airport and harbor improvements. In 1969, voters refused to increase the power and authority of the Mayor and rejected nomination and election of Councilmen by districts, instead of nomination by district and election City-wide. Voters also began rejecting school bond issues by which old structures would be replaced with earthquake-proof buildings.

Some of the old names were beginning to disappear from the scene, or from active roles in industries they had helped raise from bare ground. But the time for the collapse of the empires of Smith and others, who had built in a fever of unrestricted ambition during the soaring 1960's, was not yet at hand.

T. Claude Ryan, one of aviation's pioneers, had seen his control of Ryan Aeronautical slipping away, after it had ventured into public financing, and in 1968 it became a wholly-owned subsidiary of Teledyne, Inc., of Los Angeles. Robert C. Jackson was elevated to chairman of the Ryan board and Frank Gard Jameson became president of Teledyne Ryan.

Frederick H. Rohr, an immigrant's son whose techniques revolutionized the airframe-aerospace industry during over a period of forty-one years, died in 1965 at the age of sixty-nine. The former Mayor, Charles C. Dail, who had left his mark on so many of San Diego's civic problems as well as achievements, died in 1968 at the age of fifty-nine.

Solar Aircraft, which had begun life as a manufacturer of gliders, long since had been taken from its founder, Edmund T. Price, and with Herbert Kunzel as its new head, had become a division of International Harvester and was succeeding in expanding sales of its gas turbine engines. Price, who had come to San Diego from New Bedford, Massachusetts, died while in London in 1968. He was seventy-three.

Bishop Buddy, the first Bishop of the Catholic Diocese of San Diego, who had inspired the rise of the University of San Diego, died in 1966. He was succeeded by the Most Rev. Francis J. Furey. Ewart W. Goodwin, a native son, died in 1967 at the relatively young age of fifty-nine. Guilford Whitney, who had been born in Cedar Rapids, Iowa, and founded a variety store that could not successfully be expanded into a chain, died in 1968 at the age of eighty.

John Bate, who had dreamed the great dreams about the

harbor, was forced to announce his "retirement" as Port Director, presumably because of illness. He had guided the formation of the Unified Port District, but had not foreseen that the Commissioners in many situations would choose to represent the communities from which they came more than the port as a whole as envisioned by Bate. Sometimes, however, they did not.

But an area of disagreement had widened and Bate left to become honored in retirement as "Mr. San Diego Bay." Don L. Nay, Bate's assistant, was named as Port Director. Though the cities surrounding the bay had surrendered their tidelands to the new District, they could maintain a control on what would be done with them through appointments of the Commissioners. Thus the idea of a separate unified port under a central direction was not fully realized. Even San Diego City struggled to impose its will on the District.

Herbert Kunzel

Bate always would believe that had he been able to force the creation of a separate Board of Commissioners elected by the people, he might have retained a more direct control over bay development.

Don L. Nay

The concept of the bay as an industrial base was coming under attack, however. At a hearing on the General Plan, which embraced the future possibilities of the harbor, the local chapter of the American Institute of Architects and a civic beautification group, Citizens Coordinate, charged that under the Plan the beauty and recreational possibilities of the bay as a whole could be sacrificed to industrial development and high-rise apartments. Roy Drew, president of the architects, said:

> "The San Diego Harbor is the one great and unique natural resource of the San Diego metropolitan area ... and its function as a shipping port should not be allowed to overcome the harbor as a natural center of the recreational, social, cultural and residential environment of an otherwise sprawling metropolis."

Telltale signs were beginning to appear. During Bate's administration, port tonnage grew from 50,000 tons a year to its all-time high of 1,121,000 tons in 1966. This figure was not to be matched again in the next few years, despite an increase in coast-wide shipping. Los Angeles was becoming an ever-greater center of distribution.

The waterfront of downtown San Diego, no longer needed for commerce, was sought for tourist interests. Robert M. Golden, now directing his father's construction company, and his associates proposed a $35,000,000 "total concept" development. His plan was rejected by Port Commissioners who, instead, granted a long-term lease to Earl Gagosian's Royal Inns of America for a hotel complex. The new Harbor Island had its first tenant and tall hotels were in prospect. A park along the Lindbergh Field side of the harbor was completed and dedicated in 1968 as Spanish Landing Park.

In 1969, the Port District eliminated its traffic and marketing departments and Bate broke his silence and said the action "may well be the beginning of a giant leap backward and San Diego may become a 'landlord port' more concerned with property management than the development of shipping." Nay denied the departments were being abolished entirely but would be expanded and their functions reinstated as proved necessary. The port had prospered, however, and had gone off the tax rolls in 1968. But the port would soon be faced with the prospect that it could be cheaper to unload a ship at the port of Los Angeles, and truck goods to San Diego, than to make a separate call at San Diego.

Bay communities would begin to lose some of their interest in having their tidelands converted into industrial parks. Why did San Diego City have to have all those yachts and marinas and hotels?

When the Bartholomew grand plan for Balboa Park was being drawn up, and being considered by the Planning Commission and the City Council, all were aware that two new wings were to be added to the Fine Arts Gallery and that they would replace two of the original 1915 Exposition buildings of Spanish-Colonial architecture.

One of the wings would be built for the gallery through private donations and funds from the City's Accelerated Public Works Program. The other would be built by the Timken estate and designed to house a collection of old masters valued at about two million dollars and owned by the estate of the Putnam sisters. Foundations granting the money, and administering the estates, were dominated by the banker, Allen J. Sutherland, and the attorney, Walter Ames.

It had been a Timken – Mrs. Appleton Bridges – who with her husband, had built the existing Fine Arts Gallery as a gift for the City. The Putnam sisters were brought to San Diego in 1913, from New England, by their father, and two of the three, Amy and Annie, became collectors of art and benefactors of the Fine Arts Society. None of them married. The last of the three died in 1962.

The architectural design of the proposed Timken gallery drew protests from those who had envisioned building replacements as closely following the tradition of Spanish-Colonial architecture of the 1915 Exposition as they presumed had been implied in the Bartholomew report. Its design was a classic one, and inside and out it had Travertine marble with bronze trim.

While the new wings were considered, by themselves, as architecturally excellent, and perfect for art display, the conception of Spanish architecture had proved to be a broad one. The City Council, under pressure from civic groups, approved the designs as required under the Bartholomew plan.

The West wing of the gallery — with its James S. Copley auditorium — did not meet with the same resistance though its design left the Spanish-Colonial enthusiasts dissatisfied. Now, with the Natural History Museum building there were four versions of Spanish architecture grouped together in the park. Park Commissioners then postponed the erection of additional arcades along the Prado, which would have partially concealed

Gone from the park was another Spanish-Colonial building, to be replaced with a new West Wing of the Fine Arts Gallery. Though in the "spirit" of the same style of architecture, its appearance did not satisfy everyone.

the two new wings, and instead voted to use the money to build four more public tennis courts at Morley Field. James Britton, who wrote about artistic and civic endeavors in San Diego, described the Prado as "the boulevard of broken dreams."

Not all San Diegans were defenders of the decaying Spanish-Colonial buildings and believed, as did their creator, Bertram G. Goodhue, that they should have been torn down with the close of the first Exposition, as mere "fantasies" of a dream city. Philip L. Gildred, president of the Fine Arts Society, wanted the three structures of the Fine Arts complex to dominate the central park in a setting of green, open spaces.

A group quickly formed to resist the introduction of any addi-

Mrs. Bea Evenson

tional architectural styles and to assure the replacement of deteriorated buildings with ones of Spanish-Colonial design. It was named the Committee of 100 and was led by Mrs. Frank, or Bea, Evenson. The committee centered its attention on the next building to be logically removed or replaced, the Food and Beverage building, an L-shaped structure facing the Prado and the Natural History Museum.

A replacement was designed by the architect, Richard G. Wheeler, with Samuel Wood Hamill as consultant, and the issue of its construction was taken directly to the people. A faithful — as far as possible — reproduction was promised, with most of the ornate adornments to be re-cast and re-placed on the new structure. A $3,500,000 bond issue was placed on the ballot by City Council action and was approved by the voters on November 7, 1968.

Ever since the struggle to restore the vitality of downtown, and to bring the people back once again, had been begun, various pedestrian Malls had been discussed, planned, and rejected. Once the Downtown Association had envisioned many tree-lined streets closed to the auto, with sidewalk cafes, flower carts, and uniformed information boys.

By 1969, plans for a Mall had been reduced to five blocks on C Street and two blocks on Fifth Avenue, to touch on Broadway. Evan V. Jones, president of San Diegans, Inc., told the City

A City Council with some trepidation approved the building of the privately-endowed Timken gallery on the site of one of the old Spanish-Colonial buildings in the central portion of Balboa Park. This is a model as San Diegans saw it in 1961.

Council that in 6,000 cities downtown areas had been doomed by the failure of civic leaders to take necessary action. The suggested Mall would be a charge upon benefitting property owners and a design was ordered by the City Council in 1970 – thirteen years after a Mall had been first proposed and studied.

When two Spanish-Colonial buildings were replaced with more modern design art gallery wings, some citizens arose to defend the past and led a successful bond issue to replace a del Prado building in almost identical style, as suggested in this first architect's sketch.

CHAPTER TWELVE

LLOYD HARTING

The first overland group of the Portola-Serra Expedition saw the Port of San Diego after three months of walking up from Loreto in Baja California. Exactly 200 years later man was walking on the moon after a journey of a half million miles in eight days.

The Future — Renewing the 'City Beautiful'

Though the tax burden of supporting two great parks, one a cultural as well as a recreational center, and the other an aquatic park – and they still had not been completed – was considerable, San Diego was looking to a future in the general nation-wide rising concern over the "quality of life."

Hotels and motels were locating in Mission Valley or in San Diego Bay where marinas and clubs beckoned to yachting enthusiasts from the entire Southwest. Visitors had become a $356,000,000 business by the end of 1968. They came seeking what San Diegans already had.

The great hopes for Mission Bay had not yet been all fulfilled though its reputation as a vacation playground was spreading. On Perez Cove, an oceanarium known as Sea World opened in 1964, with lagoons, a sea grotto building, porpoise and whale training tanks, a tropical island, dining patio and Japanese village. The disappointment left by the Del Webb organization when it had failed to build a high-rise hotel on its choice highway site had been forgotten by 1968. The low-level hotel complex had been sold to an investor who in turn leased the property to the Hilton Hotels. The longed-for high-rise appeared in

1968. Additions to other existing hotels also would soar above the bay, as had been desired. And an inn for the "working man" and his family was begun in 1968. There were not as many hotels or yacht clubs, perhaps, as had been hoped for, and there were no shaded walks or grand bay and ocean connections.

In Southern California, where once the concentration of building had been eastward, now available coastal lands were being swept up by builders and speculators, and a pressure was increasing for adjustments to preserve their availability for more public uses. In San Diego, efforts to save many canyons, for parks or open spaces, would be made; and attempts would be considered to block the invasion of the ocean and erosion at Sunset Cliffs.

Some of the man-made changes in the balances of nature were being set right. Years of experimentation found the answer to what had seemed the certain disappearance of the kelp beds off Point Loma. To replace the effect of the vanished sea otters, which once fed on them, sea urchins were brought under control by the spreading of quicklime in the kelp beds. Urchins deserted the areas of growth but in time found new sources of food in the drifting kelp from the harvesting. Even the sea otters soon began to re-appear on the California coast.

Some of the bird life that once frequented Mission Bay was returning, to rest and feed in the long flood control channel which partly filled and then partly emptied through tidal action. But the springs from which they had once obtained fresh water had long since disappeared from the area north of Mission Bay.

The restrictions of the metropolitan sewer system had not been as effective in controlling development as some might have anticipated. Outlying subdivisions arose with their own sewage disposal systems that in many cases would plague the City. Subdivisions were being thrown up without adequate provisions for public services, particularly schools, and taxpayers in other areas were being asked to help pay the bills.

While its appearance had not been as insidious as in the Los Angeles basin, smog, the price of growth, was becoming a concern, and efforts to reduce it, or at least halt its spread, after years of indecision and dispute, began in earnest in 1968.

In the world of advancement which had not been foreseen by so many educators in the days of the Great Depression was a nuclear power generating plant at San Onofre, placed in operation in 1967 by the San Diego Gas & Electric Company and the Southern California Edison Company. The San Diego Gas & Electric Company itself moved uptown in 1968, into a high-rise of its own in the 100 block on Ash Street, not far from the old Cedar Street area, and at night it appeared as a beacon in a

In three decades the world had changed drastically. Once it was feared the nation had reached its "last frontier." Now an age of science had brought a nuclear power plant to the Southland, at San Onofre, shown under construction.

blaze of lights. The lights of El Cortez Hotel, high on the hill, which had once beckoned to ships approaching by sea, now were merely faint stars in a new sky of progress.

General Atomic had become property of a major oil company. Those who had seen the possibility of a clothing industry rising in San Diego, because of its position as a port for the transshipment of cotton, would have been pleased to note that 3,200 persons were engaged in manufacturing clothing in 1968.

There were 12,000 engaged in agriculture. But government was the biggest employer — 73,300 were employed in Federal, State and local jobs, including those as civilian workers at military installations. In all manufacturing there were 58,000. By the close of 1968, there were 402,300 on widely diversified payrolls in the County, and there were twenty-six specifically-zoned industrial parks and areas. The number of unemployed had declined to less than four percent.

Retired citizens were estimated at 108,000, many of them former military personnel who had remembered the shining city and had returned to spend the rest of their lives. There were far more horses in the County than in the days when they provided the primary source of locomotion. Here there was still room to live and ride, and most areas of the County were accessible by new freeways and highways.

Fourteen miles of new freeways had been built in 1968, raising the total freeway mileage to 170. The goal for 1980 was set at 527 miles. A Federally-supported highway program was recasting the principal State system into Interstate freeways. Highway 80 was becoming Interstate 8, a wide and sweeping roadway over to the mountains to the Imperial Valley, and east from there, long after the time San Diegans had considered its improvement vital to its future commerce.

No longer a community whose fate rested with a single source of income, the City's economy had in fact, in the words of economist Irvine W. Reynolds, president of Copley International Corporation, been growing for forty years at a pace faster than the Gross National Product, despite a period adjustment in the early 1960's. "San Diego's economy is probably better diversified today than seventy-five percent of the other important cities around the country."

However, more and more economic and financial, as well as political power, was being diffused with the advent of corporate interests with headquarters elsewhere.

In a sense San Diego once again felt it was a "branch line" town, at the end of the corporate line, as it had been in the days of the dominance of the railroads. But many businesses and industries were expanding outward from San Diego. C. Arnholt Smith's United States National Bank began reversing the trend of banking, picking up branches northward, beyond San Diego

The Auto was King in Southern California and cities and suburbs were shaped to meet its demands. This time exposure in the middle 1960's weaves strings of light through Mission Valley to Mission Bay.

County. His far-flung interests now concerned taxi cab companies in many cities as well as farming operations in California's Central Valley, and he had complex financial ties into the Midwest.

A post-war generation, too, was beginning to take over. Robert O. Peterson had led in expanding a fast-food and family-type restaurant chain across the country. In 1967 he hired San Diego's City Manager, Thomas Fletcher. Fletcher was succeeded by Walter H. Hahn who had been an assistant for three and a half years. But the waning of the power of the City Manager was accelerating as political pressures in the City mounted.

Robert O. Peterson

At the time the First National Bank was also expanding out of the County, and renamed the Southern California First National, effective working control was purchased by a group led by Peterson, which had sold the fast-food chain. Anderson Borthwick bowed out of San Diego's oldest banking institution which once had been the stronghold of John D. Spreckels.

The TraveLodge motel chain started by Scott King had almost 400 establishments across the country, by 1967. Earl Gagosian was expanding his own chain of Royal Inns; George Scott was still moving department stores northward, now to Palm Springs. Newly-born San Diego financial conglomerates were reaching out for distant investments.

Scott King

The racial wounds of World War II had been forgotten. By 1969 there were 7,500 Japanese-Americans in San Diego County, 5,500 more than in 1940, and there was a Sister-City relationship between San Diego and Yokohama. On the tip of Shelter Island was a gift from Yokohama, a huge replica of a Buddhist bell. It was called a Bell of Friendship from Japan. To Yokohama went a full-size replica of the Donal Hord statue, Guardian of the Waters, which stood on the bayside of the County Administration building.

An ethnic diversity embraced more than 150,000 residents. By 1970, Mexican-Americans would number 88,600, more than twelve percent of the population. Blacks would total 53,000, still less than eight percent, but they were becoming a political factor. The Reverend George W. Smith sat on the Board of Education.

Floyd Andrews

San Diegans, whose fondness for civic slogans had enlivened the years of promotional efforts with "Heaven-on-Earth" back in the Thirties, and then with "Air Capital of the West" and "Educational Center of the Southwest," now felt they had some reasons for justifying their boasts. Seven air carriers served San Diego and in 1969 it was expected that the City would have direct service to Hawaii and thus become a "Gateway to the Pacific." San Diego even could boast of its own airline, Pacific Southwest, which under Floyd Andrews had been expanding

into the nation's largest intra-state airline.

There were also those who referred to San Diego as a "City of Champions." Nine San Diego athletes had won gold medals over the years in the international Olympic Games. In the 1950's, Maureen Connolly had become the world's greatest woman tennis player and Florence Chadwick had swum the English Channel four times.

And with sixty-five golf courses in the County, San Diego often was referred to in civic promotional efforts as "Golfland, USA." Now, surely, there was civic pride in assurance that San Diego truly had become a "City in Motion."

Though observance of California's 200th birthday was to be a statewide celebration, San Diegans, or those who recalled the successes of the Old Expositions – and overlooked the problems of Fiesta del Pacifico – felt that 1969 belonged to them. After all, California had had its "birth" at San Diego, on Presidio Hill.

In 1964, Assemblyman James Mills had introduced a resolution in the Legislature for a State study of the possibilities of creating a State Historical Park at Old Town, with a view toward having some restoration work completed by the 200th anniversary. Mills' interest in Old Town came from his experience, before election to public office, as director of the San Diego Historical Society and the Junipero Serra Museum on Presidio Hill.

This action was the first step toward finally resolving disputes between land owners, and between the City and property owners, which had existed ever since the Eliot Plan first suggested the possibilities of Old Town as an historic park, for preservation as well as for tourism.

Agreements on courses to follow had been difficult to reach. But by 1964, Old Town had begun to revive, with the ascending interest of persons who did not reside or own property directly in Old Town. One of the first restorations by private contributions was that of the first home of *The San Diego Union*, and it was offered as a gift to the park of James S. Copley. Legler Benbough, son of the former Mayor, bought the historic Estudillo House, erroneously labeled over the years as Ramona's Marriage Place, and it, too, would be a gift to the State. County Supervisors restored the Whaley House of the early American period. New restaurants and a motel moved into the area.

C. Arnholt Smith and a group of associates had tried to save a building known as Casa de Lopez, one of Old Town's historic residences, which had been in the path of the new Crosstown freeway. But its crumbling adobe walls were too fragile to be moved, and a replica had to be built in a new location.

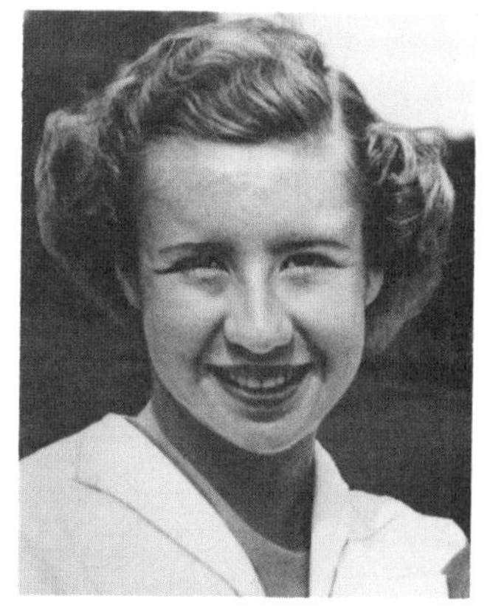

Maureen Connolly

Florence Chadwick

The millions who came to Southern California, and the thousands to San Diego, were seeking more freedom of movement and a more benign climate. And even the philosophy of Zoos was changing and a Wild Animal Park was created to provide the open space of ancestral existences. The first animals were turned out in 1969.

James R. Mills

Not so enthusiastic about State restoration of the historic aspects of Old Town was a former Democrat State Senator from San Diego and now Administrator of the State Resources Agency. He was Hugo Fisher and he was convinced that restoration should be a local project, though it would have to be directed primarily by the City and County. It could not flourish, he said, as a "honky-tonk operation for rooking tourists."

As a result of Mills' action, the State Board of Park Commissioners in 1965 singled out nineteen structures that could be restored. Support came from San Diego's City Council, the Board of Supervisors, the Chamber of Commerce, and even property owners who were represented before the State Park Board by Douglas Giddings, chairman of San Diego's own Park Commissioners. The State Commissioners agreed to approve diversion of $3,500,000 in statewide park and recreation bonds for acquisition of Old Town as a historic park as well as for acquisition of Torrey Pines park lands.

Tom Ham

San Diegans were ready to proceed. A Shelter Island restaurant operator, Tom Ham, was named to lead a large committee to plan for San Diego's participation in the 200th celebration and he announced that for this, Old Town was a "must." In 1966, the State Legislature voted in favor of appropriating $2,500,000 to begin land acquisitions, and the City instituted some architectural control over the area surrounding Old Town, but it wasn't until the following year that funds were made available.

Mills, a Democrat, was now a State Senator, but Republicans controlled the State government. Appeals had to be made to a new Governor, Ronald Reagan, but finally the State Public Works Board made an appropriation to begin actual purchases, and the State Park Commission declared eighteen acres in Old Town as a State Historical Park.

Ronald Reagan

By 1969, ninety percent of the land had been purchased, but nothing much could be done about extensive restorations in time for the 200th celebration. That did not phase San Diego's 200th Anniversary organization, which with Hugh A. Hall as director, threw up hasty improvisations in an effort to recapture some of the atmosphere of Old Spain, Mexico, and early California. Craftsmen were to be imported from Mexico to make the wares and gifts that still connected 1969 with the moods and life of 1769. When the celebration began, Charles Cordell was president.

The celebration was to last the entire year, with opening ceremonies on January 1. Public events were listed for every day of the year, not just at Old Town but all over the City. The big day would be July 16, 1969, the time when Father Junipero Serra raised the first cross in 1769 to mark the founding of California's first mission and settlement.

In the Spring of the same year, major league baseball came to San Diego, on the night of April 8, and the San Diego-Coronado Bay bridge opened at midnight of August 2. National League membership had taken the City into a new era. While San Diego sought to recall its ties to one past, the opening of the two-mile long bridge cut one of the last links with another past, a nostalgic Victorian one. The California Toll Bridge Authority purchased and retired the five ferries to remove a competing service across the bay, and the last ferry made its run at midnight of the day the bridge was opened to traffic. Ferries had connected Coronado with San Diego for eighty-three years.

The bridge itself, designed by Robert Mosher of La Jolla,

The last ferry between San Diego and Coronado in reality crossed at midnight of the day the bridge was to open for traffic. But Artist Robert J. Landry captured the feeling of the end of an era with his "Last Crossing."

swept across the bay to a height of 200 feet above the water, in a long and graceful arch, a blue ribbon in the sky.

Several thousand persons gathered on Presidio Hill on July 16 to observe the ceremonies marking the 200th anniversary of the founding of Western civilization on the West Coast.

It had taken Father Junipero Serra three months to ride his mule 600 miles up from Loreto, on the Gulf coast of Baja California, to San Diego. The day before the ceremony, three astronauts had been launched into space from Cape Canaveral, Florida, and were on their way to walk on the moon. They would travel a half million miles in eight days in an inspiring achievement of a space program that in a way had its inception in a

The auto and shopping center had combined to produce a new and more leisurely way of retail buying and selling. The centers provided some of the atmosphere which old-time city planners had suggested could still be achieved in America.

small corner of the Convair plant about twenty-five years before.

A million visitors had been expected during the year. There was considerable disappointment over Spain's failure to participate in a major way though it did award medals to Mayor Curran, Charles Cordell, the celebration president, and Philip L. Gildred, a commissioner-general. However, there was a delegation to the Bicentennial from Spain's Island of Mallorca, the birthplace of Father Serra. Portugal, whose son in the 1500's had been the first White explorer to enter the Port of San Diego, sent Vice Admiral Armando de Roboedo, its Chief of Naval Operations, to present another medal to the Mayor who accepted it on behalf of the City.

When the year had ended, and the show had closed, taxpayers learned it had cost them a million dollars and there were some of them who wondered, once again, if it all had been worth it. Expenditures by visitors rose in 1969 to more than $408,000,000, up from the more than $356,000,000 of the year before. But the increase from 1967 to 1968 had been almost as much, without a celebration.

Though nothing permanent had been left behind to mark the Bicentennial of the founding of the settlement on Presidio Hill and of California itself, the celebration had crystalized the efforts to restore Old Town to a semblance of its appearance when it was a Mexican town that had succeeded Spain's original settlement on Presidio Hill.

Though the City was approaching a population of 700,000, and all civic plans may not have materialized as had been anticipated, nor had all the ships and the trains arrived as so many had expected, or longed for, the future still beckoned to those who believed they could shape events to their desires.

To the hundreds of thousands, however, who had come seeking a new way of life, a "City Beautiful" was still represented by climate and space, and the riches of variety. They did not always remember, or even know, that it had been the dreamers who raised a town out of the dust, who broke hard ground and planted the groves and gardens, who brought the water, who set aside a great park in the heart of a town struggling for life, and envisioned the future of Mission Bay.

The experience of passing history was revealing that the grouping of public buildings, and towering downtown structures, did not necessarily create the "City Beautiful," and civic centers, unless integrated with the daily activities of the people, could become, as had happened in so many other cities, architectural backyards.

The comparison that John Nolen had offered, of a San Diego re-constituted in the manner of European cities, with broad streets and wide plazas for "open" city living, was captured in a way in the more spacious shopping centers. There was freedom from the pressures of traffic, rows of attractive shops and restaurants and sidewalk cafes, bookstores, and benches for relaxation, and shaded walkways, and even film houses. They were little "cities" isolated from each other, and so were those who used them.

But as John Nolen, the city planner, had done so long ago, a new generation of San Diegans, with a new concept of the "City Beautiful," would look again at the bay but, instead of facing the City only toward the west, would face it also toward the south, and bring back to life a section that time had passed

While the "City Beautiful," as conceived by city planners, might still be in the future, some San Diego civic leaders took another look at their City and began to think about turning it back toward the bay, once again, this time, however, to look south, toward Coronado. This is a view of the City from across the bay. They remembered that only big plans stirred men's imagination.

by. Then the people, the stores and the restaurants would surely come back.

When the plans for the World's Columbian Exposition and its new "White City" were being considered, Daniel Burnham had summoned to his architectural offices in Chicago what was described as "the greatest meeting of artists since the Fifteenth Century." Burnham had a slogan: "Make no little plans. They have no magic to stir men's blood."

When the Exposition plans were shown to a Chicago banker, Lyman J. Gage, a former Secretary of the U.S. of the Treasury, who later was to become a resident of Point Loma in San Diego, he greeted them with disbelief: "Oh, gentlemen, this is a dream. You have my good wishes. I hope the dream can be realized."

CHRONOLOGY

1940 – Census gives San Diego City a population of 203,321 and the County, 289,348.

1940 – Franklin D. Roosevelt re-elected President of the United States, for the third time.

1941 – President Roosevelt sets production goal of 60,000 airplanes for 1941 and 125,000 for the following year.

1941 – Naval bases in San Diego in swift expansion, with rise of war in Europe.

1941 – Japanese planes bomb Pearl Harbor on December 7.

1941 – Blackouts ordered in City. Enemy submarines attack coastal shipping and appear off San Diego.

1942 – Western Defense Command begins removal of Japanese from California areas, including almost 2,000 from San Diego.

1942 – Percy J. Benbough dies in office; succeeded temporarily by Dr. Howard B. Bard.

1942 – Navy Department purchases Santa Margarita y Las Flores Rancho for huge new Marine Base, Camp Pendleton.

1942 – Vessels of San Diego's tuna fleet volunteered by owners for wartime duty in Pacific.

1942 – Earl Warren, Republican, defeats Democrat Governor Culbert L. Olson.

1943 – San Diego City's population set at 390,000, not including military personnel, and in the County, 500,000.

1943 – Consolidated Aircraft formally merged with Vultee Aircraft Corporation, to become Convair.

1943 – Harley E. Knox, a Southwest San Diego dairy operator, and City Councilman, elected Mayor.

1944 – Franklin D. Roosevelt re-elected President, for his fourth term, defeating Governor Thomas Dewey of New York.

1944 – City Manager Walter Cooper killed in airplane accident; Mayor Harley E. Knox injured. Cooper succeeded by Fred A. Rhodes.

1944 – Water shortage threatens San Diego. Navy, with Presidential approval, begins emergency construction of aqueduct to bring Colorado River water to San Diego.

1944 – San Diego County Water Authority formed.

1945 – President Roosevelt dies in office and is succeeded by Vice President Harry S Truman.

1945 – United States Senate ratifies treaty giving portion of Colorado River water to Mexico and casts shadow over City's future.

1945 – San Diego voters approve bond issue of $2,000,000 to begin development of Mission Bay.

1945 – War in Europe ends and then war in Pacific following dropping of atomic bombs on Japan.

1945 – San Diego experiences a recession though not as severe as had been feared.

1946 – San Diego City assumes responsibility of financing completion of San Diego Aqueduct.

1946 – Governor Earl Warren re-elected.

1946 – Voters approve annexation of County Water Authority to Metropolitan Water District, and transfer of City-Navy aqueduct contract to Authority.

1946 – George White Marston, who stood second only to "Father" Alonzo Horton in the history of modern San Diego, dies at age 95.

1947 – People given choice of grouping public buildings along Cedar Street, or in Balboa Park. Both propositions defeated.

1947 – San Diego Aqueduct completed; first Colorado River water arrives.

1948 – Harry S Truman elected President in his own right, defeating Thomas H. Dewey.

1948 – City Manager Fred Rhodes fired by City Council. O. W. Campbell of San Jose becomes Manager.

1949 – The last electric street car begins its run from Union Depot.

1949 – Mission Bay aquatic park formally dedicated.

1950 – North Korean troops cross a dividing line in Korea and U.S. troops ordered into action.

1951 – Passenger service discontinued by San Diego & Arizona Railway.

1951 – John D. Butler first native son to be

elected Mayor of San Diego.

1952 – Dwight D. Eisenhower elected President of the United States.

1952 – Construction of second pipeline of San Diego Aqueduct initiated.

1953 – Goodwin J. Knight becomes governor of California when Earl Warren appointed Chief Justice of the United States.

1954 – Public buildings scattered; new Library opens and bonds for new Courthouse approved.

1955 – Bonds voted for construction of new Tenth Avenue Marine Terminal.

1955 – Councilman Charles C. Dail elected Mayor of San Diego.

1955 – The tuna boat Anthony M. revolutionizes tuna industry by using a nylon purse seine and power block.

1956 – Dwight D. Eisenhower re-elected President.

1956 – Convair taken over by General Dynamics and John Jay Hopkins leads San Diego's successful appeal for branch of the University of California on Torrey Pines.

1956 – Fiesta del Pacifico staged as tourist attraction; runs four summers.

1957 – George Bean of Peoria, Ill., selected to succeed O. W. Campbell as San Diego's City Manager.

1957 – First Atlas missile built at San Diego successfully test-fired.

1958 – City Council approves zone change to allow May Department Stores Company to build shopping center in Mission Valley.

1958 – Construction begins on second San Diego Aqueduct.

1959 – San Diego's City's population estimated to be 554,000.

1960 – State proposition to deliver northern California water as far south as San Diego approved.

1960 – John F. Kennedy elected President though Richard M. Nixon wins majority in San Diego.

1961 – City Council moves to acquire downtown land to centralize public buildings without voter approval.

1962 – Voters of five communities surrounding Bay of San Diego approve formation of a Unified Port District.

1962 – Incumbent Edmund G. Brown defeats Richard M. Nixon for Governor.

1962 – Voters approve $12,600,000 in bonds for Mission Bay.

1963 – President Kennedy assassinated in Dallas, Texas. Lyndon B. Johnson assumes Presidency.

1963 – Frank Curran elected Mayor in civic political struggle over city planning.

1964 – Downtown Community Concourse dedicated.

1964 – Lyndon B. Johnson elected President though Republican Barry Goldwater leads in San Diego voting.

1964 – Bonds approved for improvement of Lindbergh Field as major jet airport.

1965 – San Diego becomes the sixteenth largest city in the United States.

1966 – Voters approve City acquisition of local transit system, with expected Federal financial assistance.

1966 – Voters of County Water Authority approve financing for distribution of Feather River water in San Diego County.

1966 – Ronald Reagan elected Governor of California over Edmund G. Brown.

1966 – Voters approve $30,000,000 to construct second pipeline of second San Diego Aqueduct.

1966 – Construction of a $27,000,000 sports stadium in Mission Valley approved by voters.

1967 – Frank Curran re-elected Mayor.

1967 – A modified General Plan as a guide for the growth of San Diego approved after it had been defeated two years before.

1968 – Richard M. Nixon elected President.

1969 – San Diego begins year-long fiesta to celebrate 200th anniversary of the founding of California on Presidio Hill.

1970 – San Diego becomes the fourteenth largest city in the United States with a population of 696,769. County population reaches 1,357,854.

NOTES TO TEXT

In researching and writing the Seventh Volume of the History of San Diego heavy reliance was placed on the index to *The San Diego Union* prepared by the California Room of the San Diego Public Library, with financial assistance in the past from The Union-Tribune Publish Company. Thousands of cards lead the researcher to every event which took place from 1868 to the present, and to the role individuals played in these events.

As this volume deals with modern times few books are available to ease another author's way; many of the people who played leading roles have left few personal recollections. In preparation for this work, before the 1970's, *The Evening Tribune* conducted a series of oral interviews with leading citizens of the time, and committed their recollections to tape and print. Among those interviewed were John S. Alessio, Anderson Borthwick, Joseph Brennan, Reuben H. Fleet, Charles K. Fletcher, Frank G. Forward, Morley H. Golden, Roscoe E. Hazard, Fred A. Heilbron, Joseph Jessop, Sr., Scott King, Herbert Kunzel, Manuel O. Medina, Lawrence Oliver, Edmund T. Price, Manuel E. Rosa, George A. Scott, Max Streicher, Don M. Stewart, Allen Sutherland, Jacob Weinberger. In addition, the author sought personal clarifications of incidents from those in a position to remember them: Captain E. Robert Anderson, U.S.N.R., Ret., Glenn C. Rick, Samuel Wood Hamill, John Bate, Pauline Des Granges and former Mayor Frank Curran.

The author was fortunate in that he lived through this period and in a position where he was familiar with events and the people who shaped them. The City was a great part of his life. In the following notes the author seeks to refer the reader to sources of supplemented information from which the main themes have been developed in this volume of the History of San Diego.

In addition to access to the microfilm files of *The San Diego Union*, with its daily reports on the progress of civic affairs, the issues of *San Diego Magazine*, beginning after the close of World War II, provided detail and points of view available nowhere else. While the articles on civic affairs often were argumentative, they did present, as magazines should, points of views of passing events. Facts were brought together, in perspective, and the writers were knowledgeable.

The continuity of the history leading to the events from 1940 to 1970 are, of course, set down in the author's previous Copley Books on the History of San Diego, from pre-historic times to the beginning of World War II. They are "The Explorers," 1960, the discovery of California by Europeans, and its settlement in 1769; the "Time of the Bells," 1961, the experiences of the mission period; "The Silver Dons," 1963, the era of the great ranchos and the United States-Mexican war and its effect on California; "The Glory Years," 1964, the beginnings of modern San Diego; "Gold in the Sun," 1965, the period of the first Exposition, 1915-16, and the conviction that climate was a saleable product; and "The Rising Tide," 1967, the period between the Great Wars, the first auto migrations, and the Boom and Depression, and the beginning of a new surge to California.

General

Among the books and papers on California history the following are most helpful and informative for the general historian: "California," by John Walton Caughey, 1953; The Correspondence and Papers of Hiram Johnson, Bancroft Library, University of California, Special Collection. "The Governors of California; from Peter H. Burnett to Edmund G. Brown," by H. Brett Melendy and Benjamin F. Gilbert, 1965. "California: A History," by Andrew F. Rolle, 1963.

Valuable reference sources on the city, and urban and rural society, are: "The Shaping of Urban Society, a History of City Forms and Functions," by Janet Roebuck, 1974; "The Highway and the City," by Lewis Mumford, 1964; "Modern American Cities," edited by Ray Ginger, 1969; "A History of Urban America," by Charles N. Glabb and Theodore S. Brown, 1967; "The City of Man: A New Approach to the Recovery of Beauty in American Cities," Christopher Tunnard, 1971.

The general despair of the middle 1930's, as a result of the Depression, and an educational belief that the profit system may have come to its end is expressed for general readers and students in "The United States. A Graphic History," by three authors, Louis M. Hacker, Rudolf Modley, George R. Taylor. This is a dramatic illustration of the failure to foresee developments then unfolding which would change the face of the United States and the Earth.

War with Japan

In 1976 the existing literature of the effect of the war on San Diego was scanty and often casual. Information on daily events was assembled from the files of *The San Diego Union.* The early military aspects were drawn from newspaper reports as well as from unpublished and at one time confidential reports on San Diego's defense capabilities, prepared by the Department of the Navy, part of which is in the writer's possession, and the other, without attribution but obviously authoritative, in the archives of the San Diego Historical Society.

The first material is from the "History of the Eleventh Naval District," prepared by the U.S. Naval History Division, for the U.S. Naval Administration in the Second World War. It was written by 1945 but not published. The second manuscript, unidentified, details the reasons for the defensives which were hastily improvised in the early days of the war and describes how Japanese submarines could have approached without warning or observation. More additional detail on the lack of a defensive capability is described in "A History of the United States Air Force, 1907-1957," edited by Alfred Goldberg, 1957.

Publications on the history of information on Naval establishments in the San Diego area are numerous, as well as on Marine Corps establishments.

The statistics of the times are scattered through the archives of many Federal Departments, some now vanished, or in the National Archives, and the problems of assembling all of them would be insurmountable and not necessary. The experiences of San Diego relating to wartime rationing and housing were not much different than elsewhere, though San Diego's military and seacoast position posed special problems not found in some American cities. Many of the reports of the times were prepared by the author while a Copley Washington Bureau representative.

There is a large amount of literature on the evacuation of the Japanese from California at the beginning of the war, much of it, however, written with indignation. At times authors omitted the names of people who played important roles in the evacuation, in deference, apparently, to political ideology. Among the most helpful material were an unpublished master's thesis, "The Internment of the Japanese of San Diego County," by Gerald Schlenker, 1968; an unpublished essay by Sister Marleen Brasefield, a graduate student of the University of San Diego, titled "An Analysis of *The San Diego Union* on Japanese Internment," submitted to the San Diego Historical Society, and undated; an unpublished paper titled "The Japanese and San Diego County," by Iona Talkington, San Diego State University, prepared for Prof. J. W. Taylor, 1972. These papers are in the files of the San Diego Historical Society.

Among the publications dealing with the evacuation are "America's Concentraion Camps," by Allan R. Bosworth, 1967; "America Betrayed," by Morton Grodzins, 1949; "Prejudice – Japanese-Americans. Symbol of Racial Intolerance," by Carey McWilliams, 1944; "Executive Order 9066. The Internment of 110,000 Japanese-Americans," by Maisie and Richard Conrat, California Historical Society, 1972; "Concentration Camps U.S.A.," by Roger Daniels, 1971; "Uprooted Americans: The Japanese-Americans and the War Relocation Authority," by Dillon S. Myer, 1971.

An interesting summary of the various attitudes represented in books about the evacuation, and the attitudes of indignation or justification, is offered by William Petersen, of Ohio State University, in an article published in 1972 in *National Review*, titled "A Myth Re-Examined. The Incarceration of the Japanese-Americans."

When Defense Department records on the Japanese evacuation were declassified, historians rushed to examine them and discovered that contrary to much general opinion, the decision to remove the Japanese from the West Coast, whether right or wrong, was strictly a military one, undertaken in the context of unusual times, and not a result of racial or economic pressures.

Though no sabotage in the Hawaiian Islands or the American mainland was recorded before and during the war with Japan by visiting Japanese or secret agents, espionage was evident and widely reported by various authorities. One of the best accounts of espionage details can be found in "The Broken Seal," by Ladislas Farago, a former Naval Intelligence officer, published in 1967. In addition, Captain Ellis M. Zacharias, U.S.N., who served in San Diego and later became chief of Naval Intelligence, published "Secret Missions – The Story of an Intelligence Officer," in 1946. He later was promoted to a rear admiral.

Activities of the Japanese Navy during the war have become widely known as American scholars go deeper into a study of available records. Probably the best summary of Japanese submarine action along the West Coast was in a report in the Pacific Historical Review by Clark G. Reynolds, of Duke University, published in May of 1974. Attacks on shipping are a matter of record. The revelation of the failure of an Army B-26 to attack a Japanese submarine off the coast, because of altitude restrictions, was reported in *The San Diego Union*, in 1966, by Captain W. W. Lowrey, U.S.N., Ret. The relationship of California to Mexico during the war was described by Michael Mathes, a specialist in Mexican history and then Special Collections Librarian at the University of New Mexico, in an article, "The Two Californias During World War II," in the California Historical Society Quarterly.

City Planning

The files of the Chicago Historical Society are replete with information on the great "White City" known as the World's Columbian Exposition of 1893.

How the "White City" influenced planners throughout the country, including John Nolen, as well as Daniel Burnham who created San Francisco's "City Beautiful" plan and Charles Robinson who conceived "Los Angeles – the City Beautiful," has been described by Gordon Edwards, who was a senior planner for San Diego County before he went to Washington and a Federal post. Some of his views were published in the *San Diego Magazine* of March, 1962.

One of those inspired was John Nolen of New England, who twice drew plans of a "City Beautiful" for San Diego, some of which actually found their way into the City that San Diego became. The researcher is referred to the 1926 plan of John Nolen, available in City records. Many copies also exist of the Eliot plan of Old Town, which was drawn by Charles W. Eliot with the cooperation of the City's Planning Director, Glenn A. Rick. This was in 1946.

In the years from World War II to 1970 City planning became a crucial issue, not as to a particular plan but as to whether city planning was to exist at all. The issue had two focal points, Mission Valley and the grouping of public buildings. The election of mayors and other City officials was directly tied to positions on planning. Daily newspaper files cover almost fifteen years of dispute. The following issues of *San Diego Magazine* have pertinent summaries, though generally from a stated point of view: October and November of 1956; January, February and November of 1957; May, February, July and August of 1958; December of 1959; February, April and December of 1960; February, March and November of 1961; March, July, September and December of 1962; and May of 1963.

Balboa Park also was a center of controversy, not as to its existence but as to its uses. The report that finally gave guidance to the park in a new post-Exposition era was the Bartholomew report which recommended de-commercialization and a devotion to civic, cultural and recreational pursuits. As with all plans, it was not specific enough in some instances and the arguments over replacement of Exposition buildings, and their style of architecture, has persisted ever since. Details of the losses of land in Balboa Park, for schools and highways and other non-park uses, are described in reports of the Citizens Coordinate, particularly in May of 1966.

Water

The story of water for San Diego is a continuing one, and the researcher is referred to earlier volumes of the History of San Diego for additional background information. A number of publications, however, are invaluable in the general tracing of the development of water and the organized efforts to bring it to San Diego. One of the most useful ones is "San Diego's Quest for Water," which was issued by the Citizens Aqueduct Celebration Committee and which details the work of the San Diego County Water Authority and the Metropolitan Water District in bringing Colorado River water to San Diego. It was published in 1947. It carries an excellent chronology. In July of 1962 the Metropolitan District published "Water for The People" which provided details of the existing supplies from the Colorado and of the necessity of going even further, to Northern California, for additional water.

Other helpful publications are: "California's Stake is the Colorado River," published by the Colorado River Board of California. The fifth revision was available in 1961. "Water in San Diego County" was published by the San Diego Water Authority and is undated, but carries a detailed chronology of important dates in San Diego County Water History up through 1966, and descriptions of all member agencies. In addition, a valuable contribution was Lloyd Charles Fowler's "A History of the Dams and Water Supply of San Diego County," a University of California thesis of 1953. A basic report is that of Lester S. Ready, Louis C. Hill and J. P. Buwalda made for the City in 1937. The Twelfth Annual Report of the San Diego County Water Authority published in 1958 was important in detailing the changes that had taken place regarding the supply of water and the annexations of land and the addition of new agencies.

A number of interviews were available, with Harley Knox while he was Mayor of San Diego and led in the fight to have the Federal Government through the Navy complete the first San Diego Aqueduct, and with Fred A. Heilbron, probably the leading figure in San Diego's historic struggle for water. The interviews are available through reference cards in the California Room of the San Diego Public Library.

The author was in Washington and attended the Senate hearings and debate on the United States-Mexico treaty dividing water of the Colorado River, and his reports to *The San Diego Union* are available. In the general history of water in the West three books are invaluable: "Dividing the Waters," by J. Norris Hundley, Jr., 1966; Remi A. Nadeau's "The Water Seekers," 1960, and Erwin Cooper's "Aqueduct Empire. A Guide to Water in California. Its Turbulent History. Its Management Today," 1968.

The Harbor

The basic study of the port and its possibilities is Herbert J. Nelson's "The Port of San Diego," a San Diego State College thesis of 1956. He brings together all earlier efforts to create a major port and the influence of location and population growth on the potential market. In addition, the annual reports of the City's original Harbor Department and then the Unified Port District are available. A Master Plan for port development was prepared and issued in 1964 and it was modified in 1972. Newspaper files are replete with the dreams of greatness and the heavy reliance which had been placed on development of the cotton trade with the Imperial Valley and the Southwest. In the 1960's various articles in *The San Diego Union* described progress and one on May 22, 1960, proclaimed that "The Port of San Diego Has Grown Up." The *San Diego Magazine* in July of 1958 printed an article crediting John Bate with much that had been done, and in that same year, the magazine carried an address by George Killian, president of the American President Lines, on what the port could become. The commissioned report of Booz, Allen & Hamilton detailing a program for the port's future is available at the Port District offices.

Tuna

Tuna and tuna fishing is a complex subject which at this writing was still unfolding in a welter of new troubles for the industry. The *National Fisherman* of September 1970 in a special edition carried a good summary of the history of the tuna fleet of California, and San Diego in particular, and the conversion from pole fishing to purse seining. The same issue in an article by John Bunker detailed the wartime experiences of San Diego's tuna fleet. John Springer in the *Pan-American Fisherman* of July 1951 hailed San Diego as the tuna capital of the world and provided statistics to justify the claim. "An Economic Analysis of the Tuna Canning Industry" by Robert M. Roesti was published in 1963 in the magazine *Journal of the West*. It traced economic factors from the 1890's to the 1960's. George W. Sears, a San Diego banker, published a thesis in 1950 on financing of the tuna fleet, which he undertook for the Graduate School of Banking, the American Bankers Association, at Rutgers University. In the late 1950's Rembert James undertook for the Copley News Service a study of Japanese competition, and what could be done about it, and at the time visited Japan and discussed the problem with Japanese fishermen and business leaders. The problem of imports was never really solved to the satisfaction of San Diego fishermen, who, however, later encountered more problems from the zealousness of environmentalists concerned over sea life.

Mission Bay

Mission Bay has been argued about more than any other subject in San Diego with perhaps the exception of the fate of downtown. Various plans for development accompanied various bond issues. Details were settled with a new master plan adopted in 1958. Many public hearings were held in 1957 and 1958. Probably the most detailed suggestions for its future appearance were carried in the report of the Community Facilities Planners of Pasadena in 1960. Little of it, however, has had a direct influence on the park. A copy of the report is in the files of the Park and Recreation Department. A comprehensive view of the report with illustrations is contained in the February 1960 issue of the *San Diego Magazine*, titled "A Splendid Vision of Mission Bay." A 68-page report on how Mission Bay could become America's finest playground was prepared by the San Diego Tourist and Convention Bureau, at the request of the Mission Bay Park Commission, in 1962. Another report was that of William L. Pereira and Associates which was designed to update the original 1958 Master Plan. However, the report eventually was not acted upon and instead the original 1958 plan was adjusted for new circumstances.

Aviation

San Diego has been a center of aviation since John Montgomery flew the first glider on Otay Mesa long before the age of powered flight. The histories of San Diego's major industries devoted to airplane building or parts manufacturing have been detailed in three volumes. Two of them were written by William Wagner, once director of public relations for Ryan Aeronautical Company. One volume was "The Aviator. Being the Ventures of Pioneer Airman and Businessman, T. Claude Ryan." It was written in collaboration with Lee Dye and published in 1971. His second book was on Major Reuben H. Fleet, who founded Consolidated Aircraft and brought it to San Diego. This story ends, however, with Fleet's disposing of interests in the company at the start of World War II, under pressure from the Roosevelt Administration. It is titled "Reuben Fleet and the Story of Consolidated Aircraft," 1976. Both books are in the nature of biographies, and have some drawbacks, as they were subsidized by their subjects, but nevertheless provide valuable information on them as individuals as well as their contributions to aviation. The third book was "Rohr. The Story of a Corporation," by Edward T. Austin, published in 1969. Austin was an official of the corporation, and his work is therefore limited but, again, valuable as to the problems of industry in swiftly changing times.

In more recent years public records have been available on the progress of the aviation industry in San Diego, as well as from company reports. One of the finest was a publication on the fiftieth anniversary of the founding of Consolidated, or Convair, which was issued for 1973. It is a dramatic presentation with a useful chronology.

The role of Convair-built airplanes in World War II is detailed in "A History of the United States Air Force, 1907-1957," edited by Alfred Goldberg. For the history of Naval aviation, and historic events that took place in San Diego, a good source is "Golden Wings, a Pictorial History of the United States Navy and Marine Corps in the Air," by Martin Caidans, in cooperation with the United States Navy, 1960.

Other Material

The airport situation is familiar to all San Diegans. A summary of efforts to establish a major international airport for San Diego, is detailed in a thesis for San Diego State College by Floyd Roscoe Moore, 1960. It also provides a brief history of all military landing fields in the area. Of later interest are the daily newspaper files and issues of the *San Diego Magazine*, particularly of May and September of 1956; and in October of 1969. The history of banking in San Diego, from 1933 to 1958, can be found in Frank A. Milikan's thesis, "A Survey of the Development of Commercial Banking in San Diego County," 1960. Also among the papers at San Diego State College, or at San Diego State University as it is now known, is a thesis "The Pueblo Lands of the City of San Diego," 1769-1950, by Harold Guy Hevener, 1950. Kenneth A. Stevenson also submitted a thesis on "A History of San Diego Real Estate," 1948, while William Thomas Wootton wrote of "Urban Transportation in San Diego: The San Diego Electric Railway Company, 1922-1949," prepared in 1966. In this field also of interest is "Rails of the Silvergate" by Richard V. Dodge, and published by the *Pacific Railway Journal* in 1960. A comprehensive study of the Metropolitan Coast of Southern California was prepared for the Bureau of Governmental Research, the University of California, Los Angeles, by Richard Bigger, James D. Kitchen, Lyndon R. Musolf and Carolyn Quinn, in 1958. It deals primarily with San Diego and Orange Counties, as to growth and problems. In this can be found the municipal histories of communities in the County. Details are provided on the many annexations in the growth of the City of San Diego.

Statistics of all kinds were readily available. They did not always agree, in minor ways. Other than those of the United States Census Bureau, the reports of the Copley International Corporation were the most usable, in later years. Other statistics on population, business, finance, agriculture, tourists, and so forth came from publications of the San Diego Chamber of Commerce, The Union-Tribune Business Index, reports of the Port of San Diego and the Unified Port District, and the Population and Land Use Bulletin of the City Planning Department.

A more detailed summary of what happened to San Diego's economy as a result of the war was prepared by a San Diego banker, Glenn C. Erickson, a fulfillment of graduation requirements from the Graduate School of Business at Stanford University, in 1954. It was titled "The Effect of the Military Establishment and the Aviation Industry on the Need for a More Balanced Economy in San Diego."

The annual editions of *The San Diego Union*, on January of 1967 and 1969, brought together reports on all phases of the economy, and comments on many leading businesses and industries. The one of 1969 was most helpful in that it dealt in detail with the progress of San Diego in 200 years, from an industrial and cultural emphasis.

The material on the ecology of San Diego came from some of the writings of the late Bryant Evans, Science Editor of *The San Diego Union* who was commissioned to prepare a book on the ecology of the region but was unable to complete it.

Of interest in the developing story of Mission Valley is a thesis by Virgil Raymond Hanson, "A Study in Changing Land Use, 1769-1960." This was done at the University of California, Los Angeles, in 1960.

Besides reports of the Federal Census, LeRoy E. Harris has contributed to the general knowledge of "The Settlement Patterns of Negroes and Spanish-Americans on the West Coast" in his dissertation for Carnegie-Mellon University in 1974, and it is found at the San Diego Historical Society.

The Cities

Books on cities, and even on the histories of cities, are often fragmented or episodic. A City often is too large to embrace with a single volume of a serious nature. Among the newer works on cities are "Los Angeles, Biography of a City," edited by John and LaRee Caughey, which brings together the comments and thoughts of many explorers and writers who have passed that way, or remained or lived there. Gunther Barth has published "Instant Cities, The Urbanization and the Rise of San Francisco and Denver." The prolific writer and historian Remi Nadeau also has "Los Angeles from Mission to Modern City," which he brought out in 1960. It is a comparatively thin book for so large a subject.

Illustrations

The publishers of the "City of the Dream" were fortunate in having access to the photographic and negative files of *The San Diego Union* and *The Evening Tribune*. All but a half dozen illustrations were taken by photographers of the two newspapers over a thirty-year period. Among the photographers represented are Charles Sick, chief photographer; Stan Griffin, retired; Ed Neil, Roger Wrenn, Joe Flynn, Bob Redding, Thane McIntosh, Dan Tichonchuk, John Godwin, Phil McMahan, Ted Winfield, George Smith, Jerry Rife, John Price, Jerry Windle, Dennis Huls, Joe Holly, Rick McCarthy, Bob Ivins, Tim Wilson, Tony Doubek and Larry Armstrong.

The painting reproduced for the dust jacket and for background purposes on the title page, and, in part, for chapter pages, was taken from a collection by Rex Brandt, the noted water colorist, of Corona del Mar, for the Copley book, "Rex Brandt's San Diego — Land of the Sundown Sea," which was published by Best-West, of Palm Springs. All of the paintings in his book are in the collection of Helen K. Copley.

A painting by the Japanese artist, K. (Joe) Sugaya, who was interned in 1942, at Poston, Arizona, of his internment camp, was loaned for the book by Rhoda Kruse, head of the California Room of the San Diego Public Library. The painting of the "Last Crossing" by Robert J. Landry is owned by Mrs. Ilma Pourade. The painting of "Father" Alonzo Horton is by David Wayne Millsap and was done for the Copley Book "The Glory Years" in 1964. The Title and

Insurance Company's Historical Collection provided photographs of San Diego, the Camp Lockett mounted patrol, and a Fort Rosecrans soldier awaiting inspection. Photos of the Lindbergh Field runway and Convair plant, before the war, and the air view of wartime camouflage, are from General Dynamics. The California State Library provided the early map of San Diego showing location of the first airfields. Exposi-Books. The photo of a man on the moon is from the National Aeronautical Space Administration. Coastal wartime defense photos are from The Associated Press.

The Beginning

In the Winter of 1916, W. D. Waffot wrote in the Mentor publication's Department of Travel: "On the Cabrillo Bridge, in Balboa Park, in San Diego, I met two middle-aged people who had gone out to the Coast, and could not make up their minds – and hearts – to leave. 'We came to see Southern California two years ago, and we are still here. There are thousands like us.' And indeed my own feelings were much like theirs, for I found it hard to turn my back on that fair summerland. I was glad that I left on a night train, for then there was no looking back. Under the folds of darkness the beauty of it all passes away 'like a dream that is told.'". Imagine what happened when the auto and the airplane disgorged their millions into Southern California. The task of telling how it was in the early days, and how time unfolded the drama of an awakening land, was proposed by the late James S. Copley, and undertaken by this writer at the urging of his wife, Ilma Pourade, who, too, came before the "flood." Out of this grew Copley Books which have been continued by Helen K. Copley.

INDEX